Record of a Girlhood, Volume III

Frances Ann Kemble

BIBLIOLIFE

RECORD OF A GIRLHOOD.

BY

FRANCES ANN KEMBLE.

IN THREE VOLUMES.

VOL. III.

LONDON:

RICHARD BENTLEY AND SON,

Publishers in Ordinary to Her Majesty the Queen.

1878.

RECORD OF A GIRLHOOD.

JOURNAL, 1831.

Thursday, April 21st.—Walked in the square, and studied Lady Teazle. The trees are thickly clothed with leaves, and the new-mown grass, even in the midst of London, smelt fresh and sweet; I was quite alone in the square, and enjoyed something like a *country* sensation. I went to Pickersgill, and Mrs. Jameson came while I was sitting to him; that Medora of his is a fine picture, full of poetry. We dined with the Harnesses; Milman and Croly were among the guests (it was a sort of *Quarterly Review* in the flesh). I like Mr. Milman; not so the other critic.

Friday, 22nd.—Visiting with my mother; called on Lady Dacre, who gave me her pretty little piece of " Wednesday Morning," with a view to our doing it for my father's benefit. It is really very pretty, but I fear will look in our large theatre as a lady's water-colour sketch of a landscape would by way of a

41

scene. I walked in·the square in the afternoon, and
studied Lady Teazle, which I do not like a bit, and
shall act abominably. At the theatre to-night the
house was not very full, and the audience were un-
pleasantly inclined to be political; they took one of
the speeches, " The king, God bless him," and applied
it with vehement applause to his worthy Majesty,
William IV.

Saturday, 23rd.—After my riding lesson, went and
sat in the library to hear Sheridan Knowles's play of
" The Hunchback." Mr. Bartley and my father and
mother were his only audience, and he read it himself
to us. A real play, with real characters, individuals,
human beings, it is a good deal after the fashion of
our old playwrights, and does not disgrace its models.
I was delighted with it; it is full of life and originality;
a little long, but that's a trifle. There is a want of
clearness and coherence in the plot, and the comic
part has really no necessary connection with the rest
of the piece; but none of that will signify much, or,
I think, prevent it from succeeding. I like the woman's
part exceedingly, but am afraid I shall find it very
difficult to act.

After dinner there was a universal discussion as to
the possibility and probability of Adorni's self-sacrifice
in " The Maid of Honour," and as the female voices
were unanimous in their verdict of its truth and likelihood, I hold it to be likely and true, for Dante says
we have the " intellect of love," and Cherubino (a very
different kind of authority) says the same thing; and
I suppose we are better judges of such questions than
men. The love of Adorni seems to me, indeed, more

like a woman's than a man's, but that does not tell
against its verisimilitude. Our love is characterized
generally by self-devotion and self-denial, but the
qualities which naturally belong to our affection were
given to Adorni by his social and conventional position. He was by birth and fortune dependent on and
inferior to Camiola, as women are by nature dependent
on and inferior to men; and so I think his love for
her has something of a feminine quality.

In the evening went with my mother to a party
at old Lady Cork's. We started for our assembly
within a few minutes of Sunday morning. Such
rooms—such ovens! such boxes full of fine folks and
foul air! in which we stood and sat, and looked and
listened, and talked nonsense and heard it talked,
and perspired and smothered and suffocated. On
our arrival, as I was going upstairs, I was nearly
squeezed flat against the wall by her potent grace,
the Duchess of St. Albans. We remained half an
hour in the steaming atmosphere of the drawing-
rooms, and another half-hour in the freezing hall
before the carriage could be brought up; caught a
dreadful cold and came home; did not get to bed till
two o'clock, with an intolerable face-ache and tooth-
ache, the well-earned reward of a well-spent evening.

[The career of the Duchess of St. Albans was, as
far as worldly circumstances went, a curious one. As
Miss Mellon she was one of my mother's stage con-
temporaries; a kind-hearted, good-humoured, buxom,
rather coarse actress, with good looks, and good
spirits of a somewhat unrefined sort, which were not
without their admirers; among these the old banker,

Mr. Coutts, married her, and dying, left her the sole
possessor and disposer of his enormous .wealth. My
mother, who had always remained on friendly though
not intimate terms with her old stage-mate, went
to see her in the early days of her widowhood, when
Mrs. Coutts gave her this moderate estimate of her
"money matters:" "Ah, I assure you, dear Mrs.
Charles, the reports of what poor, dear Mr. Coutts
has left me are very much exaggerated—not, I really
believe, more than a few hundred thousand pounds.
To be sure" (after a dejected pause), "there's the
bank—they say about fifty thousand a year."

This small fortune and inconsiderable income
proved sufficient to the moderate desires of the young
Duke of St. Albans, who married this destitute widow,
who thenceforth took her place (and a large one) in
the British aristocracy, and chaperoned the young
Ladies Beauclerc, her husband's sisters, in society.
She was a good-natured woman, and more than once
endeavoured to get my father and mother to bring me
to her balls and magnificent parties. This, however,
they steadily declined, and she, without resenting it,
sent her invitations to my youngest brother alone,
to whom she took a great fancy, and to whose accepting her civilities no objection was made. At her
death she left her great wealth to Mr. Coutts's grand-
daughter, Miss Burdett Coutts, the lady whose excellent use of her riches has made her known all over
the world as one of the most munificently charitable
of Fortune's stewards.

The Duchess of St. Albans was not without shrewd
sense and some humour, though entirely without

education, and her sallies were not always in the best possible taste. Her box at Covent Garden could be approached more conveniently by crossing the stage than by the entrance from the front of the house, and she sometimes availed herself of this easier exit to reach her carriage with less delay. One night when my father had been acting Charles II., the Duchess of St. Alban's crossing her old work-ground, the stage, with her two companions, the pretty Ladies Beauclerc, stopped to shake hands with him (he was still in his stage costume, having remained behind the scenes to give some orders), and presenting him to her young ladies, said, " There, my dears ; there's your ancestor." I suppose in her earlier day she might not have been a bad representative of their " ancestress.".

Monday, April 25th. — Finished studying Lady Teazle. In the evening at the theatre the house was good, but the audience was dull and I was in wretched spirits and played very ill.

Dall was saying that she thought in two years of hard work we might, that is, my father and myself, earn enough to enable us to live in the south of France. This monstrous theatre and its monstrous liabilities will banish us all as it did my uncle Kemble. But that I should be sorry to live so far out of the reach of H——, I think the south of France would be a pleasant abode: a delicious climate, a quiet existence, a less artificial state of society and mode of life, a picturesque nature round me, and my own dear ones and my scribbling with me,—I think with all these conditions I could be happy enough in the south of France or anywhere.

The audience were very politically inclined, applied all the loyal speeches with fervour, and called for " God save the King " after the play. The town is illuminated, too, and one hopes and prays that the " Old Heart of Oak " will weather these evil days, but sometimes the straining of the tackle and the creaking of the timbers are suggestive of foundering even to the most hopeful. The lords have been vindicating their claim to a share in *common* humanity by squab- bling like fish-wives and all but coming to blows; the bishops must have been sacred and scandalized, lords spiritual not being fighting men nowadays.

After the play Mr. Stewart Newton, the painter, supped with us,—a clever, entertaining man and charming artist; a little bit of a dandy, but probably he finds it politic to be so. He told us some comical anecdotes about the Royal Academy and the hanging of the pictures.

The poor, dear king [William IV.], who it seems knows as much about painting as *una vacca spagnuola*, lets himself, his family, and family animals be painted by whoever begs to be allowed that honour. So when the pictures were all hung the other day, somebody discovered in a wretched daub close to the ceiling a portrait of Lady Falkland [the king's daughter], and another of his Majesty's favourite *cat*, which were im- mediately *lowered* to a more honourable position, to accomplish which desirable end, Sir William Beechey [then president of the academy] removed some of his own paintings. On a similar occasion during the late King George IV.'s life, a wretched portrait of him having been placed in one of the most conspicuous

situations in the room, the Duke of Wellington and
sundry other distinguished *cognoscenti* complimented
Sir Thomas Lawrence on it *as his;* this was rather a
bitter pill, and must have been almost too much for
Lawrence's courtierly equanimity.

Wednesday, April 27th.—To the riding school, where
Miss Cavendish and I discoursed on the *stay-at-home*
sensation, and agreed that it is bad to encourage it
too far, as one may narrow one's social circle till at
last it resolves itself into *one's self.*

Wrote to thank Dr. Thackeray [provost of King's
College, Cambridge, and father of my life-long friend
A—— T——] for the Shakespeare he has sent me,
and Lady Dacre for her piece of "Wednesday Morning."
In the evening they all drove out in the open carriage
to see the illuminations; I stayed at home, for the
carriage was full and I had no curiosity about the
sight.   The town is one blaze of rejoicing for the
Reform Bill triumph; the streets are thronged with
people and choked up with carriages, and the air is
flashing and crashing with rockets and squibs and
crackers, to the great discomfort of the horses.   So
many *R*'s everywhere that they may stand for reform,
revolution, ruin, just as those who run may choose to
read, or according to the interpretation of every individual's politics; the most general acceptation in
which they will be taken by the popular understanding
will assuredly be *row.*

Friday, 29th.—Went off to rehearsal without any
breakfast, which was horrible! but not so horrible as
my performance of Lady Teazle promises to be.   If
I do the part according to my notion, it will be mere

insipidity, and yet all the traditional pokes and pats
with the fan and *business* of the part, as it is called,
is so perfectly unnatural to me that I fear I shall
execute it with a doleful bad grace. It seems odd that
Sir Peter always wears the dress of the last century,
while the costume of the rest of the *dramatis personæ*
is quite modern. Indeed, mine is a ball dress of the
present day, all white satin and puffs and clouds of
white tulle, and garlands and wreaths of white roses
and jasmine; it is very anomalous, and makes Lady
Teazle of no date, as it were, for her manners are
those of a rustic belle of seventeen hundred and something, and her costume that of a fine lady of the
present day in the height of the present fashion,
which is absurd.

Mrs. Jameson paid me a long visit; she threatens
to write a play; perhaps she might; she is very
clever, has a vast fund of information, a good deal of
experience, and knowledge and observation of the
world and society. She wanted me to have spent the
evening with her on the 23rd, Shakespeare's birth and
death day, an anniversary all English people ought
to celebrate. Lady Dacre called, in some tribulation,
to say that she had committed herself about her little
piece of "Wednesday Morning," and that Lady Salisbury, who wants it for Hatfield, does not like its being
brought out on the stage.

Lady Dacre says Lady Salisbury is "afraid of comparisons" (between herself and me, in the part). *I*
think Lady Salisbury would not like "our play" to
be made "common and unclean" by vulgar publicity.
In the evening I went to the theatre to see a new

comedy by a Spaniard. The house was literally empty, which was encouraging to all parties. The piece is slightly constructed in point of plot, but the dialogue is admirably written, and, as the work of a foreigner, perfectly surprising. I was introduced to Don Telesforo de Trueba, the author, an ugly little young man, all hair and glare, whiskers and spectacles; he must be very clever and well worth knowing. Mr. Harness took tea with us after the play.

[The comedy, in five acts, of "The Exquisites" was a satirical piece showing up the ridiculous assumption of affected indifference of the young dandies of the day. The special airs of impertinence by which certain officers of a "crack" regiment distinguished themselves had suggested several of the most telling points of the play, which was in every respect a most remarkable performance for a foreigner.]

Saturday, April 30th.—Received a letter from John; he has determined not to leave Spain at present; and were he to return, what is there for him to do here? In the evening to Mrs. C——'s ball; it was very gay, but I am afraid I am turning "exquisite," for I didn't like the music, and my partners bored me, and the dancing tired me, and my journal is getting like K——'s head—full of naked facts, unclothed with a single thought.

Sunday, May 1st.—As sulky a day as ever *glouted* in an English sky. The "young morn" came picking her way from the east, leading with her a dripping, draggled May, instead of Milton's glorious vision.

After church, sundry callers: Mr. C—— bringing prints of the dresses for "Hernani," and the W——s,

who seem in a dreadful fright about the present state
of the country. I do not suppose they would like to
see Heaton demolished.

In the evening we went to the Cartwrights'. It is
only in the morning that one goes there to be tor-
tured; in the evening it is to eat delicious dinners and
hear delightful music.

Hummel, Moscheles, Neukomm, Horsley, and Sir
George Smart, and how they did play! *à l'envi l'un de
l'autre*. They sang, too, that lovely glee, "By Cecil's
Arbour." The thrilling shudder which sweet music
sends through one's whole frame is a species of acute
pleasure, very nearly akin to pain. I wonder if by
any chance there is a point at which the two are one
and the same thing!

Tuesday, May 3rd.—I wrote the fourth scene of the
fifth act of my play ["The Star of Seville"], and acted
Lady Teazle for the first time; the house was very
good, and my performance, as I expected, very bad;
I was as flat as a lady amateur. I stayed after the
play to hear Braham sing "Tom Tug," which was a
refreshment to my spirit after my own acting; after
I came home, finished the fifth act of "The Star of
Seville." "Joy, joy for ever, my task is done!" I
have not the least idea, though, that "heaven is
won."

Wednesday, May 4th.—A delightful dinner at the
B——s', but in the evening a regular crush; however,
if one is to be squeezed to death (though 'tis an
abolished form of torture), it may as well be in good
company, among the fine world, and lots of pleasant people besides: Milman, Sotheby, Lockhart,

Sir Augustus Calcott, Harness, Lady Dacre, Joanna
Baillie, Lady Calcott, etc.

Friday, May 6th.—Real March weather: cold, piercing, damp, wretched, in spite of which I carried
Shakespeare to walk with me in the square, and read
all over again for the fiftieth time all the conjectures
of everybody about him and his life. How little we
know *about him*, how intimately we seem to know *him*!
I had the square all to myself, and it was delicious:
lilac, syringa, hawthorn, lime blossoms, and new-
mown grass in the midst of London,—and Shakespeare to think about. How grateful I felt for so
much enjoyment! When I got home, corrected the
proof-sheets of "Francis I.," and thought it looked
quite pretty in print.

Out so late dancing, Wednesday and Thursday
nights, or rather *mornings*, that I had no time for
journal-writing. What a life I do lead!

Friday, May 13th.—At twelve o'clock to Bridgewater
House for our first rehearsal of "Hernani." Lady
Francis wants us to go down to them at Oatlands.
I should like of all things to see Weybridge once more;
there's many a nook and path in those woods that
I know better than their owners. The rehearsal lasted
till three, and was a tolerably tidy specimen of amateur acting. Mr. Craven is really very good, and I
shall like to act with him very much, and Mr. St.
Aubin is very fair. Was introduced to Mrs. Bradshaw, whose looks rather disappointed me, because
she "did contrive to make herself look so beautiful"
on the stage, in Clari and Mary Copp and everything
she did; I suppose her exquisite acting got into her

face, somehow. Henry Greville is delightful, and I like him very much. When we left Bridgewater House we drove to my aunt Siddons's. Every time I see that magnificent ruin some fresh decay makes itself apparent in it, and one cannot but feel that it must soon totter to its fall.

What a price she has paid for her great celebrity!— weariness, vacuity, and utter deadness of spirit. The cup has been so highly flavoured that life is absolutely without savour or sweetness to her now, nothing but tasteless insipidity. She has stood on a pinnacle till all things have come to look flat and dreary; mere shapeless, colourless, level monotony to her. Poor woman! what a fate to be condemned to, and yet how she has been envied, as well as admired!

After dinner had only just time to go over my part and drive to the theatre. My dear, delightful Portia! The house was good, but the audience dull, and I acted dully to suit them; but I hope my last dress, which was beautiful, consoled them. What with sham business and real business, I have had a busy day.

Saturday, May 14*th.*—Received a note from Theodosia [Lady Monson], and a whole cargo of delicious flowers from Cassiobury. She writes me that poor old Forster [an old cottager who lived in Lord Essex's park and whom my friend and I used to visit] is dying. The last I saw of that "Old Mortality" was sitting with him one bright sunset under his cottage porch, singing to him and dressing his hat with flowers, poor old man! yet after walking this earth upwards of ninety-seven years the spirit as well as the flesh must be weary. His cottage will lose half its picturesque-

ness without his figure at the door; I wonder who
will take care now of the roses he was so fond of, and
the pretty little garden I used to forage in for lilies of
the valley and strawberries! I shall never see him
again, which makes me sad; I was often deeply struck
by the quaint wisdom of that old human relic, and
his image is associated in my thoughts with evening
walks and summer sunsets and lovely flowers and
lordly trees, and he will haunt Cassiobury always to
me. I went with my mother to buy my dresses for
" Hernani " which will cost me a fortune and a half.

Great Russell Street, Saturday.

MY DEAREST H——,

You see I have taken your advice, and,
moreover, your paper, in order that, in spite of the
dispersion of Parliament and the unattainability of
franks, our correspondence may lose nothing in bulk,
though it must in frequency. I think you are be-
having very shabbily in not writing to me. Are you
consulting your own pleasure, or my purse? I dedicate so much of my income to purposes which go
under the head of " money thrown away; " don't you
think the cost of our correspondence may be added
to that without seriously troubling my conscience?
What shall I say to you? "Reform" is on the tip
of my pen, and great as are our private matters of
anxiety, they scarcely outweigh in our minds the
national interest that is engrossing almost every
thinking person throughout the country. You know
I am no politician, and my shallow causality and want
of adequate information alike unfit me from under-

standing, much less discussing, public questions of
great importance; but the present crisis has aroused
me to intense interest and anxiety about the course
events are taking. You can have no conception of
the state of excitement prevailing in London at this
moment. The scene in the House of Lords immediately preceding the dissolution the papers will have
described to you, though if the spectators and par-
ticipators in it may be believed, the tumult, the
disorder, the Billingsgate uproar on that occasion
would not be easy to describe. Lord Londonderry,
it seems, thought that the days of *faust-recht* had
come back again, and I fancy more than he are of
that opinion.

An illumination was immediately ordered by the
Lord Mayor Donkin (or *key*, as "t'other side" call
him); but, owing to the shortness of the notice he
gave, it seems the show of light was not satisfactory
to the tallow chandler part of the population, so
another was appointed two nights after. My mother
and the two Harrys went out in the open carriage to
drive through the streets. I was depressed and dis-
inclined for sight-seeing, and did not go, which I
regretted afterwards, as all strong exhibitions of
public feeling are curious and interesting. They
say the crowd was immense in all the principal
thoroughfares, and of the lowest order. They testified
their approbation of the various illuminated devices
by shouts and hurrahs and applause; their dis-
pleasure against the various non-illuminators was
more violently manifested by assailing their houses
and breaking their windows.

Sundry were the glass sacrifices offered at the shrine of consistent Tory patriotism at the West End of the town. The mottoes and sentences on some of the illuminations were noteworthy for their democratic flavour: "The king and the people," "The people of England," "The glorious dissolution," "The glorious reform," "The people and the press," "The people's triumph." A man who seemed by his dress to belong to the very lowest class (a cross apparently between a scavenger and a ragseller), with a branch of laurel waving in his tattered hat, stopped before this last sentence and exclaimed, "No—they don't yet; but they will."

I have been having quite a number of holidays at the theatre lately. They have brought out a comedy in which I do not play, and are going to bring out a sort of historical melodrama on the life of Bonaparte, so that I think I shall have easy work, if that succeeds, for the rest of the season. I have just finished correcting the proof-sheets of "Francis I.," and think it looks quite pretty in print, and have dedicated it to my mother, which I hope will please her. . . .

Dear H——, this is Saturday, the 14th, and 'tis now exactly three weeks since I began this letter. I know not what you will think of this, but, indeed, I am almost worn out with the ceaseless occupations of one sort and another that are crowded into every day, and the impossibility of commanding one hour's quiet out of the twenty-four. . . .

I am afraid we shall not come to Ireland this summer, after all, my dear H——. The Dublin

manager and my father have not come to terms, and
I hear Miss Inverarity (a popular singer) is engaged
there, so that I conclude we shall not act there this
season. This is so great a disappointment to me
that I cannot say anything whatever about it. I
have been acting Lady Teazle for Mr. Bartley and
my father's benefit. It seems to have pleased the
public very well. Without caring for it much myself,
I find it light and amusing work, and much easier
for me than Lady Townley, because it is a natural
and that an entirely artificial character; the whole
tone and manners, too, of Sheridan's rustic belle
are much more within my scope than those of the
woman of fashion of Sir John Vanbrugh's play.

On Friday we had our first rehearsal of "Hernani,"
at Bridgewater House, and I was greatly surprised
with some of the acting, which, allowing for a little
want of technical experience, was, in Mr. Craven's
instance, really very good. He is the grandson of old
Lady Craven, the Margravine of Auspach, and enacts
the hero of the piece, which I think he will do very
well. The whole play, I think, will be fairly acted for
an amateur performance. Lord and Lady Francis
have pressed my mother very much to go down for a
little while to Oatlands, the beautiful place close to
Weybridge, which belonged to the Duke of York, and
of which they have taken a lease. My mother has
accepted their invitation, and looks forward with
great pleasure to revisiting her dear Weybridge.
I know a good deal more of that lovely neighbourhood and all its wild haunts than the present proprietors of Oatlands. Lady Francis is a famous

horsewoman, and told me by way of inducement to go there that we would gallop all over the country together, which sounded very pleasant. . . .

I called on my aunt Siddons the other day, and was shocked to find her looking wretchedly ill; she has not yet got rid of the erysipelas in her legs, and complained of intense headache. Poor woman! she suffers dreadfully. . . . Cecilia's life has been one enduring devotion and self-sacrifice. I cannot help wishing, for both their sakes, that the period of her mother's infirmity and physical decay may be shortened. I received a charming letter from Theodosia yesterday, accompanying a still more charming basketful of delicious flowers from dear Cassiobury—how much nicer they are than human beings! I don't believe I belong to man (or woman) kind, I like so many things —the whole material universe, for example—better than what one calls one's fellow-creatures. She told me that old Foster (you remember the old cottager in Cassiobury Park) was dying. The news contrasted sadly with the sweet, fresh, living blossoms that it came with. The last time that I saw that old man I sat with him under his porch on a bright sunny evening, talking, laughing, winding wreaths round his hat, and singing to him, and that is the last I shall ever see of him. He was a remarkable old man, and made a strong impression on my fancy in the course of our short acquaintance. There was a strong and vivid *remnant* of mind in him surviving the contest with ninety and odd years of existence; his manner was quaint and rustic without a tinge of vulgarity; he is fastened to my memory by a certain wreath of flowers and sunset light upon the brook that ran in front of his cottage, and the smell of some sweet roses that grew over it, and I shall never forget him. . . .

I went to the opera the other night and saw Pasta's " Medea " for the first time. I shall not trouble you with any ecstasies, because, luckily for you, my admiration for her is quite indescribable; but I have seen grace and majesty as perfect as I can conceive, and so saying I close my account of my impressions. I fancied I was slightly disappointed in Taglioni, whose dancing followed Pasta's singing, but I suppose the magnificent tragical performance I had just witnessed had numbed as it were my power of appreciation of her grace and elegance, and yet she seemed to me like · a *dancing flower;* so you see I must have liked her very much. . . .

God bless you, dear; pray write to me very soon. I want some consolation for not seeing you, nor the dear girls, nor the sea. I could think of that fresh, sparkling, fresh-looking, glassy sea till I cried for disappointment.

Ever yours,

F. A. K.

The Miss Inverarity mentioned in this letter was a young Scotch singer of very remarkable talent and promise, who came out at Covent Garden just at this time. She was one of the tallest women I ever saw, and had a fine soprano voice as high as herself, and sang English music well. She was a very great favourite during the short time that I remember her on the stage.

MY DEAREST H——,

My mother has just requested me to talk with A—— about her approaching first communion, and it troubles me because I fear I cannot do so satisfactorily to her (I mean my mother) and myself. I think my feeling about the sacrament, or rather the preparation necessary for receiving it, is different from hers. It is not so much to me an awful as a merciful institution. One goes to the Lord's Table because one is weak and wicked and wretched, not because one is, or even has striven to be, otherwise. A holy reverence for the holy rite is indispensable, but not, I think, such a feeling as would chill us with fear, or cast us down in despondency. The excess of our poverty and humility is our best claim to it, and therefore, though the previous "preparations," as it is rather technically called, may be otherwise beneficial, it does not seem to me necessary, much less indispensable. Our Lord did not say, "Cleanse yourselves, amend yourselves, strip yourselves of your own burdens and come to me;" but, "Come to me and I will cleanse you, I will cure you, I will help you and give you rest." It is remembering this that I venture to take the sacrament, but I know other people, and I believe my mother among them, think a much more specific preparation necessary, and I am afraid, therefore, that I might not altogether meet my mother's views in what I might say to A—— upon the subject. I wish you would tell me what your opinion and feeling is about this.

Your affectionate,

F. A. K.

Sunday, May 15th.—Walked home from church with Mrs. Montague and Emily and Mrs. Proctor, discussing among various things the necessity for "preparation" before taking the sacrament. I suppose the publican in the parable had not prepared his prayer, and I suppose he would have been a worthy communicant.

They came in and sat a long time with my mother talking about Sir Thomas Lawrence, of whom she spoke as a perfect riddle. I think he was a dangerous person, because his experience and genius made him delightfully attractive, and the dexterity of his flattery amounted in itself to a fine art. The talk then fell upon the possibility of friendship existing between men and women without sooner or later degenerating, on one part or the other, into love. The French rhymster sings—

> "Trop tot, hélas, l'amour s'enflamme,
>   Et je sens qu'il est mal aisé;
>   Que l'ami d'une belle dame,
>   Ne soit un amant déguisé."

My father came in while the ladies were still here, and Mrs. Procter behaved admirably well about her husband's play. . . .

I do think it is too bad of the management to have made use of my name in rejecting that piece, when, Heaven knows, so far from *rejecting*, I never even *object* to anything I am bidden to do; that is, never visibly or audibly. . . .

Mrs. P—— called, and the talk became political and lugubriously desponding, and I suddenly found myself inspired with a contradictory vein of hopeful-

ness, and became vehement in its defence. In spite
of all the disastrous forebodings I constantly have, I
cannot but trust that the spread of enlightenment
and general progress of intelligence in the people of
this country—the good judgment of those who have
power and the moderation of those who desire improvement—will effect a change without a *crash* and
achieve reform without revolution.

Wednesday, May 18th.—My mother and I started
at two o'clock for Oatlands. The day was very
enjoyable, for the dust and mitigated east wind were
in our backs; the carriage was open, and the sun was
almost too powerful, though the earth has not yet
lost its first spring freshness, nor the trees, though
full fledged, their early vivid green. The turf has
not withered with the heat, and the hawthorn lay
thick and fragrant on every hedge, like snow that
the winter had forgotten to melt, and the sky above
was bright and clear, and I was very happy. I had
taken " The Abbot " with me, which I had never read;
but my mother did not sleep, so we chatted instead
of my reading. She recalled all our former times at
Weybridge. . . . It was a great pleasure to retrace
this well-known road, and again to see dear old
Walton Bridge and the bright, broad Thames, with
the noble chestnut trees on its banks, the smooth,
smiling fields stretching beyond it, and the swans
riding in such happy majesty on its bosom. I really
think I do deserve to live in the country, it is so
delightsome to me. We reached Oatlands an hour
before dinner-time and found the party just returned
from riding. We sauntered through part of the

grounds to the cemetery of the Duchess of York's
dogs. . . . We had some music in the evening. Lady
Francis sang and I sang, and was frightened to death,
as I always am when asked to do so. . . .

Thursday, 19*th*.—A bright sunny morning, the
trees all bowing and bending, and the water chafing
and crisping under a fresh, strong, but not cold, wind.
I lost my way in the park and walked towards
Walton, thinking I was going to Weybridge, but,
discovering my mistake, turned about, and crossing
the whole park came out upon the common and our
old familiar cricketing ground. I flew along the dear
old paths to our little cottage, but "Desolate was the
dwelling of Morna,"—the house closed, the vine torn
down, the grass knee-deep, the shrubs all trailing
their branches and blossoms in disorderly luxuriance
on the earth, the wire fence broken down between the
garden and the wood, the gate gone; the lawn was
sown with wheat, and the little pine wood one tangled
maze, without path, entrance, or issue. I ran up the
mound to where John used to stand challenging the
echo with his bugle. . . .

O tempo passato!—the absent may return and
the distant be brought near, the dead be raised and in
another world rejoin us, but a day that is gone is gone,
and all eternity can give us back no single minute of
the past! I gathered a rose and some honeysuckle
from the poor dishevelled shrubs for my mother, and
ran back to Oatlands to breakfast. After breakfast
we went over "Hernani," with Mrs. Sullivan for
prompter, and when that was over everybody went
out walking; but I was too tired with my morning's

tramp, and sat under a tree on the lawn reading
a very good little book on the sacrament, which went
over the ground of my late discussion with Mrs. Mon-
tagu and Mrs. Procter on the subject of "preparation" for taking it.

After lunch there was a general preparation 'for
riding, and just as we were all mounted it began
to rain, and persevered till, in despair, Mr. and Mrs.
Sullivan rode off without our promised escort.   Mr.
C—— arrived just as we had disequipped, and the
gentlemen all dispersed.   Lady Francis and I sang
together for some time, and suddenly the clouds
withholding their tears, she and I, in one of those
instants of rapid determination which sometimes
make or mar a fate, tore on our habits again, jumped
on our horses, and galloped off together over the
park.   We had an enchanting, grey, soft afternoon,
with now and then a rain-drop and sigh of wind, like
the last sob of a fit of crying.   The earth smelt
deliciously fresh, and shone one glittering, sparkling,
vivid green.   Our ride was delightful, and we galloped
back just in time to dress for dinner.

In the evening, sauntering on the lawn and pleasant,
bright talk indoors.   Lord John (the present venerable
Earl Russell) would be quite charming if he wasn't
so afraid of the rain.   I do not think he is made
of sugar, but, politically, perhaps he is the salt of
the earth; he certainly succeeds in keeping himself
dry.

Friday, Oatlands.—Walked out before breakfast;
the night's rain had refreshed the earth and revived
every growing thing, the east wind had blown itself

away, and a warm, delicious western breeze came
fluttering fitfully over the new-mown lawn. After
breakfast we rehearsèd Mr. Craven's and Captain
Shelley's and my scenes in "Hernani." I think
they will do very well if they do not shy at the
moment of action, or rather acting. We had some
music, and then the gentlemen went out shooting.
I took "The Abbot" and established myself on a hay-
cock, leaving Lady Francis to her own indoor devices.
By-and-by the whole party came out, and we sat on
the lawn laughing and talking till the gentlemen's
carriage was announced, and our rival heroes took
their departure for town, cheek by jowl, in a pretty
equipage of Mr. Craven's in the most amicable mood
imaginable. As soon as they were off we mounted
and rode out, past our old cottage, down by Brook-
lands, through the second wood, and by the Fairies'
Oak. O Lord King, Lord King (we were riding
through the property of the Earl of Lovelace, then
Lord King), if I was one of those bishops whom
you do not love, I would curse, excommunicate, and
anathematize you for cutting down all those splendid
trees and laying bare those deep, dark, leafy nooks,
the haunts of a thousand "Midsummer Night's
Dreams," to the common air and the staring sun.
The sight of the dear old familiar paths brought the
tears to my eyes, for, stripped and thinned of their
trees and robbed of their beauty, my memory restored
all their former loveliness. On we went down to
Byefleet to the mill, to Langton's through the sweet,
turfy meadows, by hawthorn hedges musical as sweet,
over the picturesque little bridge and along that deep,

dark, sleepy water flowing so silently in its sullen smoothness. On we went a long way over a wide common, where the coarse-grained peaty earth and golden glory of the flowering gorse reminded me of Suffolk's motto—

> "Cloth of gold, do not despise
> That thou art mix'd with cloth of frieze;
> Cloth o. frieze, be not too bold
> That thou art mix'd with cloth of gold."

Back by St. George's Hill, snatching many a leaf and blossom as I rode to carry back to A—— mementoes of our dear Weybridge days, and so home by half-past seven, just time to dress for dinner. As we rode along, Lord Francis and I discussed poets and poetry *in general*—more particularly Byron, Keats, and Shelley; it was a very pretty and proper discourse for such a ride.

In the evening heard all manner of delicious ghost stories; afterwards made music, Lady Francis and I trying all sorts of duets, my mother keeping up a "humming" third and Lord Francis listening and applauding with equal zeal and discretion. . . .

Saturday, May 21st.—My brother John come home from Spain. . . .

Sunday, 22nd.—What a very odd process dreaming is! I *dreamt* in the night that John had come home, and flung myself out of bed in my sleep to run down-stairs to him, which naturally woke me; and then I remembered that he was come home and that I had seen and welcomed him, which it seems to me I might as well have dreamed too while I was about it, and saved myself the jump out of bed. I hate dreaming;

it's like being mad—having one's brain work without the control of one's will.

Dear A—— took the sacrament for the first time at the Swiss church. On my return from church in the afternoon found Sir Ralph and Lady Hamilton and Don Telesforo de Trueba. I like that young Spaniard; he's a clever man. It was such fun his telling me all the story of the Star of Seville, little imagining I had just perpetrated a five-act tragedy on that identical subject.

Tuesday, May 24th.—Drove down to Clint's studio to see Cecilia's (Siddons's) portrait. It's a pretty picture of a " fine piece of a woman," as the Italians say, but it has none of the very decided character of her face. . . .

Wednesday, May 25th.—After dinner went over my part, dressed and set off for Bridgewater House for our dressed. rehearsal of " Hernani." Found the stage in a state of. *unfinish,* the house topsy-turvy, and everybody to the right and left. Sat for an hour in the drawing-room while our very specially small and select audience arrived. Then heard Lady Francis, Henry Greville, Mrs. Bradshaw, and Mr. Mitford try their glee—one of Moore's melodies arranged for four voices—which they sang at the top of their lungs in order to hear themselves, while the carpenters and joiners hammered might and main at the other end of the gallery finishing the theatre.

About nine they were getting under weigh, and we presently began the rehearsal. The dresses were all admirable; they (not the clothes, but the clothes pegs)

were all horribly frightened. I was a little nervous
and rather sad, and I felt strange among all those
foolish lads, taking such immense delight in that
which gives me so very little, dressing themselves up
and acting. To be sure, "nothing pleaseth but rare
accidents." Mr. M——, our prompter, thought fit
by way of prompting to keep up a rumbling bass
accompaniment to our speaking by reading every
word of the play aloud, as the singers are prompted
at the opera house, which did not tend much to our
assistance. Everything went very smoothly till an
unlucky young "mountaineer" rushed on the stage
and terrified me and Hernani half to death by in-
articulating some horrible intelligence of the utmost
importance to us, which his fright rendered quite
incomprehensible. He stood with his arms wildly
spread abroad, stuttering, sputtering, madly ejaculating and gesticulating, but not one articulate word
could he get out. I thought I should have exploded
with laughter, but as the woman said who saw the
murder, "I knew I mustn't (faint), and I didn't."
With this trifling exception it all went off very well.
Either I was fagged with my morning's ride or the
constitution of the gallery is bad for the voice; I
never felt so exhausted with the mere effort of speaking, and thought I should have died prematurely
and in earnest in the last scene, I was so tired.
When it was over we adjourned with Lord and
Lady Francis and the whole *dramatis personæ* to
Mrs. W————'s magnificent house and splendid
supper. . . .
While we were at table everybody suddenly stood

up, my mother and myself reverently with the rest,
when the whole company drank my health, and I col-
lapsed down into my chair as red and as *limp* as a
skein of scarlet wool, and my mother with some confusion expressed my obligation and her own surprise
at the compliment.   I talked a good deal to Captain
Shelley, who is a nice lad, and, considering his
beauty, and the admiration bestowed on him by all
the fine ladies in London, remarkably unaffected.
We are asked down to Oatlands again, and I hope my
work at the theatre will allow of my going.   What a
shocking mess those young gentlemen actors did make
of their green room this evening, to be sure! rouge,
swords, wine, moustaches, soda water, and cloaks
strewed in every direction.   I wonder what they
would say to the drawing-room decorum of our
Covent Garden green room.

  Thursday, May 26th.—Tried on dresses with Mrs.
Phillips, and talked all the while about the characteristics of Shakespeare's women with Mrs. Jameson,
who had come to see me.   I pity her from the bottom
of my heart; she has a heavy burthen to carry, poor
woman. . . . Went in the evening to rather a dull
dinner, after which, however, I had the pleasure of
hearing Mrs. Frere sing, which she did very charmingly, and so as quite to justify her great society
musical reputation.   After our dinner at the F——s'
we went to Mrs. W——'s evening party, where I sat
alone, heard somebody sing a song, was introduced to
a man, spoke incoherently to several people, got up,
was much jostled in a crowd of human beings, and
came home—and that's society.   We are asked to a

great supper at Chesterfield House, after a second representation which is to be given of "Hernani." My mother thinks it is too much exertion and dissipation for me, and as it is not a ball I do not care to go.

Friday, May 27th.—At eight o'clock drove with my mother to Bridgewater House. We went into the library, where there was nobody, and Lady Francis, Henry Greville, and Lady Charlotte came and sat with us. I was literally crying with fright. Lady Francis took me to my dressing-room, my mother rouged me, blessed me, and went off to join the audience assembled in the great gallery. I went over my part once and my room a hundred times in every direction. At nine they began; the audience very wisely were totally in the dark, which threw out the brilliantly illuminated stage to great advantage, and considering that they were the finest folk in England they behaved remarkably well—listened quietly and attentively, and applauded like Covent Garden galleries. It all went well except poor Mr. Craven's first speech, in which he got out. I don't know whether Lady L—— was among the spectators, and gave him *des éblouissements*. It all went off admirably, however, and oh, how glad I was when it was over!

Saturday, May 28th.—I was awakened by a basket of flowers from Cassiobury, and a letter from Theodosia. Old Foster is dead. I wish he might be buried near the cottage. I should like to know where to think of his resting-place, poor old man! . . .

In the evening Mrs. Jameson, the Fitzhughs, R——P——, and a Mr. K——, a friend of John's, and sundry and several came. . . . We acted charades, and they all went away in high good humour.

Sunday, May 29th.—An " eternal, cursed, cold, and heavy rain," as Dante sings. My mother, A——, and I went to the Swiss church; the service is shorter and more unceremonious than I like; that sitting to sing God's praise, and standing to pray to Him, is displeasing to all my instincts of devotion.

After church my mother was reading Milton's treatise on Christian doctrine, and read portions of it aloud to me. I always feel afraid of theological or controversial writings, and yet the faith that shrinks from being touched lest it should totter is certainly not on the right foundation. I suppose we ought, on the contrary, to examine thoroughly the reason of the faith that is in us. Declining reading upon religious subjects may be prudent, but it may be indolence, cowardice, or lack of due interest in the matter. I think I must read that treatise of Milton's.

Great Russell Street, May 29th, 1831.

MY DEAREST H——,

I have but little time for letter-writing, getting daily " deeper and deeper still " in the incessant occupations of one sort and another that crowd upon and almost overwhelm me ; and now my care is not so much whether I shall have time to write you a long letter, as how I shall get leisure to write to you at all. You complain that, in spite of the present interest I profess in public affairs, I have given you no details of my opinion about them—my hopes or fears of the result of the Reform movement. I have other things that I care more to write to you about than politics, and am chary of my space,

because, though I can cross my letter, I can only
have one sheet of paper. "The Bill," modified as
it now is, has my best prayers and wishes, for to say
that the removal of certain abuses will not give the
people bread which they expect is nothing against it;
but, at the same time that I sincerely hope this measure will be carried, I cannot conceive what Government will do *next*, for though trade is at this moment
prosperous, great poverty and discontent exist among
large classes of the people, and as soon as these needy
folk find out that Reform is really not immediate
bread *and* cheese *and* beer, they will seek something
else which they may imagine will be those desired
items of existence, and that is what it may be difficult
to give them. In the mean time party spirit here has
reached a tremendous pitch; old friendships are
broken up and old intimacies cease; former cordial
acquaintances refuse to meet each other, houses are
divided, and the dearest relations disturbed, if not
destroyed. Society is become a sort of battle-field,
for every man (and woman too) is nothing if not
political. In fact, there really appears to be no middle
or moderating party, which I think strange and to be
deplored. It seems as if it were a mere struggle
between the nobility and the mobility, and the middle-
class—that vast body of good sense, education, and
wealth, and efficient to hold the beam even between
the scales—throws itself man by man into one or the
other of them, and so only swells the adverse parties
on each side.

Parliament meets again in a few days, and then
comes the tug of war. Lord John Russell was at

Oatlands while we were there, and as the Francis
Egertons and their guests were all anti-Reformers,
they led him rather a hard life. He bore all their
attacks with great good humour, however, and with
the well-satisfied smile of a man who thinks himself
on the right, and knows himself on the safe side, and
wisely forbore to reply to their sallies. Our visit there
was delightful.

As the distance is but one and twenty miles, my
mother and I posted down in the open carriage. The
only guests we found on our arrival were Mr. and
Mrs. Sullivan (she is a daughter of Lady Dacre's,
and a charming person), Lord John Russell, and two
of our *corps dramatique*, Mr. Craven and Captain
Shelley, son of Sir John Shelley, a handsome,
good-humoured, pleasant young gentleman, who
acts Charles V. in "Hernani." I got up very
early the first morning I was there and went down
before breakfast to our little old cottage. In the lane
leading to it I met a poor woman who lived near us,
and whom we used to employ. I spoke to her, but
she did not know me again. I wonder if these four
years can have changed me so much? The tiny
house had not been inhabited since we lived there. . . .
My aunt Siddons is better, and Cecy very well.

Your affectionate

F. A. K.

[The beautiful domain of Oatlands was only rented
at this time by Lord Francis Egerton, who delighted
so much in it that he made overtures for the purchase
of it. The house was by no means a good one, though

it had been the abode of royalty; but the park was charming, and the whole neighbourhood, especially the wooded ranges of St. George's Hill, extremely wild and picturesque. . . . Lord Francis Egerton bought St. George's Hill, at the foot of which he built Hatchford, Lady Ellesmere's charming dower house and residence after his death, and the house of Oatlands became a country inn, very pleasant to those who had never known it as the house of former friends, and therefore did not meet ghosts in all its rooms and garden walks; and the park was cut up into small villa residences and rascally inclined citizen's boxes. Hatchford, the widowed home of Lady Ellesmere and burial-place of her brother, to whose memory she erected there an elaborate mausoleum, has passed out of the family possessions and become the property of strangers. One son of the house lives on St. George's Hill, and has his home where I have so often drawn rein while riding with his father and mother to look over the wild, wooded slopes to the smiling landscape stretching in sunny beauty far below us.]

Monday, May 30*th.* . . . The Francis Egertons called, and sat a long time discussing " Hernani." . . . I must record such a good pun of his, which he only, alas, *dreamt.* He dreamt Lord W—— came up to him, covered with gold chains and ornaments of all sorts, and that he had called him the " Chain Pier." . . . In the evening to Bridgewater House. As soon as we arrived, I went to my own private room, and looked over my part. We began at nine. Our audience

43

was larger than the last time. The play went off
extremely well; we were all improved. I was very
anxious to play well, for the Archbishop of York
was in the front row, and he (poor gentleman!) had
never had the happiness of seeing me, the playhouse being forbidden ground to him. [This seems
rather inconsistent, as all the lesser clergy at this
time frequented the theatre without fear or reproach.
Dr. Hughes, the Very Reverend Prebend of St. Paul's,
Milman, Harness, among our own personal friends,
were there constantly, not to speak of my behind-the-
scenes acquaintance, the Rev. A. F.] I should like
to seduce an old Archbishop into a liking for the
wickedness of my mystery, so I did my very best to
edify him, according to my kind and capacity. . . .
At the end of the play, as I lay dead on the stage,
the king (Captain Shelley) was cutting three great
capers, like Bayard on his field of battle, for joy his
work was done, when his pretty dancing shoes
attracted, in spite of my decease, my attention, and
I asked, with rapidly reviving interest in existence,
what they meant, on which I was informed that the
supper at Mrs. Cunliffe's was indeed a ball. I jumped
up from the dead, hurried off my stage robes, and
hurried on my private apparel, and followed my
mother into the saloon. Here I had delightful talk
(though I believe I was dancing on my mind's feet all
the while) with Lord John Russell, Miss Berry, Lady
Charlotte Lindsay, and that charming person, James
Wortley, and I got a glimpse of Lord O——'s lovely
face, who is a beautiful creature. After being duly
stared at by the crowds of my exalted fellow-beings

who filled the room, Lady Francis said she would send them away, and we adjourned to Mrs. Cunliffe's, and had a very fine ball; that is to say, we had neither room to dance, nor space to sit, nor power to move.

"Oh, pleasure is a very pleasant thing," as Byron sings and H—— for ever says, and certainly a good ball is a pleasant thing, and in spite of the above drawbacks I was enchanted with everything. Such shoals of partners! such nice people! such perfect music! such a delightful floor! Danced till the day had one eye wide open, and then home to bed—what a good thing it is to have one under the circumstances! I hope I have not been very tipsy to-night, but it is difficult with so many stimulants to keep *quite* sober: Broad daylight! Six o'clock!

Tuesday, May 21st.—My feet ache so with dancing that I can hardly stand. Did not some traditional princesses of German fairyland dance their shoes and stockings to pieces?

Going into the drawing-room I found my darling Dr. Combe there, and if I had not been so tired I must have made a jump at his neck, I was so very glad to see him. He brought me a letter from Mr. Combe, whom I love only one step lower. He sat with us but a short time, and leaves town to-morrow, which I am sorry for, first, because I should like to have seen him again so very much, and next, because I should have been glad that my mother became better acquainted with the mental charms and seductions of the man whose outward appearance seems to have allayed some of her apprehensions for the safety

of my heart and those of my Edinburgh cousins.
Mrs. W—— called soon after. She is intent upon
my acting Mlle. Mar's part in "Henri Trois." I can
do nothing with any French part in Covent Garden.
If they can find a theatre of half that size to get it up
in, well and good ; but seen from a distance, which
defies discrimination of objects, a thistle is as good as
a rose, and in that enormous frame refinement is
mere platitude, and finish of detail an unnecessary
minutia.

We went to the theatre to see a new piece, I believe
by Mrs. Norton.   The pit and galleries were very
indifferent ; the dress circle and private boxes full of
fine folk.   Lady St. Maur (Georgiana Sheridan, Mrs.
Norton's youngest sister, afterwards Duchess of
Somerset and Queen of Beauty) and her husband,
with Corinne and Mr. Norton, in a box opposite ours.
What a terrible piece ! what atrocious situations and
ferocious circumstances !—tinkering, starving, hanging—like a chapter out of the Newgate Calendar.
But, after all, she's in the right; she has given the
public what they desire, given them what they like.
Of course it made one cry horribly; but then of
course one cries when one hears of people reduced by
sheer craving to eat nettles and cabbage-stalks.   Desti-
tution, absolute hunger, cold and nakedness, are no
more subjects for artistic representation than sickness,
disease, and the *real* details of idiotcy, madness, and
death.   All art should be an idealized, elevated representation (not imitation) of nature ; and when beggary
and low vice are made the themes of the dramatist,
as in this piece, or of the poet, as in the works of

Crabbe, they seem to me to be clothing their inspira-
tions in wood or lead, or some base material, instead
of gold or ivory. The clay of the modeller is more
real, but the marble of the sculptor is the clay glorified.
In Crabbe's writings one has at least the comfort and
consolation of a high moral sense, charming versifica-
tion, and an occasional tender, exquisite expression of
the beauties of nature. Our play to-night could not
boast of these *alleviations*.

Wednesday, June 1st.—At the riding school saw
Miss C——, who wants me to get the play changed at
Covent Garden *for this evening*—"rien que cela !"
What a fine thing it is to be "one of those people !"
They fancy that anybody's business of any sort can be
postponed to the first whim that enters their head.
My mother came with Dr. Combe in the carriage to
fetch me from the riding school. At home found a
note from Lady Francis and the epilogue Lord Francis
has written to "Hernani," which I am certainly
bound to like, for it is highly complimentary to me.

I went to the real theatre in the evening to do real
work. The house was good, but I played like a
wretch—ranted, roared, and acted altogether infa-
mously. The fact was I was tired to death, and of
course violence always has to supply the place of
strength. Unluckily all the F——s were there, and
I felt sorry for them. To be sure, they had never
seen "The Hunchback" before, and I should think
would heartily desire never to see it again ; my performance was shameful.

Thursday, June 2nd.—Mr. Hayter called. Lord
Francis has spoken to him about the picture he

wishes him to do of me, and he came to take the
position, and I gave him his choice of three or four.
I dare say he will make a very pretty picture. As for
my likeness, that *I* am not hopeful about. I have
gone through the operation in vain so very often.
Murray has sent me some beautiful and delightful
books. . . . A third representation of "Hernani"
is called for, it seems, and, as far as I am concerned,
they are welcome to it; but Lady Francis came to
say that the Duchess of Gloucester wants it to be
acted on the 23rd, and I am afraid that will not do
for my theatre arrangements; they must try and
have it earlier, if possible. Lady Francis has half
bribed me with a ball. They want us to go down to
Oatlands for Saturday and Sunday, and I hope we
may be able to manage it. . . . After Lady F——
was gone, my mother had a visit from Mrs. B——;
her manner is bad, her matter is good. She is
clever and excellent, and I have a great respect for
her. She interested me immensely by her account of
Mrs. Fry's visits to Newgate. What a blessed, happy
woman to do so much good; to be the means of
comfort and consolation, perhaps of salvation, to such
desolate souls! How I did honour and love what I
heard of her. Mrs. B—— said Mrs. Fry would be
delighted to take me with her some day when she went
to the prison. My mother laughingly said she was
afraid Mrs. Fry would convert me—surely not to
Quakerism. I do not think I need a new faith, but
power to act up to the one I profess. I need no
Quaker saint to tell me I do not do that.

[I had the great honour of accompanying Mrs. Fry

in one of her visits to Newgate, but from various
causes received rather a painful impression instead of
the very different one I had anticipated. Her divine
labour of love had become *famous*, and fine ladies of
fashion pressed eagerly to accompany her, or be
present at the Newgate exhortations. The unfortunate women she addressed were ranged opposite
their less excusable sister sinners of the better class,
and I hardly dared to look at them, so entirely did I
feel out of my place by the side of Mrs. Fry, and so sick
for their degraded attitude and position. If I had
been alone with them and their noble teacher I would
assuredly have gone and sat down amongst them.
On the day I was there a poor creature sat in the
midst of the congregation attired differently from all
the others, who was pointed out to me as being under
sentence of transportation for whatever crime she
committed. Altogether I felt broken-hearted for *them*
and ashamed for *us*.]

. My mother has had a letter from my father (he
was acting in the provinces), who says he has met
and shaken hands with Mr. Harris (his co-proprietor of
Covent Garden, and antagonist in our ruinous lawsuit
about it). I wonder what benefit is to be expected
from that operation with—such a person.

Sunday, June 5th. . . . On my return from afternoon
service found Mr. Walpole with my mother; they
amused me extremely by a conversation in which they
ran over, as far as their memories would stretch (near
sixty years), the various fashions and absurd modes
of dress which have prevailed during that period.
Toupees, fêtes, toques, bouffantes, hoops, bell hoops,

sacques, polonaises, levites, and all the parapher-
nalia of horsehair, powder, pomatum, and pins,
in the days when court beauties had their heads
dressed over-night for the next day's drawing-room,
and sat up in their chairs for fear of destroying the
edifice by lying down. No wonder they were obliged
to rouge themselves,—the days when once in a fortnight was considered often enough for ridding the hair
of its horrible paste of flour and grease. We are
certainly cleaner than our grandmothers, and much
more comfortable, though it is not so long since my
own head was dressed *à la giraffe*, in three bows
over pins half a foot high, so that I could not sit up-
right in the carriage without knocking against the top
of it. My mother's and Mr. Walpole's recollections
and descriptions were like seeing a set of historical
caricatures pass before one.

Monday, June 6th.—The house was very full at the
theatre this evening, and Miss C—— sent me round a
delicious fresh bouquet. I acted well, I think; the
play was "Romeo and Juliet." It is so very pleasant
to return to Shakespeare, after *reciting* Bianca and
Isabella, etc. I revelled in the glorious poetry and
the bright, throbbing *reality* of that Italian girl's existence; and yet Juliet is nothing like as nice as Portia,
—*nobody* is as nice as Portia. But the oftener I act
Juliet the oftener I think it ought never to be acted at
all, and the more absurd it seems to me to try to act
it. After the play my mother sent a note with the
carriage to say she would not go to the ball, so I
dressed myself and drove off with my father from the
theatre to the Countess de S——'s. At half-past

eleven the ball had not begun. Mrs. Norton was there in splendid beauty; at about half-past twelve the dancing began, and it was what is called a very fine ball. While I was dancing with Mr. C——, I saw my father talking to a handsome and very magnificent lady, who my partner told me was the Duchess of B——; after our quadrille, when I rejoined my father, he said to me, " Fanny, let me present you to——" here he mumbled something perfectly inaudible, and I made a curtsy, and the lady smiled sweetly and said some civil things and went away. " Whose name did you mention," said I to my father with some wickedness, "just now when you introduced me to that lady ? " " Nobody's, my dear, nobody's; I haven't the remotest idea who she is." " The Duchess of B——," said I, glibly, strong in the knowledge I had just acquired from my partner. " Bless my soul ! " cried the poor man, with a face of the most ludicrous dismay, "so it was ! I had quite forgotten her, though she was good enough to remember me, and here I have been talking cross questions and crooked answers to her for the last half-hour ! "

Was ever anything so terrible ! I feared my poor father would go home and remain awake all night, sobbing softly to himself, like the eldest of the nine Miss Simmonses in the ridiculous novel, because in her nervous flurry at a great dinner party she had refused instead of accepting a gentleman's offer to drink wine with her. Lady G—— then came up, whom he did remember, and who was " truly gracious;" and I left him consoled, and, I hope, having forgotten his dreadful duchess again. All the world, as the

saying is, was at this ball, and it certainly was a very
fine assembly. We danced in a splendid room hung
with tapestry—a magnificent apartment, though it
seemed to me incongruous for the purpose ; dim burning lights and flitting ghosts and gusts of wind and
distant footfalls and sepulchral voices being the proper
furniture of the " tapestried chamber," and not wax
candles, to the tune of sunlight and bright eyes and
dancing feet and rustling silks and gauzes and laughing voices, and all the shine and shimmer and flaunting
flutter of a modern ball. . . .

At half-past two, though the carriage had been
ordered at two, my father told me he would not " spoil
sport," and so angelically stayed till past four.   He is
the best of fathers, the most affectionate of parents,
the most benevolent of men !   There is a great difference between being chaperoned by one's father instead
of one's mother : the latter, poor dear ! never flirts, gets
very sleepy and tired, and wants to go home before she
comes ; the former flirts and talks with all the pretty,
pleasant women he meets, and does not care till what
hour in the morning—a frame of mind favourable to
much dancing for the *youngers*.   After all, I had to
come away in the middle of a delightful mazurka.

Tuesday, June 7th. . . . We had a very pleasant
dinner at Mr. Harness's.   Moore was there, but
Paganini was the chief subject discussed, and we
harped upon the one miraculous string he fiddles on
without pauses. . . . After dinner I read one of Miss
Mitford's hawthorny sketches out of " Our Village,"
which was lying on the table ; they always carry one
into fresh air and green fields, for which I am grateful
to them.

Wednesday, June 8th.—While I was writing to H—— my mother came in and told me that Mrs. Siddons was dead. I was not surprised; she has been ill, and gradually failing for so long. . . . I could not be much grieved for myself, for of course I had had but little intercourse with her, though she was always very kind to me when I saw her. . . . She died at eight o'clock this morning—peaceably, and without suffering, and in full consciousness. . . . I wonder if she is gone where Milton and Shakespeare are, to whose worship she was priestess all her life—whose thoughts were her familiar thoughts, whose words were her familiar words. I wonder how much more she is allowed to know of all things now than she did while she was here. As I looked up into the bright sky to-day, while my father and mother were sadly recalling the splendour of her day of beauty and great public power, I thought of the unlimited glory she perhaps now beheld, of the greater holiness and happiness I trust she now enjoys, and said in my heart, "It must be well to be as she is." I had never thought it must be well to be as she *was*. . . .

As soon as the news came my father went off to see what he could do for Cecilia, poor thing, and to bring her here, if she can be persuaded to leave Baker Street. He was not much shocked, though naturally deeply grieved by the event; my aunt has now been ill so long that any day might have brought the termination of the protracted process of her death. When he returned he said Cecilia was composed and quiet, but would not leave the house at present. I have written to Lady Francis to decline going to Oatlands, which we were to have done this week.

At dinner my father told me some of the arrangements he has made for the summer. We are to act at Bristol, Bath, Exeter, Plymouth, and Southampton. He then said, "Suppose we take steamer thence to Marseilles, and so on to Naples?" My heart jumped into my mouth at the thought; but how should I ever come back again? . . . Everything here is *so ugly*, even without comparison with that which is beautiful elsewhere; from Italy how should one come back to live in London?

Thursday, June 9th. . . . And so I am to act Lady Macbeth! I feel as if I were standing up by the great pyramid of Egypt to see how tall I am! However, it must be done; perhaps I may even do it less ill than Constance,—the greater intensity of the character may perhaps render majesty less *indispensable*. Power (if one had enough of it) might atone for insufficient dignity. Lady Macbeth made herself a queen by dint of wickedness; Constance was royal born—a radical difference, which ought to be in my favour. But dear, dear, dear, what a frightful undertaking for a poor girl, let her be never so wicked!

And *the* Lady Macbeth will never be seen again! I wish just now that in honour of my aunt the play might be forbidden to be performed for the next ten years. My father and myself have a holiday at the theatre—but only for the week—because of Mrs. Siddons's death, and we are to go down to Oatlands—nobody being there but ourselves, that is my brother and I—for the rest and quiet and fresh air of these few days.

Friday, June 10*th.*—Before three the carriage was announced, and we started for the country. We dropped Henry at Lord Waldegrave's and had a very pleasant drive, though the day was as various in its moods as if we were in April instead of June. We arrived at about six, and found Mr. C—— had been made an exception to the "positively nobody" who was to meet us. . . .

Saturday, June 11*th.*—Read the French piece called " Une Facete," which half killed me with crying. It is exceedingly clever, but altogether *too* true, in my opinion, for real art. It is not dramatic truth but absolute imitation of life, and instead of the mitigated emotion which a poetical representation of tragic events excites, it produces a sense of positive suffering too acutely painful for an artistic result; it is a perfectly prosaical reproduction of the familiar vice and its inseparable misery of modern everyday life ; it wants elevation and imagination—aerial perspective; it is close upon one, and must be agonizing to see well acted. My studies were certainly not of the most cheerful order, for after finishing this morbid anatomy of human hearts I read an article in the *Phrenological Journal* on Bouilland's " Anatomy of the Brain," which made me feel as if my brain was stuck full of pins and needles.

Perhaps a certain amount of experience must be attained through experiment, and if the wits of the human species are to be better understood, governed, and preserved by the results obtained by cutting and hacking the brains of living animals, *perhaps* some of our more immediate mercy is to be sacrificed to

our humanity in the lump; but if this is not the forbidden doing evil that good may come of it, I do not
know what is. One of the effects of Mr. Bouilland's
excruciating experiments on his victims was to turn
me already sick and give me an agonizing pain in *my*
brain. I hope their beneficial consequences did not
end there.

I did all this reading before breakfast, and when I
left my room it was still too early for any one to be
up, so I set off for a run in the park. The morning
was lovely, vivid, and bright, with soft shadows flitting
across the sky and chasing one another over the
sward, while a delicious fresh wind rustled the trees
and rippled the grass; and unable to resist the temptation, bonnetless as I was, I set off at the top of my
speed, running along the terrace, past the grotto, and
down a path where the syringa pelted me with showers
of mock orange blossoms, till I came under some
magnificent old cedars, through whose black, broad-
spread wings the morning sun shone, drawing their
great shadows on the sweet-smelling earth beneath
them, strewed with their russet-coloured shedding. I
thought it looked and smelt like a Russia leather
carpet. Then I came to the brink of the water, to a
little deserted fishing pavilion surrounded by a wilderness of bloom that was once a garden, and then I ran
home to breakfast. After breakfast I went over the
very same ground with Lady Francis, extremely demure, with my bonnet on my head and a parasol in
my hand, and the utmost propriety of decorous de-
meanour, and said never a word of my mad morning's
explorings. A girl's run and a young lady's walk are

very different things, and I hold both pleasant in their
way. The carriage was ordered to take my mother to
Addlestone to see poor old Mrs. Whitelock, and
during her absence Lady Francis and I repaired to
her own private sitting-room, and we entertained
each other with extracts from our respective journals.
I was struck with the high esteem she expressed for
Lord Carlisle; in one place in her journal she said she
wished she could hope her boys would grow up as
excellent men as he is, and this in spite of her party
politics, for she is a Tory and he a Whig, and she is
really a partisan politician. . . .

In the afternoon, after a charming meandering ride,
we determined to go to Monks Grove, the place Lady
Charlotte Greville has taken on St. Anne's Hill. . . .
In the evening we had terrifical ghost stories, which
held us fascinated till *one o'clock in the morning*.

> "The stories done, to bed they creep,
> By whispering winds soon lull'd asleep."

Sunday, June 12th. . . . It's nearly five years since
I said my prayers in that dear old little Weybridge
church. . . .

On our return, as the horses are never used on
Sunday, we went down to the water and got into the
boat. The day was lovely, and as we glided along the
bright water my mother and Lady Francis and I
murmured, half voice, all sorts of musical memories,
which made a nice accompaniment to Lord Francis'
occasional oar dip that just kept the boat in motion.
When we landed, my mother returned to the house,
and the rest of us set off for a long delightful stroll to

the farm, where I saw a monstrous and most beautiful
dog whom I should like to have hugged, but that he
looked so grave and wise it seemed like a liberty.
We walked on through a part of the park called
America, because of the magnificent rhododendrons
and azaleas and the general wildness of the whole.
The mass was so deep one's feet sank into it; the sun,
setting, threw low, slanting rays along the earth and
among the old tree trunks. It was a beautiful bit of
forest scenery; how like America I do not know.
Upon the race-course we emerged into a full, still
afternoon atmosphere of brilliant and soft splendour;
the whole park was flooded with sunshine, and little
creeks of light ran here and there into the woods we
had just left, touching with golden radiance a solitary
tree, and glancing into leafy nooks here and there,
while the mass of woodland was one deep shadow. . . .

Much discussion as to the possibilities and pro-
babilities of our being able to stay here another day.
When we came back from our afternoon ride at near
eight, found Mr. Greville and Lady Charlotte here,
and a letter from my father, saying that I could be
spared from my work at the theatre a little longer,
and promising to come down to us. . . . In the evening
Mr. C—— and I acted some of Racine's "Andro-
maque" for them; my old school part of Hermione
which I have not forgotten, and then two scenes from
Scribe's pretty piece of "*les premières Amours.*" He
acts French capitally, and moreover bestowed upon
me the two following ridiculous conundrum puns, for
which I shall be for ever grateful to him—

"Que font les Vaches à Paris?"

" Des Vaudevilles " (dès Veaux de Ville).

" Quelle est la sainte qui n'a pas lesoin de Jarretières ? "

Ste. Sébastienne " (ses bas se tiennent).

What absurd, funny stuff!

Tuesday, June 14th.—Gardening on the lawn—haymaking in the meadow—delightful ride in the afternoon, the beginning of which, however, was rather spoiled by some very disagreeable accounts Mr. C—— was giving us of Lord and Lady ——'s *ménage.* What might, could, would, or *should* a woman do in such a case ? Endure and endure till her heart broke, I suppose. Somehow I don't think a man would have the heart to *break* one's heart; but, to be sure, I don't know. . . .

We did not return home till near nine, and so, instead of dinner, all sat down to high tea, at which everybody was very cheerful and gay, and the talk very bright. . . .

I wish I could have painted my host and hostess this morning as they stood together on the lawn; she with her beautiful baby in her arms, her bright, fair forehead and eyes contrasting so strikingly with his fine, dark head. I never saw a more charming picture. (Landseer has produced one version of it in his famous " Return from Hawking.") Are not all such groups " Holy Families ? " They looked to me holy as well as handsome and happy. . . .

Wednesday, June 15th. . . . The races in the park were to begin at one, and we wished, of course, to keep clear of them and all the gay company ; so at twelve my mother and I got into the pony carriage, and drove

44

to Addlestone to my aunt Whitelock's pretty cottage
there. It rained spitefully all day, and the races and
all the fine racing folk were drenched. At about six
o'clock my father came from London, bringing me
letters ; the weather had brightened, and I took a long
stroll with him till time to dress for dinner. . . . In
the evening music and pleasant talk till one o'clock.

Thursday, June 16th.—At eight o'clock my mother
and I walked with my father to meet the coach, on the
top of which he left us for London. After breakfast
took my mother down to my "Cedar Hall," and established her there with her fishing, and then walked up
the hill to the great trees and amused myself with
bending down the big branches, and, seating myself on
them, let them spring up with me. Climbing trees, as
poor Combe would say, excites one's "wonder" and
one's "caution" very agreeably, and I like it. I
took Lord Francis' translation of "Henri Trois" back
to the "Cedar Hall," where my mother was still
watching her float. I was a good deal struck with it.
He has not finished the whole of the first act yet, but
there is one scene between the Duchess of Guise and
St. Megrin that I should think ought to be very
effective on the stage ; and I can imagine how charming Mdlle. Mars must have been in her sleep-walk-
ing gestures and intonations. The situation, which
is highly dramatic, is, I think, quite new ; I cannot
recollect any similar one in any other play. . . .

After lunch my mother, Lady Charlotte, and Mr.
Greville drove off to Monks Grove, and we followed
them on horseback ; it is a little paradise of a place,
with its sunny, smooth sloping lawns and bright,

sparkling piece of water, the masses of flowers
blossoming in profuse beauty, and the high, overhanging, sheltering woods of St. Anne's Hill rising behind
it. . . . On our way home much talk of Naples. I
might like to go there, no doubt; the question is how I
should like to come back to London after Naples, and
I think not at all. In the evening read the pretty
French piece of " Michel et Christine " which my
father had sent me.

Friday, June 17th. . . . My mother, Mr. C——,
and I drove together back to town; so good-bye,
Oatlands.

Monday, June 20th.—Went to rehearsal at half-past
ten for John Mason, who is to come out in Romeo to-
night; he had caught a dreadful cold and could hardly
speak, which was terribly provoking, poor fellow!
After my theatre rehearsal of " Romeo and Juliet "
drove to Bridgewater House to rehearse " Hernani."
In the evening the house was very good at Covent
Garden; I played well. John Mason was suffering
dreadfully from cold and hoarseness; the audience
were very good natured, however, and he got through
uncommonly well. My mother said I played " beautifully," which was saying much indeed for her. I
was delighted, especially as the Francis Levesons and
—— were all there.

Tuesday, June 21st.—Went to Bridgewater House
to rehearse. Charles Young was among our morning
audience; I was so glad to see him, for dear old
acquaintanceship. The king was going to the House
of Parliament, and Palace Yard was thronged with
people, and we sat round one of the Bridgewater

House windows to see the show. At about one the royal carriages set out—such lovely cream-coloured horses, with blue and silver trappings; such splendid, shining, coal-black ones, with coral-coloured trappings. The equipages looked like some enchanted present in a fairy story. The king—God bless him!—cannot, I should think, have been much annoyed by the clamorous greetings of his people. I'm afraid that ominous, sullen silence is a bad sign of the times. We rehearsed very steadily. Lord Francis, who is taking the old duke's part because of Mr. St. Aubin going abroad, is much improved by some teaching Young has bestowed upon him; but still he is by no means so good as Mr. St. Aubin was. . . .

Wednesday, 22nd.—Read "La Chronique de Charles Neuf," which is very clever, but the history of that period in France is so revolting that works of fiction founded upon it are as disagreeable as the history itself. Hogarth's pictures and Le Sage's novels are masterpieces, and yet admirable only as excellent representations of what in itself is odious. However, they are satirical works, and so have their *raison d'être*, which I do not think a serious novel about detestable times and people has. Drove to Bridgewater House, feeling so unwell that I could scarcely stand, and was obliged to lie down till I was called to go on the stage. We had a magnificent audience—all the grandeurs in England except the King. The Queen, the Duke and Duchess of Gloucester, the Duke and Duchess of Cumberland, Princess Elizabeth, Prince Leopold, the Duke of Brunswick. And lesser magnificoes the room full. Such very superior people

make a dull audience, of course; the presence of
royalty is always understood to bar applause, which is
not etiquette when a Majesty is by. I played very ill;
my voice was quite unmanageable, and broke twice, to
my extreme dismay. The fact is, I am fagged *half* to
death; but as I cannot give up my work and cannot
bear to give up my play, the only wonder is that I am
not fagged *whole* to death.   Mr. Craven acted really
capitally, and I wondered how he could.   They put us
out terribly in one scene by forgetting the bench on
which I have to sit down.   Hernani managed with
great presence of mind and cleverness in its absence,
but it spoilt our prettiest picture.   After the play
Lady Francis came to fetch me to be presented to the
Queen; her Majesty was most gracious in her reception of me, and so were the Princess Elizabeth and
the Duke of Gloucester, who came and had quite a
long chat with me.   When I had received my dismissal
from her Majesty I ran to disrobe, and returned to
join the crowd in the drawing-room. . . . When they
were all gone we adjourned to Lady Gower's—a most
magnificent supper, which *we* enjoyed in the perfection
of comfort, in a small boudoir opening into and commanding the whole length of the supper saloon.   Our
snuggery just held my mother, Lady Francis, myself,
Charles Greville, and three of our *corps dramatique*,
and we not only enjoyed a full view of the royal table,
but what was infinitely amusing, poor Lord Francis'
disconsolate countenance, which half killed us with
laughing.   Supper done, we all proceeded downstairs
to see the Royalty depart, and looked at a fine picture
of Lawrence's of that handsome creature, Lord Clan-

william.   Took leave of my friends for some months, I am sorry to say; took Mr. —— home in our carriage and set him down just at day-dawn. It was past four o'clock before I saw my bed; and the life I am leading is really enough to kill any one.

Thursday, June 23*rd.*—Quite unwell, and in bed all day. Mrs. Jameson came and sat with me some time. We talked of marriage, and a woman's chance of happiness in giving her life into another's keeping. I said I thought if one did not expect too much one might secure a reasonably fair amount of happiness, though of course the risk one ran was immense. I never shall forget the expression of her face; it was momentary, and passed away almost immediately, but it has haunted me ever since.

Great Russell Street.

DEAR LADY DACRE,

      I am commissioned by my mother to request your kind permission to bring my brother to your evening party on Saturday; she hopes you will have no scruple in refusing this request, if for any reason you would rather not comply with it. . . .

I have been thinking much about what you said to me both *viva. voce* and in your note upon that "obnoxious word" in my play. Let me entreat you to put aside conventional regards of age and sex, which have nothing to do with works of art or literature, and view the subject without any of those considerations, which have their own proper domain, doubtless—although I think you have in this instance admitted their jurisdiction out of it. . . . I hope as

long as I live that I shall never write anything offen-
sive to decency or morality, or their pure source,
religion; and I hope in my own manners and conversation always to preserve the decorum prescribed by
society, good taste, and good feeling; but as a dramatic
writer, supposing I am ever to be one, I shall have to
depict men as well as women, coarse and common
men as well as refined and courtly ones, and all and
each, if I fulfil my task, must speak the language that
their nature under their several circumstances points
out as individually appropriate. But I forget that I
am addressing one far better able than I am to say
what belongs to all questions of poetry and art. Forgive
me, my dear Lady Dacre, and allow me to add that,
as when I put my play into your hands I told you
that should you find it too intolerably dull and bad I
would release you from your kind promise of accepting
its dedication to yourself, I can only repeat my
readiness to do so if upon any other ground whatever
you feel reluctant to grace my title-page with your
name. Pray tell me so without hesitation, as I had
rather forego that honour than owe it to your courtesy
without your entire good will.

In any event pray accept my best acknowledgments
for your kindness, and believe me always

Your very truly obliged

F. A. K.

This letter was written in answer to some strictures
of Lady Dacre's on what appeared to her coarseness
of language in my play of "The Star of Seville,"
which she thought unbecoming a "young lady." If I

remember rightly, too, she said that the introduction
of a scene in a bedchamber might be deemed objectionable.   I had asked her permission to dedicate the play
to her, which she had granted; and though she failed
to convince me that a young-lady element had any
business whatever in a play, she very kindly allowed
her name to adorn the title-page of my *un*-young
ladylike drama.

   Soon after this my father and aunt and myself left
London for our summer tour in the provinces, which
we began at Bristol.

   Monday, July 4th, Bristol.—The play was "Romeo
and Juliet," and the nurse was a perfect farce in
herself; she really was worth any money, and her
soliloquy when she found me "up and dressed and
down again," very nearly made me scream with
laughter in the middle of my trance.   Indeed, the
whole play was probably considered an "improved
version" of Shakespeare's Veronese story, both in the
force and delicacy of the text.   Sundry wicked words
and coarse appellations were decorously dispensed
with ; many fine passages received judicious additions ;
not a few were equally judiciously omitted altogether.
What a shocking hash !

   Tuesday, July 5th.—After breakfast we sallied forth
to the market, to my infinite delight and amusement.
It is most beautifully clean; the fruit and vegetables
look so pretty, and smell so sweet, and give such an
idea of plentiful abundance, that it is delightful to
walk about among them.   Even the meat, which I
am generally exceedingly averse to go near, was so

beautifully and nicely arranged that it had none of
its usual repulsiveness; and the sight of the whole
place, and the quaint-looking rustic people, was so
pleasantly envious. We stopped to gossip with a
bewitching old country dame, whose market stock
might have sat, with her in the middle of it, for its
picture; the veal and poultry so white and delicate-
looking, the bacon like striped pink and white ribbons,
the butter so golden, fresh, and sweet, in a great basket
trimmed round with bunches of white jasmine, the
green leaves and starry blossoms and exquisite per-
fume making one believe that butter ought always to
be served, not in a "lordly dish," but in a bower of
jasmine. The good lady told us she had just come
up from "the farm," and that the next time she came
she would bring us some home-made bread, and that
she was going back to brew and to bake. She looked
so tidy and *rural*, and her various avocations sounded
so pleasant as she spoke of them, that I felt greatly
tempted to beg her to let me go with her to "the
farm," which I am sure must be an enchanting place,
neat and pretty, and flowery and comfortable, and full
of rustic picturesqueness; and *while the sun shone*, I
think I should like a female farmer's life amazingly.
Went to the theatre and rehearsed "Venice Preserved," which is an entirely different kind of thing.
Charles Mason dined with us. After dinner I finished
reading Miss Ferrier's novel of "Destiny," which I
like very much; besides being very clever, it leaves a
pleasant taste in one's mind's mouth. Went to the
theatre at six; the play was "Venice Preserved," and
I certainly have seldom seen a more shameful

exhibition. In the first place C—— did not even
know his words, and that was bad enough ; but when
he was out, instead of coming to a stop decently, and
finishing at least with his cue, he went on extem-
porizing line after line, and speech after speech, of
his own, by way of mending matters. I think I never
saw such a performance. He stamps and bellows low
down in his throat like an ill-suppressed bull ; he
rolls his eyes till I feel as if they were flying out of
their sockets at me, and I must try and catch them.
He quivers and quavers in his speech, and pulls and
wrenches me so inhumanly, that what with inward
laughter and extreme rage and pain, I was really all
but dead in earnest at the end of the play. I acted
very ill myself till the last scene, when my Jaffier,
having been done justice to by the Venetian Government, I was able to do justice to myself, and having
gone mad, and no wonder, died rather better than I
had lived through the piece.

July 6th, Bristol.—Walked out to order the horses,
and afterwards went on to look at the Abbey Church.
We examined one or two interesting old monuments ;
but were obliged to curtail our explorings, as the
doors were about to be closed. We have been talking
much lately of a remote possibility of going to America ;
and as I left this old brown pile to-day, it seemed to
me curious to think of a country which has no
cathedrals, no monuments of the Old Faith. How
venerable, in spite of its superstitions and abuses ; for
its long undisputed sway over all civilized lands ; for
the great and good men who honoured it by their lives
and works—the religion of Augustine, of Bruno,

Benedict, Francis d'Assisi, Francis de Sales, Fenelon,
and how many more—the Christianity of Europe in
its feudal, chivalrous times, those days of noble, good,
as well as fierce, evil deeds and lives, the faith that
kings and warriors bowed to when sovereignty was
absolute and military power supreme. America has
no grey abbeys, no ruined cloisters, to tell of monastic
brotherhoods — the preserves of ancient historic
chronicles, the guardians of the early wells and
springs of classic learning and genius. In America
there are no great, old, time-stained, weather-beaten,
ivy-mantled churches full of tombs, such as we saw
to-day, with curious carvings and quaint effigies, and
where the early rulers of the land embraced the faith
and received the baptism of Christ. That must be a
very strange country. But they have Plymouth Rock,
on the shore where the Protestant Pilgrims landed.

The horses having come to the door, we set off for our
ride ; our steeds were but indifferent hacks, but the
road was charming, and the evening serene and pure,
and I was with my father, a circumstance of enjoyment to me always. The characteristic feature of the
scenery of this region is the vivid, deep-toned foliage
of the hanging woods, through whose dense tufts of
green, masses of grey rock and long *scars* of warm-
coloured red-brown earth appear every now and then
with the most striking effect. The deep-sunk river
wound itself drowsily to a silver thread at the base of
steep cliffs, to the summit of which we climbed,
reaching a fine level land of open downs carpeted with
close, elastic turf. On we rode, up hill and down
dale, through shady lanes full of the smell of lime-

blossom, skirting meadows fragrant with the ripe
mellow hay and honey-sweet clover, and then between
plantations of aromatic, spicy fir and pine, all exhaling
their perfumes under the influence of the warm
sunset. At last we made a halt, where the road,
winding through Lord de Clifford's property, com-
manded an enchanting view. On our right, rolling
ground rising gradually into hills, clothed to their
summits with flourishing evergreens, firs, larches,
laurel, arbutus—a charming variety in the monotony of
green. On the farthest of these heights Blaise Castle,
with two grey towers, well defined against the sky,
looked from its bosky eminence over the whole
domain, which spread on our left in sloping lawns,
where single oaks and elms of noble size threw their
shadows on the sunlit sward, which looked as if none
but fairies' feet had ever pressed it. Beyond this,
through breaks and frames, and arches made by the
trees, the broad Severn glittered in the wavy light.
It was a beautiful landscape in every direction. We
returned home by sea wall and the shore of the
Severn, which seemed rather bare and bleak after the
soft loveliness we had just left. . . .

Thursday, July 7th.—Went to the theatre to rehearse
" The Gamester." In the afternoon strolled down to
the river with my father and Dall. We took boat
and rowed towards the cliffs. Our time, however, was
limited ; and just as we reached the loveliest part of
the river, we were obliged to turn home again. . . .
At dinner, as we were talking about America, and I
was expressing my disinclination ever to go thither,
my father said: " If my cause (our Chancery suit)

goes ill before the Lords, I think the best thing I can
do will be to take ship from Liverpool and sail to the
United States." I choked a little at this, but presently
found voice to say, "Ebben son pronta;" but he
replied, "No, that he should go alone." That you
never should, my own dear father! . . . But I do
hate the very thought of America.

Saturday, July 9th. . . . In the afternoon drove out
in an open carriage with Dall to Shirehampton, by the
same road my father and I took in our ride the other
day.

Bristol, July 10th, 1831.

MY DEAR MRS. JAMESON,
            I can neither bid you confirm nor deny any
"*reports* you may hear," for I am in utter ignorance,
I am happy to say, of the world's surmisings on my
behalf, and had indeed supposed that my time for
being honoured by its notice in any way was pretty
well past and over.

I am glad you are having rest, as you speak of it
with the enjoyment which those alone who work hard
are entitled to. I trust, too, that in the instance of
your eyes no news is good news, for you say nothing
of them, and I therefore like to hope that they have
suffered you to forget them.

I'm disappointed about your Shakespeare book. I
should like to have had it by my next birthday, which
is the 27th of November, and to which I look forward
with unusually mingled feelings. However, it cannot
be helped; and I have no doubt the booksellers are
right in point of fact, for we are embarked on board

too troublous times to carry mere *passe temps* literature
with us. "We must have bloody noses and cracked
crowns," I am afraid, and shall find small public
taste or leisure for *polite letters*.

I like this place very well; it is very quiet, and my
life is always a happy one with my father. He always
spoils me, and that is always pleasant, you know.

The Bristol people are rather in a bad state just
now for our purposes, for trade here is in a very
unprosperous condition; and the recent failure of
many of their great mercantile houses does no good
to our theatrical ones. The audiences are very
pleasant, however, and the company by no means
bad. We are here another week, and then take ship
for Ilfracombe, and thence by land to Exeter; after
that Plymouth and Southampton. . . . I wish I could
be in London for " Anna Bolena." I cannot adequately
express my admiration for Madame Pasta; I saw her
in Desdemona the Saturday night on which I scrawled
those few lines to you. I think if you knew how
every look and tone and gesture of hers affects me,
you would be satisfied. She is almost equal to an
imagination; more than that I cannot say. If you
rate " imagination " as I think you must, I need say
nothing more. We shall certainly be back in London
by the end of September, if not before. In the mean
time believe me ever yours most truly,

F. A. K.

Sunday, July 10*th.*—My father wickedly *dawdled*
about till we were nearly late for church, and had to
scamper along the quays and up the steep street, to poor

dear Dall's infinite discomfiture, who grumbled and
puffed, and shuffled and shambled along, while I
plunged on, breathlessly ejaculating, "It is so hateful
to be late for church!" The cathedral (which I
believe it is not) was quite full, but we obtained seats
in the organ gallery, where we could not hear very well,
but had a very fine view of the *coup d'œil* presented
by the choir and church below us. The numerous and
many-coloured congregation, the white surpliced
choristers, the charity school children in their uniforms
surrounding the altar, all framed in by the dark old
oak screens with their quaint readings, and partially
vividly illuminated by occasional gleams of strong
sunlight which poured suddenly through the coloured
windows, presented a beautiful picture. The service
was very well performed : the organ is a remarkably
good one, and one or two of the boys' voices were
exquisitely soft and clear. It is a fine service, and
yet I do not like it by way of religious worship. It
does not make me devout, in the proper form of the
term ; it appeals too much to my senses and my
imagination ; it is religion *set* to music and painting,
and artistic religion does not suit me. The incessant
passing of people through the church, too, disturbs
one, and gives an unpleasant air of irreverence to the
whole. . . . I think I might like to go to a cathedral for
afternoon service, much as I like to spend my Sunday
leisure in reading Milton, though I should not be
satisfied to make my whole devotional *exercises* consist
in reading "Paradise Lost." A wretchedly weak,
poor sermon ; how strange that such a theme should
inspire nothing better than such a discourse ! How-

ever, I suppose this sort of ministering is the inevitable result of a " ministry " embraced merely as a
means of subsistence.   No one could paint pictures or
compose music, *only* because they wanted bread, so I
do not see why any one should preach sermons fit to
be heard, only because they want bread.   If I was a
despot, I would suppress hebdomadal writing of
sermons, and people should be *forbidden* instead of
bidden to talk nonsense upon sacred subjects.

Monday, 11*th.*—At night the theatre was very full,
and the audience pleasant.   During supper my father,
Charles Mason, and I had a long discussion about
Kean.   I cannot help thinking my father wrong about
him.   Kean *is* a man of decided genius, no matter
how he neglects or abuses nature's good gift.   He has
it.   He has the first element of all greatness—power.
No taste, perhaps, and no industry, perhaps; but let
his deficiencies be what they may, his faults however
obvious, his conceptions however erroneous, and his
characters, each considered as a whole, however imperfect, he has the one atoning faculty that compensates
for everything else, that seizes, rivets, electrifies all
who see and hear him, and stirs down to their
very springs the passionate elements of our nature.
Genius alone can do this.

As an actor, one whose efforts are the result of
study, of mental research, reflection, and combination ;
as an intellectual anatomist, whose knowledge must
dissect, and then re-form and reproduce again in
beauty and harmony the image he has taken to pieces ;
as an artist, who is bound to conceal both the first
and last processes, the dismembering of the parts

and the re-uniting them in a whole, and whose business is to make the most deliberate mental labour and the most studied personal effects appear the spontaneous result of unpremeditated passion and emotion (feigned passion and emotion, which are to appear real),—in capacity for all this Kean may be defective. He may not be an actor, he may not be an artist, but he *is* a man of genius, and instinctively with a word, a look, a gesture, tears away the veil from the heart of our common humanity, and lays it bare as it beats in every human heart, and as it throbs in his own. Kean speaks with his whole living frame to us, and every fibre of ours answers his appeal.

I do not know that I ever saw him in any character which impressed me as a *whole work of art;* he never seems to me to intend to be any one of his parts, but I think he intends that all his parts should be *him.* So it is not Othello who is driven frantic by doubt and jealousy, nor Shylock who is buying human flesh by its weight in gold, nor Sir Giles Overreach who is selling his child to hell for a few years of wealth and power; it is Kean, and in every one of his characters there is an intense personality of his *own* that, while one is under its influence, defies all criticism— moments of such overpowering passion, accents of such tremendous power, looks and gestures of such thrilling, piercing meaning, that the excellence of those *parts* of his performances more than atones for the want of greater unity in conception and smooth- ness in the entire execution of them.

The discussion about Kean led naturally to some talk about his most famous parts, particularly Shy-
45

lock.   My father's conception of Shylock seems to me
less the right one than Kean's; but then, if my father
took what *I* think the right view of the part, he would
have to give up acting it.   The real Shylock—that is,
Shakespeare's—is a creature totally opposite in his
whole organization, physical and mental, to my
father's; and as my father cannot force his nature in
any particular into uniformity with that of Shylock,
he endeavours to persuade himself that the theory by
which he tries to bring it into harmony with his
individuality, and within the compass of his powers,
is the right one; but I think him entirely mistaken
about it.   Kean did with the part exactly what my
father wants to do—adapted his conceptions to his
means of execution; but Kean's physical constitution
was much better suited to express Shylock as
Shylock should be expressed than my father's.   My
father attempts to make Shylock "poetical" (in the
superficial sense), because that is the bias of his own
mind in matters of art.   Classical purity and refinement of taste are his specialties as an actor, and
neither power nor intensity.

Shylock's master passion is not revenge, which is
a savage, but avarice, which is a sordid motive.   His
hatred is inspired more by defeated hope of gain and
positive losses and threatened ventures, than by the
personal insults and contumely he has received.

Avarice is an absolutely base passion, and a grand
poetical character cannot consistently be raised upon
such a foundation, nor can a nature be at once grovelling and majestic.   Besides, Shakespeare has not
made Shylock "poetical."   The concentrated venom

of his passion is prosaic in its vehement utterance—
close, concise, vigorous, logical, but not imaginative;
and in the scenes where his evil nature escapes the
web of his cunning caution, and he is stung to fury
by his complicated losses, there is intense passion but
no elevation in his language.

There is a vein of humour in Shylock. A grim,
bitter, sardonic flavour pervades the part, that blends
naturally with the sordid thrift and shrewd, watchful,
eager vigilance of the miser. It infuses a terrible
grotesqueness into his rage, and curdles one's blood
in the piercing, keen irony of his mocking humility to
Antonio, and adds poignancy to the ferocity of his
hideous revenge.   This Kean rendered admirably, and
in this my father entirely fails, but it is an important
element of the character.

My father is hard upon Kean's defects because
they are especially antagonistic to his artistic taste
and tendency, but I think, too, there is a slight
infusion of the vexation of unappreciated labour in
my father's criticism of Kean. He forgets that power
is universally felt and understood, and refinement
seldom the one or the other, and for a thousand who
applaud Kean's " What, wouldst thou have a serpent
sting thee twice ? " probably not ten people are aware
of his exquisite "nevertheless" in the reading of
Antonio's letter. Most eyes can " see a church by
daylight ; " not many stop to look at the lights and
shadows that are for ever varying and adding to the
beauty of its aspect. I wonder how, being as well
aware as my father is of all the fine work that escapes
the eyes of the public, he can care for this kind of
thing as he does.

Tuesday, 12*th*.—We are having events at the theatre, and not of a pleasant sort. Mr. Brunton, the manager, is in "difficulties" (civilized plural for debt), and it seems that last night during the play one of his creditors put an execution into the theatre, and laid violent hands upon the receipts, which, as it was my father's benefit, rather dismayed us. So after breakfast this morning, having put out my dresses for my favourite Portia for to-night, I went to the theatre to ascertain if there was to be a rehearsal or not. My father had gone in search of Mr. Brunton to see how matters could be arranged, and at all events to represent that we could not go on acting unless our money was secured to us. Charles Mason, Dall, and I in the mean time found the poor actors in the theatre very much at a loss how to proceed, as it seemed extremely doubtful whether there would be any performance; so we returned home, where we found my father, who said that at all events there must be a rehearsal, for it was absolutely necessary if we did act to-night, and could do us no harm if we did not, so we repaired again to the theatre, where the scattered and scared *corps dramatique* having been got together again, we proceeded to business.

Wednesday, 18*th*.—Mr. K—— called and told us that some arrangement had been made with the truculent creditor of our poor manager by which *we* shall not lose any more in this unlucky business. My father will be quit for about a hundred pounds. I am very sorry for Mr. Brunton, but he should not have placed us in such an uncomfortable position. My father has offered to act one night beyond our

engagement for the sake, if possible, of making up to
the actors the arrears of salary Mr. Brunton owes
them.   They are all poor, hard-working people,
earning no more than the means of subsistence,
and this withholding of their due falls very heavily
on them.

   Thursday, 14*th.* . . . At the theatre the house was
very good, and the audience very pleasant.   The play
was " The Provoked Husband," and I'm sure I play
his provoking wife badly enough to provoke anybody ;
but she's not a person to my mind, which is an
artistic view of the case.

   [My modes of dealing with my professional duties
at this very unripe stage of my career irresistibly
remind me of a not very highly educated female
painter who had taken it into her head to make an
historical picture of Cleopatra.   Sending to a friend
for a few "references" upon the subject of that im-
perial gipsy's character and career, she sent them
hastily back, saying she had relinquished her purpose,
" having really no idea Cleopatra was that sort of
person."]

   Friday, July 15*th.*—Miserrima ! I have broken a
looking-glass ! and on Friday, too ! What *do* I think
will happen to me ! Had a long talk this morning
with dear Dall about my dislike to the stage. I do
not think it is the acting itself that is so disagreeable
to me, but the public personal exhibition, the violence
done (as it seems to me) to womanly dignity and
decorum in thus becoming the gaze of every eye and
theme of every tongue.   If my audience was reduced
to my intimates and associates I should not mind

it so much, I think; but I am not quite sure that I should like it then.

At the theatre the house was very full, and the audience particularly amiable. In the interval between the fourth and fifth act Charles Mason made a speech to them, informing them of Mr. Brunton's distress, and our intention of acting for him on Monday. They applauded very much, and I hope they will do more, and come. My part of the charity is certainly not small; to be pulled and pushed and dragged hither and thither, and generally " knocked about," as the miserable Belvidera, for three mortal hours, is a sacrifice of self which my conscience bears me witness is laudable. I would much rather pay with my purse than my person in this case. Unfortunately, je n'ai pas de quoi.

Sunday, July 17*th.*—To Redcliffe Church with my father and Dall. What a beautiful old building it is ! . . . What a sermon ! Has the truth, as our Church holds it, no fitter expounders than such a preacher ? Are these its stays, props, and pillars— teachers to guide, enlighten, and instruct people as cultivated and intelligent as the people of this country on the most momentous of all subjects ? Are these the sort of adversaries to oppose to men like Channing ? As for not going to church because of bad or foolish sermons, that is quite another matter, though I not unfrequently hear that reason assigned for staying away. One goes to church to say one's prayers, and not to hear more or less fine discourses; one goes because it is one's duty, and a delight and comfort, and a quite distinct duty and delight from that of

private prayer. A good sermon, Heaven knows, is a
rare blessing to be thankful for, but if one went to
church only in the expectation of that blessing, one
might stay away most Sundays in the year.

[My youthful scorn of "poor preaching" reminds
me of what I once heard Edward Everett say, who,
before becoming his country's "Minister," in the
diplomatic sense of the word, had been a powerful
and eloquent Unitarian preacher : "I hear a good
deal of criticism upon sermons which are supposed
to be religious or moral exhortations, not intellectual
exercises. I dare say many sermons are not *first rate*,
but moderate good preaching is not a bad thing, and
pretty poor preaching is better than most men's
practice."]

Monday, July 18*th.*—The theatre was crowded to-
night, which delighted me. It is pleasant to see
malicious and evil actions produce such a result. I
was very nervous and excited, and nearly went into
hysterics over one small incident of the evening.
At the close of the first separation scene—the play
was "Venice Preserved"—when Jaffier is carried out
by the nape of the neck by Pierre, and Belvidera
extracted on the other side in the arms (and iron
ones they were) of Bedamar, the audience of course
were affected, harrowed, overcome by the poignant
pathos of the situation. Charles looked woe-begone. I
called upon him in tones of the most piercing anguish
(an agony not entirely feigned, as my bruises can
bear witness). The curtain descended slowly amidst
sympathetic sobs and silence—the musicians themselves, deeply moved, no doubt, with the sorrows of the

scene, mournfully resumed their fiddles, and struck
up " ti *ti* tum *tiddle* un *ti* tum *ti* "—the jolliest jig you
ever heard. The bathos was irresistible ; we behind the
scenes, the principal sufferers (perhaps) in the night's
performance, were instantly comforted, and all but
shouted with laughter. I hope the audience were
equally revived by this grotesque sudden cheering of
their spirits. After the tragedy a Bristolian Paganini
performed a concerto on one string. Dall declares that
the whole orchestra played the whole time—but some
sounds reached me in my dressing-room that were
decidedly *unique* more ways than one, not at all unlike
our favourite French fantasia—" Complainte d'un
cochon au lait qui rêve." But the audience were trans-
ported ; they clapped and the fiddle squeaked, they
shouted and the fiddle squealed, they hurraed and the
fiddle uttered three terrific screams, and it was over
and Paganini is done for—here, at any rate. He
need never show face or fiddle here ; he hasn't a string
(even one) left to his bow in Bristol. " So Orpheus
fiddled," etc.

Tuesday, July 19*th.*—Dinner-party at the —— which
ought to have been chronicled by Jane Austen. I sat
by a gentleman who talked to me of the hanging
gardens of Semiramis and what might have been
cultivated therein (hemp perhaps), then of the deriva-
tion of languages—he still kept among roots—and
finally of *tea*, which he told me he was endeavouring
to grow on the Welsh mountains. Some of the table-
talk deserved printing *verbatim*, only it was almost
too good to be true, or at any rate believed.

Wednesday, July 20*th.*—Charles Mason came after

breakfast, and told us that there was some chance of
poor Mr. Brunton's getting out of prison (into which
his creditor has thrust him), for that the latter had
been so universally scouted for his harsh proceeding
that he probably would be shamed into liberating
him.

We shall not leave Bristol to-day. The wind is contrary and the weather quite unfavourable for a party
of pleasure, which our trip by sea to Ilfracombe was
to be. It's very disagreeable living half in one's trunks
and travelling-bags, as this sort of uncertainty compels
one to do. I studied Dante, wrote verses and
sketched, and tried to be busy; but a defeated
departure leaves one's mind and thoughts only half
unpacked, and I felt idle and unsettled, though I
worked at " The Star of Seville " till dinner time.

After dinner I studied politics in the *Examiner* and
read an article on Cobbett, which made me laugh, and
the motto to which might have been " Malvolio, thou
art sick of self-conceit.". . .

Thursday, July 21st.—At dinner a discussion, suggested by Mr. D——'s conduct to Mr. Brunton, on
the subject of returning evil for evil, and the difficulty
of not doing so, if not deliberately and in deed, upon
impulse and by thought. Nothing is easier in such
matters than to say what one would do, and nothing,
I suppose, more difficult than to do what one should
do. So God keep us all from convenient opportunities
of revenging ourselves. . . .

[Occasionally one hears in the streets voices in
which the making of a fortune lies, and when one
remembers what fortunes some voices have com-

manded, it seems bitterly cruel to think of such a
possession begging its bread for want of the chance
that might have made it available by culture. A
woman, some years ago, used to sing at night in the
neighbourhood of St. James's Street, whose voice was
so exquisite, so powerful, sweet, and thrilling, a mezzo
soprano of such pure tone and vibrating quality, that
Lady Essex, my sister, and myself at different times,
struck by the woman's magnificent gift and miserable
position, had her into our houses, to hear her sing
and see if nothing could be done to give her the full
use of her noble natural endowment. She was a plain
young woman of about thirty, tolerably decently
dressed, and with a quiet, simple manner. She said
her husband was a house paperer in a small way,
and when he was out of employment she used to go
out in the evening and see what her singing would
bring her. Poor thing! it was impossible to do anything for her; she was too old to learn or unlearn anything. No training could have corrected the low
cockney vulgarity and coarse, ignorant indistinctness
and incorrectness of her enunciation. And so in after
years, as I returned repeatedly to England, after longer
or shorter intervals of time, and always inhabited the
same neighbourhood in London, I still continued to
hear, on dark drizzly evenings (and never without
a thrill of poignant pain and pity) this angel's voice
wandering in the muddy streets, its perfect, round,
smooth edge becoming by degrees blunted and broken,
its tones rough and coarse and harsh, some of the
notes fading into feeble indistinctness—the fine, bold,
true intonation hiding its tremulous uncertainty in

trills and quavers, alternating with pitiful husky coughing, while every now and then one or two lovely, rich, pathetic notes, surviving ruin, recalled the early sweetness and power of the original instrument. The idea of what that woman's voice might have been to her used to haunt me.

It was hearing Rachel singing (barefoot) in the streets of Paris that Jules Janin's attention was first excited by her. Her singing, as I heard it on the stage in the drinking song of the extraordinary piece called "Valeria," in which she played two parts, was really nothing more than a chanting in the deep contralto of her speaking voice, and could hardly pass for a musical performance at all, any more than her wonderful uttering of the "Marseillaise," with which she made the women's blood run cold, and the men's hair stand on end, and everybody's flesh creep.

My sister and I used often to plan an expedition of street-singing for the purpose of seeing how much we could collect in that way for some charity. We were to put ourselves in "poor and mean attire"—I do not know that we were to "smirch our faces" with brown paint; we thought large battered poke-bonnets would answer the purpose, and, thus disguised, we were to go the rounds of the club windows, my father walking at a discreet distance for our protection on one side of the street, and our formidable pirate friend Trelawney on the other. We never carried out this project, though I have no doubt it would have brought us a very pretty penny for any endowment we might have wished to make.]

Friday, July 22nd.—Long and edifying talk with

dear Dall upon my prospects in marrying. " While
you remain single," says she, " and choose to work,
your fortune is an independent and ample one; as soon
as you marry, there's no such thing. Your position
in society," says she, " is both a pleasanter and more
distinguished one than your birth or real station en-
titles you to ; but that also is the result of your professional exertions, and might, and probably would, alter
for the worse if you left the stage; for, after all, it is mere
frivolous fashionable popularity." I ought to have got
up and made her a curtsy for that. So that it seems
I have fortune and fame (such as it is)—positive real
advantages, which I cannot give with myself, and
which I cease to own when I give myself away, which
certainly makes my marrying any one or any one
marrying me rather a solemn consideration; for I
lose everything, and my marryee gains nothing in a
worldly point of view—says she—and it's incontro-
vertible and not pleasant. So I took up Dante, and
read about devils boiled in pitch, which refreshed my
imagination and cheered my spirits very much.

[How far my ingenious mind was from foreseeing
the days when men of high rank and social station
would marry singers, dancers, and actresses, and be
condescending enough to let their wives continue to
earn their bread by public exhibition, and even to appropriate the proceeds of their theatrical labours ! I
have not yet made up my mind whether, in these
cases, the *gentleman* ought not to take his wife's name
in private, as a compensation for her not taking his in
public. Poor Miss Paton's noble husband was the
only Englishman, that I know of, who committed that

act of self-effacement. To go much further back in
dramatic and social history, the old, accomplished,
mad Earl of Peterborough married the famous singer
Anastasia Robinson, and refused to acknowledge the
fact till her death. To be sure, this was a more
cowardly, but a less dirty meanness. He withheld
his name from her, but did not take her money.]

It is settled now that we go to Exeter by coach, and
now that we have given up our pretty sea trip to
Ilfracombe, the weather has become lovely—perverse
creature!—but I am glad we are going away in every
way.

Saturday, Bristol, July 23rd. . . . We started at eight,
and taking the whole coach to ourselves as we do, I
think travelling by a public conveyance the best mode
of getting over the road. They run so rapidly ; there
is so little time lost, and so much trouble with one's
luggage saved. The morning was grey and soft and
promised a fine day, but broke its promise at the end
of our second stage, and began to pelt with rain, which
it continued to do the live-long blessed day. We
could see, however, that the country we were passing
through was charming. One or two of the cottages
by the roadside, half-smothered in vine and honeysuckle, reminded me of Lady Juliana,* who, when
she said she could live in a desert with her lover,
thought that it was a " sort of place full of roses."
. . . These labourers' cottages were certainly the
poor dwellings of very poor people, but there was
nothing unsightly, repulsive, or squalid about them—
on the contrary, a look of order, of tidy neatness about

* In Miss Ferrier's novel, " Marriage."

the little houses, that added the peculiarly English
element of comfort and cleanliness to the picturesqueness of their fragrant festoons of flowery drapery, hung
over them by the sweet season. The little plots of
flower garden one mass of rich colour; the tiny strip
of kitchen garden, well stocked and trimly kept, beside
it; the thriving fruitful orchard stretching round the
whole; and beyond, the rich cultivated land rolling its
waving corn-fields, already tawny and sunburnt, in
mellow contrast with the smooth green pasturages,
with their deep-shadowed trees and bordering lines of
ivied hawthorn hedgerows, marking boundary lines of
division without marring the general prospect—a
lovely landscape that sang aloud of plenty, industry,
and thrift. I wonder if any country is more blessed
of God than this precious little England ? I think it is
like one of its own fair, nobly blooming, vigorous
women ; her temper—that's the climate—not perfection, to be sure (but, after all, the old praise of it is
true; it admits of more constant and regular out-of-door
exercise than any other); the religion it professes,
pure ; the morality it practises, pure, probably by
comparison with that of other powerful and wealthy
nations. Oh, I trust that neither reform nor its
extreme, revolution, will have power to injure this
healthily, heartily constituted land. . . .

Exeter, July 24th, 1831.

DEAREST H——,

          We arrived here last night, or rather even-
ing, at half-past six o'clock, and I found your letter,
which having waited for me, shall not wait for my
answer. . . .

Thank you for John's translation of the German
song, the original of which I know and like very much.
The thoughts it suggested to you must constantly arise
in all of us. I believe that in these matters I feel all
that you do, but not with the same intensity. To
adore is most natural to the mind contemplating
beauty, might, and majesty beyond its own powers;
to implore is most natural to the heart oppressed with
suffering, or agitated with hopes that it cannot accomplish, or fears from which it cannot escape. The
difference between natural and revealed religion is
that the one worships the loveliness and power it
perceives, and the other the goodness, mercy, and
truth in which it believes. The one prays for
exemption from pain and enjoyment of happiness
for body and mind in this present existence; the
other for deliverance from spiritual evils, or the possession of spiritual graces, by which the soul is fitted
for that better life towards which it tends. . . .

I do not think " Juliet " has written to you hitherto,
and I am rather affronted at your calling me so. I
have little or no sympathy with, though much com-
passion for, that Veronese young person. . . . There
is but one sentiment of hers that I can quote with
entire self-application, and that is—

> " I have no joy of this contract to-night;
>   It is too rash, too unadvised, too sudden."

In spite of which the foolish child immediately secures
her lover's word, appoints the time for meeting, and
makes every arrangement for following up the declaration she thought too sudden by its as sudden exe-

cution.   Poor Juliet! I am very sorry for her, but
do not like to be called after her, and do not think I
am like her.   I have been working very hard every
day since you left Bristol (my belief is that Juliet was
very idle).   I am sorry to say I find my playing very
hard work; but easy work, if there is such a thing,
would not be best for me just now. . . .

Yours ever,

F. A. K.

Sunday, Exeter.—To church with Dall and my
father, a blessing that I can never enjoy in London,
where he is all but stared out of countenance if he
shows his countenance in a church, and it requires
more devotion to the deed than I fear he possesses to
encounter the annoyance attendant upon it.   We
heard an excellent sermon, earnest, sober, simple,
which I was especially grateful for on my father's
account.   Women don't mind bad preaching; they
have a general taste for sermons, and, like children
with sweeties, will swallow bad ones if they cannot
get good.   "We have a natural turn for religion,"
as A. F. said of me; but men, I think, get a not
unnatural turn against it when they hear it ill advo-
cated. . . .

The day has been lovely, and from my perch among
the clouds here I am looking down upon a lovely view.
Following the irregular line of buildings of the street,
the eye suddenly becomes embowered in a thick rich
valley of foliage, beyond which a hill rises, whose sides
are covered with ripening corn-fields, meadows of vivid
green, and fields where the rich red colour of the earth

contrasts beautifully with the fresh hedgerows and tall, dark elm trees, whose shadows have stretched themselves for evening rest down in the low rosy sunset. It is all still and bright, and the sabbath bells come up to me over it all with intermitting sweetness, like snatches of an interrupted angels' chorus, floating hither and thither about the earth.

Monday.—We contrived to get some saddle-horses, and rode out into the beautiful country round Exeter, but the preface to our poem was rather dry prose. We rode for about an hour between powdery hedges all smothered in dust, up the steepest of hills, and under the hottest of suns; but we had our reward when we halted at the top, and looked down upon a magnificent panorama of land and water, hill and dale, broad smiling meadows, and dark shadowy woodland—a vast expanse of various beauty, over which the eye wandered and paused in slow contentment. As we came leisurely down the opposite side of the hill, we met a gipsy woman, and I reined up my horse and listened to my fortune :—" I have a friend abroad who is very fond of me." I hope so. " I have a relation far abroad who is very fond of me too." I know so. "I shall live long." More is the pity. "I shall marry and have three children." Quite enough. " I shall take easily to love, but it will not break my heart." I am glad to hear that. " I shall cross the sea before I see London again." Ah ! I am afraid not. " The end of my summer will be happier than its beginning "—and that may very easily be. For that I gave my prophetess a shilling. Oh, Zingarella ! my blessing on your black

46

eyes and red-brown cheeks! May you have spoken
true! . . .

Meantime, my companions, my father and Mr.
Kean, were discussing the fortunes of Poland. If I
were a man, with a hundred thousand pounds at my
disposal, I would raise a regiment and join the Poles.
The Russians have been beaten again, which is good
hearing. Is it possible this cause should fall to the
earth? On our way home, had a nice smooth, long
canter by the river-side. We turned off our road to
visit a pretty property of Mr. F——'s, the house half-
way up a hill, prettily seated among pleasant woods.
We galloped up some fields above it to the brow of
the rise, and had three mouthfuls of delicious fresh
breeze, and a magnificent view of Exeter and the
surrounding country. . . . After dinner, off to the
theatre; it was my benefit, "The Gamester." The
house was very full, and I played and looked well;
but what a Stukely! I was afraid my eyes would
scarcely answer my purpose, but that I should have
been obliged to "employer l'effort de mon bras" to
keep him at a proper distance. What ruffianly
wooing! and not one of the actors knew their parts.
Stukely said to me in his love-speech, "Time has not
gathered the roses from your cheeks, though often
washed them." I had heard of Time as the thinner
of people's hair, but never as the washer of their
faces.

Sunday, July 31*st.*—Went to church, to St. Sid-
well's. . . . We had another good sermon; that
preacher must be a good man, and I should like to
know him. . . .

Our dinner-party this evening was like nothing but a chapter out of one of Miss Austen's novels. What wonderful books those are! She must have written down the very conversations she heard *verbatim*, to have made them so like, which is Irish. . . . How many things one ought to die of and doesn't! That dinner did come to an end. In the drawing-room afterwards, in spite of the dreadful heat, two fair female friends actually divided one chair between them; I expected to see them run into one every minute, and kept speculating then which they would be, till the idea fascinated me like a thing in a nightmare. As we were taking our departure, and had got half-way down the stairs, a general rush was made at us, and an attempt, upon some pretext, to get us back into that dreadful drawing-room. I thought of Malebranche hooking the miserable souls that tried to escape back again into the boiling pitch. But we got away and safe home, and leave Exeter to-morrow.

Exeter, July 31st, 1831.

DEAREST H——,
        I am content to be whatever does not militate against your affection for me. . . . I had a long letter from dear A——, a day ago, from Weybridge. She is quite well, and says my mother is as happy as the day is long, now she is once more in her beloved haunts. I love Weybridge too very much. . . . It seems to me that memory is the special organ of pain, for even when it recalls our pleasures, it recalls only the past, and half their sweetness becomes bitter in the process. I have a tenacious and acute memory,

and, as the phrenologists affirm, no hope, and feel
disposed to lament that, not having both, I have
either. The one seems the necessary counterpoise
of the other; the one is the source of most of the ·
pain, as the other is of most of the pleasure, which
we derive from the things that are not; and I feel
daily more and more my deficiency in the more
cheerful attribute. . . .

You have been to the Opera, and seen what even
one's imagination does not shrug its shoulders at; I
mean Madame Pasta. I admire her perfectly, and
she seems to me perfect. How I wish I had been
with you! And yet I cannot fancy you in the Opera
House; it is a sort of atmosphere that I find it difficult to think of your breathing. . . . I wish you had
not asked me to write verses for you upon that picture
of Haydon's "Bonaparte at St. Helena." Of course,
I know it familiarly through the engraving, and, in
spite of its sunshine, what a shudder and chill it
sends to one's heart! It is very striking, but I have
neither the strength nor concentrativeness requisite
for writing upon it. The simplicity of its effect is
what makes it so fine; and any poetry written upon it
would probably fail to be as simple, and therefore as
powerful, as itself. I cannot even promise you to
attempt it, but if ever I fall in with a suitable frame
of mind for so bold an experiment, I will remember
you and the rocks of St. Helena. "My Lady" (an
Italian portrait on which I had written some verses)
"Mia Donna," or "Madonna," more properly to
speak, was a most beautiful Italian portrait that I
saw, not in Augustin's gallery, but in a small collec-

tion of pictures belonging to Mr. Day, and exhibited
at the Egyptian Hall. Sir Thomas Lawrence told
me, when I described it to him, that he thought it
was a painting of Giordano's. It was a lovely face,
not youthful in its character of beauty; there is a
calm seriousness about the brow and forehead, a
clear, intellectual severity about the eye, and a sweet,
still placidity round the mouth, that united, to my
fancy, all the elements of beauty, physical, mental,
and moral. What an incomparable friend that
woman must have been! Why is it that we rejoice
that a soul fit for heaven is constrained to tarry
here, but that, in truth, the fittest for this is also
the fittest for that life? For it seems to me more
natural not to wish to detain the bright spirit from
its brighter home, and not to sorrow at the decree
which calls it hence to perfect its excellence in higher
spheres of duty. . . .

I think a blight of uncertainty must have pervaded
the atmosphere when I was born, and penetrated, not
certainly my nature, but my whole earthly destiny,
with its influence; from my plans and projects for
to-morrow on to those of next year, all is mist and in-
distinct indecision. I suppose it is the trial that suits
my temper least, and therefore fits it best. It surely
is that which "wilfulness, conceit, and egotism" find
hardest to endure. Yesterday I determined so far to
escape from, or cheat, my destiny as to have a peep
into futurity by the help of a gipsy. Riding with my
father, and the whole hour, time, day, and scene,
were in admirable harmony: the dark, sunburnt
face, with its bright, laughing eyes and coal-black

curls and flashing teeth ; the old gateway against
which she was leaning ; the blue summer sky and
sunny road skirted with golden corn-fields—the whole
picture in which she was set was charming. . . .

            "I know it is a sin to be a mocker ;"

and I am sure I need not tell you that I am sincerely
grateful for all the kindness and civility that is
bestowed upon us wherever we go. . . . What with
riding, rehearsing, and acting, my days are completely
filled. We start for Plymouth to-morrow at eight, and
act "Romeo and Juliet" in the evening, which is
rather laborious work. We play there every night
next week. When next I write I will tell you of our
further plans, which are at this moment still uncertain. . . . Affectionately yours,

                                     F. A. K.

[These were the days before railroads had run everything and everybody up to London. There were still
to be found then, in various parts of England, life
that was peculiar and provincial, and manners that
had in them a character of their own and a stamp of
originality that had often quite as much to attract as
to repel. Men and women are, of course, still the
same that sat to that enchanting painter, Jane
Austen, but the whole form and colour and outward
framing and various countenance of their lives have
merged its distinctiveness in a commonplace conformity to universal custom ; and in regard to the
more superficial subjects of her fine and gentle satire,
if she were to return among us she would find half
her occupation gone.]

Monday, August 1st.—I got some books while waiting for the coach, and we started at half-past eight.
The heat was intolerable and the dust suffocating,
but the country through which we passed was lovely.
For a long time we drove along the brow of a steep
hill. The valley was all glorious with the harvest:
corn-fields with the red-gold billows yet untouched by
the sickle; others full of sunburnt reapers sweeping
down the ripe ears; others, again, silent and deserted,
with the tawny sheaves standing, bound and dry,
upon the bristling stubble, on the ground over which
they rippled and nodded yesterday, a great rolling
sea of burnished grain. All over the sunny landscape peace and prosperity smiled, and grey-steepled
churches and red-roofed villages, embowered in thick
protecting shade, seemed to beckon the eye to rest as
it wandered over the charming prospect. The white-
walled mansions of the lords of the land glittered
from the verdant shelter of their surrounding plantations, and the thirsty cattle, beautiful in colour and
in grouping, stood in pools in the deeper parts of the
brooks, where some giant tree threw its shadow over
the water and the smooth sheltered sward round its
feet. In spite of this charming prospect I was very
sad, and the purple heather bordering the road, with
its thick tufts, kept suggesting Weybridge and the
hours I had lately spent there so happily. . . . To
shake myself I took up "Adam Blair;" and, good
gracious! what a shaking it did give me! What a
horrible book! And how could D—— have recom-
mended me to read it? It is a very fine and powerful
piece of work, no doubt; but I turned from it with

infinite relief to "Quentin Durward." Walter Scott
is quite exciting enough for wholesome pleasure; there
is no poison in anything that he has ever written: for
how many hours of harmless happiness the world
may bless him!

At Totnes we got out of the coach to shàke ourselves, for we were absolute dust-heaps, and then
resumed our powdery way, and reached Plymouth
at about four o'clock. As we walked up towards
our lodgings, we were met by Mr. Brunton, with
the pleasing intelligence that those we had be-
spoken had been let, by some mistake, to another
family. Dusty, dreary, and disconsolate, I sat down
on the stairs which were to have been ours, while
Dall upbraided the hostess of the house, and my
father did what was more to the purpose—posted off to
find other apartments for us; no easy matter, for the
town is crammed to overflowing. In the mean time a
little blue-eyed fairy, of about two years old, came
and made friends with me, and I presently had her
fast asleep in my lap. After carrying my prize into
an empty room, and sitting by it for nearly half an
hour while it slept the sleep of the blessed, I was
called away from this very new interest, for my
father had succeeded in finding house-room for us,
and I had yet all my preparations to make for the
evening.

The theatre is a beautiful building for its purpose,
of a perfectly discreet size, neither too large nor too
small, of a very elegant shape, and capitally constructed for the voice. The house was very *full;* the
play, "Romeo and Juliet."   I played abominably ill,

and did not like my audience, who must have been very good-natured if they liked me.

Tuesday, August 2nd.—Rose at seven, and went off down to the sea, and that was delightful. In the evening the play was " Venice Preserved." I acted very well, notwithstanding that I had to prompt my Jaffier through every scene, not only as to words, but position on the stage, and "business," as it is called. How unprincipled and ungentlemanlike this is ! The house was very fine, and a pleasanter audience than the first night. Found a letter from Mrs. Jameson after the play, with an account of Pasta's " Anna Bolena." How I wish I could see it !

Wednesday, August 3rd.—Rose at seven, and went down to the sea to bathe. The tide was out, and I had to wait till the nymphs had filled my bath-tub. . . . At the theatre in the evening, the play was " The Stranger." The house not so good as last night, and the audience were disagreeably noisy. . . .

Thursday, August 4th.—They will not let me take my sea-bath every morning ; they say it makes me too weak. Do they mean in the head, I wonder ? . . . " Let the sanguine then take warning, and the disheartened take courage, for to every hope and every fear, to every joy and every sorrow, there comes a last day," which is but a didactic form of dear Mademoiselle Descuillier's conjuring of our impatiences : " Cela viendra, ma chère, cela viendra, car tout vient dans ce monde ; cela passera, ma chère, cela passera, car tout passe dans ce monde." . . . I finished my drawing, and copied some of " The Star of Seville." I wonder if it will ever be acted ? I think I

should like to see a play of mine acted.   In the evening at the theatre, the play was "Isabella."   The house
was very full, and I played well.   The wretched
manager will not afford us a green baize for our
tragedies, and we faint and fall and die upon bare
boards, and my unhappy elbows are bruised black
and blue with their carpetless stage, barbarians that
they be !

 Friday, August 5th.—Down to the sea at seven
o'clock; the tide was far out, the lead-coloured strand,
without its bright foam-fringes, looked bleak and
dreary; it was not expected to be batheable till eleven,
and as I had not breakfasted, I could not wait till
then.   Lingered on the shore, as Tom Tug says,
thinking of nothing at ¦all, but inhaling the fresh air
and delicious sea-smell.   I stood and watched a party
of pleasure put off from the shore, consisting of a
basket of fuel, two baskets of provisions, a cross-look-
ing, thin, withered, bony woman, wrapt in a large
shawl, and with boots thick enough to have kept her
dry if she had walked through the sea from Plymouth
to Mount Edgecombe.   Her *tête-à-tête* companion was
a short, thick, squat, stumpy, dumpy, dumpling of a
man, in a round jacket, and very tight striped trousers.
" Sure such a pair were never seen."   The sour she,
stepped into their small boat first, but as soon as her
fat play-fellow seated himself by her, the poor little
cockle-shell dipped so with the increased weight, that
the tail of the cross-shawl hung deep in the water.   I
called after them, and they rectified the accident without sending me back a "Thank you."   I love the
manners of my country-folk, they are so unsophisti-
cated with civility.

At the theatre the play was "The Gamester," for my benefit, and the house was very fine. My father played magnificently; I, "not even excellent well, but only so-so." The actors none of them knew their parts, abominable persons; and as for Stakely —well! Mdlle. Dumesnil, in her great, furious scene in Hermione, ended her imprecations against Orestes by spitting in her handkerchief and throwing it in his face. The handkerchief spoils the frenzy. I wonder if it ever occurred to Mrs. Siddons so to wind up her abuse of Austria in "King John." By-the-by, it was when asked to give his opinion of the comparative merits of Clairon and Dumesnil, that Garrick said, "Mdlle. Clairon was the greatest actress of the age, but that for Mdlle. Dumesnil he was not aware that he had seen her, but only Phedre, Rodogund, and Hermione, when she did them." After the play the audience clamoured for my father. He thought that "l'envie leur en passerait;" and not being in a very good humour, he declined appearing. The uproar went on, the overture to the farce was inaudible, and the curtain drew up amid the deafening shouts of "Kemble! Kemble!"—they would not suffer the poor *farçeurs* to go on, even in dumb show. I was at the side scene, and thought it really a pity not to put an end to all the fuss; so I went to my father, who was standing at the stage door in the street, and requested him to stop the disturbance by coming forward at once. He turned round, and without saying anything but "Tu me le conseilles," walked straight upon the stage, and addressed the audience as follows: "Ladies and gentlemen, I had left the theatre when

word was brought to me that you had done me the
honour to call for me; as I conclude you have done so
merely in conformity to a custom which is becoming
the fashion of calling for certain performers after the
play, I can only say, ladies and gentlemen, that I
enter my protest against such a custom. It is a
foreign fashion, and we are Englishmen; therefore I
protest against it. I will take my leave of you by
parodying Mercutio's words: Ladies and gentlemen,
bon soir; there's a French salutation for you." So
saying he walked off the stage, leaving the audience
rather surprised; and so was I. I think he is labouring under an incipient bilious attack.

We had a long discussion to-day as to the possibility of women being good dramatic writers. I
think it so impossible that I actually believe their
physical organization is against it; and, after
all, it is great nonsense saying that intellect is
of no sex. The brain is, of course, of the same
sex as the rest of the creature; besides, the original
feminine nature, the whole of our training and education, our inevitable ignorance of common life and
general human nature, and the various experience of
existence, from which we are debarred with the most
sedulous care, is insuperably against it. Perhaps
some of the manly, wicked Queens Semiramis, Cleopatra, could have written plays; but they lived their
tragedies instead of writing them.

Saturday, August 6th.—After breakfast our excellent
architect came to fetch us for our expedition to the
breakwater. My father complained of being dreadfully bilious, a bad preparation for the purpose. I

wanted to stay at home with him, or at all events to put off the party for an hour or two ; but he would not hear of either plan.   So as soon as I was ready we set off.   We walked first to the M——s', and then proceeded in a body to the shore, where a Government boat was waiting for us ; and what a cargo we were, to be sure !   My father, certainly no feather ; our worthy friend, who must weigh eighteen stone, if a pound ; Mr. and Mrs. W——, thinnish bodies ; but her friend, Dall, and myself decidedly thickish ones ; then the pilot, a gaunt, square Scotchman ; and four stout sailors.   The gallant little craft curtsied and curtsied as she received us, one by one, and at length, when we were all fairly and pretty closely packed, she put off, and breasted the water bravely, rising and dancing on the back of the waves like a dolphin.   I should have enjoyed it but for my father's ghastly face of utter misery.   The day was dull, the sky and sea lead-coloured, the brown coast by degrees lost its distinctness, and became covered with a dark haze that seemed to blend everything into a still, stony, threatening iron-grey mass.   The wind rose, the sea became inky black and swelled into heavy ridges, which made our little vessel dip deep and spring high, as she toiled forward ; and then down came the rain— such tremendous rain !   Cloaks, shawls, and umbrellas were speedily produced ; but we were two miles from shore, between the rising sea and the falling clouds, sick, wet, squeezed.   Oh the delights of that party of pleasure !   My father looked cadaverous, Dall was portentously silent, I shut my eyes and tried to sleep, being in that state when to see, or hear, or speak, or

be spoken to, is equally fatal.   At length we reached
the foot of the breakwater, and I sprang out of the
boat, too happy to touch the stable rock.   The rain
literally fell in sheets from the sky, and the wind blew
half a hurricane; but I was on firm ground, and
taking off my bonnet, which only served the purpose
of a water-spout down my back, I ran, while Mr.
M——, holding my arm, strode along the mighty
water-based road, while the angry sea, turning up
black cauldrons full of boiling foam, dashed them upon
the barrier man has raised against its fury in magnificent, solemn wrath.   This breakwater is a noble
work; the daring of the conception, its vast size and
strength, and the utility of its purpose, are alike
admirable.   We do these things and die; we ride upon
the air and water, we guide the lightning and we
bridle the sea, we borrow the swiftness of the wind
and the fine subtlety of the fire; we lord it in this
universe of ours for a day, and then our bodies are
devoured by these material slaves we have controlled,
and helplessly mingle their dust with the elements
that have obeyed our will, who re-absorb the garment
of our soul when that has fled—whither?

The rain continuing to fall in torrents, and my
father being wretchedly unwell, we gave up our purpose of visiting Mount Edgecombe, and returned to
Plymouth.   The sea was horribly rough, even inside
the breakwater; but I shut my eyes that I might not
see how we heaved, and sang that I might not think
how sick I was: and so we reached shore, and I ran
up and down the steep beach while the rest were disembarking, and the wind soon dried my light muslin

clothes. The other poor things continued drenched
till we reached home. After a good rest, we went to
our dinner at Mr. W——'s; my father was all right
again, and our party, that had separated in such dismal
plight, met again very pleasantly in the evening. Mr.
W—— got quite tipsy with talking, an accident not
uncommon with eager, excitable men, and all but
overwhelmed me with an argument about dramatic
writing, in which he was wrong from beginning to
end. . . . We leave Plymouth to-morrow.

Sunday, August 7th.—Started for Exeter at seven,
and slept nearly the whole way by little bits; between
each nap getting glimpses of the pleasant land that
blended for a moment with my hazy, dream-like
thoughts, and then faded away before my closing
eyes. One patch of moorland that I woke to see was
lovely—all purple heather and golden gorze; nature's
royal mantle thrown, it is true, over a barren soil,
whose grey, cold, rifted ridges of rock contrasted
beautifully with its splendid clothing. We got to
Exeter at two o'clock, and I was thankful to rest the
rest of the day.

Monday, August 8th.—I read old Biagio's preface to
Dante, which, from its amazing classicality, is almost
as difficult as the crabbed old Florentine's own writing.
Worked at a rather elaborate sketch tolerably successfully, and was charmingly interrupted by having our
landlady's pretty little child brought in to me. She is
a beautiful baby, but will be troublesome enough by-
and-by. . . . At the theatre the house was very good;
I played tolerably well upon the whole, but felt so
fagged and faint towards the end of the play that I
could hardly stand.

Tuesday, August 9th.—I sometimes wish I was a stone, a tree, some senseless, soulless, irresponsible thing; that ebbing sea rolling before me, its restlessness is obedience to the law of its nature, not striving against it, neither is it "the miserable life in it" urging it to ceaseless turmoil and agitation. . . . We dined early, and then started for Dorchester, which we reached at half-past ten, after a most fatiguing journey. It was a still, grey day, an atmosphere and light I like; there is a clearness about it that is pleasanter sometimes than the dazzle of sunshine. Some of the country we drove through was charming, particularly the vale of Honiton. . . . I have an immense bedroom here; a whole army of ghosts might lodge in it. I hope, if there are any, they will be civil, well-behaved, and, above all, invisible.

Wednesday, August 10th. . . . At ten o'clock we started for Weymouth, where we arrived in the course of an hour, and found it basking on the edge of a lovely summer sea, with a dozen varying zones of colour streaking its rippling surface; from the deep, dark purple heaving against the horizon to the delicate pearl-edged, glassy golden-green that spreads its transparent sheets over the sparkling sand of the beach. The bold chalky cliffs of the shore send back the burning sunlight with blinding brightness, and stretch away as far as eye can follow in hazy outlines, that glimmer faintly through the shimmering mist. It is all very beautiful. . . . I got ready my things for the theatre, . . . and when I got there I was amused and amazed at its absurdly small proportions; it is a perfect doll's playhouse, and until I saw that my father

really could stand upon the stage, I thought that I
should fill it entirely by myself. How well I remembered all the droll stories my mother used to tell about
old King George III. and Queen Charlotte, who had a
passion for Weymouth, and used to come to the funny
little theatre here constantly ; and how the princesses
used to dress her out in their own finery for some of
her parts. [I long possessed a very perfect coral
necklace of magnificent single beads given to my
mother on one of these occasions by the Princess
Amelia.] The play was "Romeo and Juliet," and
our masquerade scene was in the height of the modern
fashion, for there was literally not room to stir ; and
what between my nurse and my father I suffered
very nearly total eclipse, besides much danger of being
knocked down each time either of them moved. In
the balcony, besides me, there was a cloud, which occasionally interfered with my hair, and I think must
have made my face appear to the audience like a chin
and mouth speaking out of the sky. To be sure, this
inconvenient scenic decoration made rather more
appropriate the lines which Shakespeare wrote (only
unfortunately Romeo never speaks them), "Two of the
stars," etc. I acted very well, but was so dreadfully
tired at the end of the play that they were obliged to
carry me up to my dressing-room, where I all but
fainted away ; in spite of which, as I got out of the
carriage at the door of our lodging, hearing the dear
voice of the sea calling me, I tried to persuade Dall to
come down to it with me; but she, thinking I had had
enough of emotion and exertion, made me go in and
eat my supper and go to bed, which was detestable on

47

her part, and so I told her, which she didn't mind in the least.

Thursday, August 11*th.*—A kind and courteous and most courtly old Mr. M—— called upon us, to entreat that we would dine with him during our stay in Wey-mouth; but it is really impossible, with all our hard work, to do society duty too, so I begged permission to decline.   After he was gone we walked down to the pier, and took boat and rowed to Portland.   The sky was cloudless, and the sea without a wave, and through its dark-blue transparent roofing we saw clearly the bottom, one forest of soft, undulating weeds, which, catching the sunlight through the crystal-clear water, looked like golden woods of some enchanted world within its depths; and it looks just as weird and lovely when folks go drowning down there, only they don't see it.   I sang Mrs. Hemans's "What hid'st thou in thy treasure-caves and cells?" and sang and sang till, after rowing for an hour over the hardly heaving, smooth surface, we reached the foot of the barren stone called Portland.   We landed, and Dall remained on the beach while my father and I toiled up the steep ascent.   The sun's rays fell perpendicularly on our heads, the short, close grass which clothed the burning, stony soil was as slippery as glass with the heat, and I have seldom had a harder piece of exer-cise than climbing that rock, from the summit of which one wide expanse of dazzling water and glaring white cliffs, that scorched one's eyeballs, was all we had for our reward.   To be sure, exertion is a pleasure in itself, and when one's strength serves one's courage, the greater the exertion the greater the

pleasure. We saw below us a railroad cut in the rock
to convey the huge masses of stone from the famous
quarries down to the shore. The descent looked
almost vertical, and we watched two immense loads
go slowly down by means of a huge cylinder and
chains, which looked as if the world might hang upon
them in safety. I lay down on the summit of the
rock while my father went off exploring further, and
the perfect stillness of the solitude was like a spell.
There was not a sound of life but the low, drowsy
humming of the bees in the stone-rooted tufts of
fragrant thyme. On our return we had to run down
the steep, slippery slopes, striking our feet hard to
the earth to avoid falling; firm walking footing there
was none. When we joined Dall we found, to our
utter dismay, that it was five o'clock; we bundled ourselves *pêle-mêle* into the boat and bade the boatman
row, row, for dear life; but while we were indulging in
the picturesque he had been indulging in fourpenny,
which made him very talkative, and his tongue went
faster than his arms. I longed for John to make our
boat fly over the smooth, burnished sea; the oars came
out of the water like long bars of diamond dropping
gold. We touched shore just at six, swallowed three
mouthfuls of dinner, and off to the theatre. The play
was "Venice Preserved." I dressed as quick as
lightning, and was ready in time. The house was not
very good, and I am sure I should have wondered if
it had been, when the moon is just rising over the
fresh tide that is filling the basin, and a delicious salt
breeze blows along the beach, and the stars are
lighting their lamps in heaven; and surely nobody

but those who cannot help it would be breathing the gas and smoke and vile atmosphere of the playhouse. I played well, and when we came home ran down and stood a few minutes by the sea ; but the moon had set, and the dark palpitating water only reflected the long line of lights from the houses all along the curving shore.

Friday, August 12*th, Portsmouth.* . . . The hotel where we are staying is quite a fine house, and the Assembly balls used to be held here, and so there is a fine large " dancing-hall deserted " of which I avail myself as a music-room, having entire and solitary possession of it and a piano. . . . At the theatre the house was good, and I played well. . . .

Monday, August 15*th, Southampton.*—After breakfast practised till eleven, and then went to rehearsal ; after which Emily Fitzhugh came for me, and we drove out to Bannisters. Poor Mrs. Fitzhugh was quite over-come at seeing my father, whom she has not seen since Mrs. Siddons's death ; we left her with him to talk over Campbell's application to her for my aunt's letters. He has behaved badly about the whole business, and I hope Mrs. Fitzhugh will not let him have them. . . . When we came in I went and looked at Lawrence's picture of my aunt in the dining-room (now in the National Gallery ; it was painted for Mrs. Fitzhugh). It is a fine rich piece of colouring, but there is a want of ease and grace in the figure, and of life in the countenance, and altogether I thought it looked like a handsome dark cow in a coral necklace. O ox-eyed Juno ! forgive the thought. . . . At the theatre the house was good ; the play was " Romeo and Juliet,"

and I played well. While I was changing my dress
for the tomb scene—putting on my grave-clothes, in
fact—I had desired my door to be shut, for I hate that
lugubrious funeral dirge. How I do hate, and have
always hated, that stage funeral business, which I
never see without a cold shudder at its awful unfitness.
I can't conceive how that death's pageant was ever
tolerated in a theatre. [I think Mrs. Bellamy, in her
" Memoirs," mentions that it was first introduced as a
piece of new sensation when she and Garrick were
dividing the town with the .efforts of their rival
managership.] At present the pretext for it is to give
the necessary time for setting the churchyard scene
and for Juliet to change her dress, which she has no
business to do according to the text, for it expressly
says that she shall be buried in all her finest attire,
according to her country's custom. In spite of which
I was always arrayed in long white muslin draperies
and veils, with my head bound up, corpse fashion, and
lying, as my aunt had stretched me, on the black bier
in the vault, with all my white folds drawn like carved
stone robes along my figure and round my feet, with
my hands folded and my eyes shut. I have had some
bad nervous minutes, sometimes fancying, " Suppose
I should really die while I am lying here, making
believe to be dead ! " and imagining the surprise and
dismay of my Romeo when I didn't get up ; and at
others fighting hard against heavy drowsiness of over
fatigue, lest I should be fast asleep, if not dead, when
it came to my turn to speak—though I might have
depended upon the furious bursting open of the doors
of the vault for my timely waking. Talking over this

with Mrs. Fitzhugh one day she told me a comical
incident of the stage life of her friend, the fascinating
Miss Farren. The devotion of the Earl of Derby to
her, which preceded for a long time the death of Lady
Derby, from whom he was separated, and his marriage
to Miss Farren, made him a frequent visitor behind
the scenes on the nights of her performance. One
evening, in the famous scene in Joseph Surface's
library in "The School for Scandal," when Lady
Teazle is imprisoned behind the screen, Miss Farren,
fatigued with standing, and chilled with the dreadful
draughts of the stage, had sent for an armchair and
her furs, and when this critical moment arrived, and
the screen was overturned, she was revealed, in her
sable muff and tippet, entirely absorbed in an eager
conversation with Lord Derby, who was leaning over
the back of her chair.

Tuesday, 16th, Southampton.—After breakfast walked
down to the city wall, which has remnants of great
antiquity they say, as old as the Danes, one bit being
still heroically called "Canute's Castle."

Wednesday, August 17th.—Went to the theatre,
and rehearsed "The Stranger." On my return found
Emily waiting for me, and drove with her to Bannisters. . . . In the evening, at the theatre, the
house was very good, but I played only so-so, and not
at all excellent well. . . .

Thursday, August 18th.—While I was practising I
came across that pretty piece of ballad pathos, "The
Banks of Allan Water," and sang myself into sobbing.
Luckily I was interrupted by Dall and my father, who
came in with a little girl, poor unfortunate! whose

father had brought her to show how well she deserved an engagement at Covent Garden. She sat down to the piano at his desire, and panted through the great cavatina in the "Gazza Sadra." Poor little thing! I never heard or saw anything that so thoroughly impressed me with the brutal ignorance of our people; for there is scarcely an Englishman of that man's condition, situated as he is, who would not have done the same thing. A child of barely ten years old made to sing her lungs away for four hours every day, when it is not possible yet to know what the character and qualities of her voice will be, or even if she will have any voice at all. Wasting her health and strength in attempting "The Soldier Tired" and "Di piacer," it really was pitiful. We gave her plenty of kind words and compliments, and sundry pieces of advice to him, which he will not take, and in a few months no doubt we shall hear of little Miss H—— singing away as a prodigy, and in a few years the voice, health, and strength will all be gone, and probably the poor little life itself have been worn out of its fragile case. Stupid barbarian! After rehearsal drove to Bannisters. . . . In the evening, at the theatre, the play was "The Provoked Husband." The house was very full; I played fairly well. I was rather tired, and Lady Townley's bones ached, for I had been taking a rowing lesson from Emily, and supplied my want of skill, tyro fashion, with a deal of unnecessary effort.

Friday, August 19th. . . . It sometimes occurs to me that our spirits, when dwelling with the utmost intensity of longing upon those who are distant from us, must create in them some perception, some con-

sciousness of our spiritual presence, so that not by
the absent whom I love thinking of me, but by my
thinking of them, they must receive some intimation
of the vividness with which my soul sees and feels
them. It seems to me as if my earnest desire and
thought must not bring those they dwell on to me, but
render me in some way perceptible, if not absolutely
visible, to them.

> "Though thou see me not pass by,
> Thou shalt feel me with thine eye."

I fancy I must create my own image to their senses
by the clinging passion with which my thoughts dwell
on them. And yet it would be rather fearful if one
were thus subject, not only to the disordered action of
one's own imagination, but to the ungoverned imagin-
ations of others; and so, upon the whole, I don't
believe people would be allowed to pester other people
with their presence only by dint of thinking hard
enough and long enough about them. It would be
intolerable, and yet I have sometimes fancied I was
thinking myself visible to some one. . . . In the
evening, at the theatre, the house was very good; the
play was " The Gamester," and I played very ill. I
felt fagged to death; my work tires me, and I am
growing old.

Saturday, 20th.—At Bannisters all the morning.
Emily gave me two charming Italian songlets, and
then they drove us down to Southampton. At the
theatre this evening the house was all but empty,
owing to some stupid blunder in the advertisement.
The play was " The School for Scandal," and I played

well. . . . To-morrow I shall be at home once more
in smoky London.

Southampton, August 19th, 1831.

MY DEAREST H——,

I do not like to defer answering you any
longer, though I am not very fit to write, for I am half
blind with crying, and have a torturing side-ache, the
results of bodily fatigue and nervous anxiety; but if I
do not write to you to-night I know not when I shall
be able to do so, for I shall have to rehearse every
morning and to act every night, and I expect the
intermediate hours will be spent on the road to and
from Bannisters, the Fitzhughs' place near here. I
have been travelling ever since half-past eight to-day,
and have hardly been three hours out of the coach
which brought us from Weymouth, where we have been
acting for the last week. Your letter followed me
from Plymouth, and right glad I was to get it. . . .
I do not know what I can write you of if not myself,
and I dare say, after all, my thoughts are more amusing
to you, or rather, perhaps, more useful, in your processes of observing and studying human nature in
general, through my individual case, than if I wrote
you word what plays we had been acting, etc., etc. . . .
To meet pain, no matter how severe, the mind girds
up its loins, and finds a sort of strength of resistance
in its endurance, which is a species of activity. To
endure helplessly prolonged suspense is another matter
quite, and a far heavier demand upon all patient power
that is in one. . . .

So you have seen the railroad; I am so glad

you have seen that magnificent invention. I wish
I had been on it with you. I wish you had seen
Stephenson; you would have delighted in him, I
am sure. The hope of meeting him again is one of
the greatest pleasures Liverpool holds out to me. . . .
With regard to what are called "fine people," and
liking their society better than that of "not fine
people," I suppose a good many tolerable reasons
might be adduced by persons who have that pre-
ference. They do not often say very wise or very witty
things, I dare say; but neither do they tread on one's
feet or poke their elbows into one's side (figuratively
speaking) in their conversation, or commit the numerous solecisms of manner of less well-bred people. For
myself, my social position does not entitle me to mix
with the superior class of human beings generally
designated as "fine people." My father's indolence
renders their society an irksome exertion to him, and my
mother's pride always induces her to hang back rather
than to make advances to anybody. We are none of
us, therefore, inclined to be very keen tuft-hunters.
But for these very reasons, if "fine people" seek me,
it is a decided compliment, by which my vanity is
flattered. A person with less of that quality might be
quite indifferent to their notice, but I think their
society, as far as I have had any opportunity of
observing it, has certain positive merits, which attract
me irrespectively of the gratification of my vanity.
Genius and pre-eminent power of intellect, of course,
belong to no class, and one would naturally prefer the
society of any individual who possessed these to that
of the King of England (who, by-the-by, is not, I

believe, particularly brilliant). I would rather pass a
day with Stephenson than with Lord Alvanley, though
the one is a coal-digger by birth, who occasionally
murders the king's English, and the other is the
keenest wit and one of the finest gentlemen about
town. But Stephenson's attributes of genius, industry, mental power, and perseverance are his
individually, while Lord Alvanley's gifts and graces
(his wit, indeed, excepted) are, in good measure, those
of his whole social set. Moreover, in the common
superficial intercourse of society, the minds and
morals of those you meet are really not what you
come in contact with half the time, while from their
manners there is, of course, no escape; and therefore
those persons may well be preferred as temporary
associates whose manners are most refined, easy, and
unconstrained, as I think those of so-called "fine
people" are. Originality and power of intellect belong
to no class, but with information, cultivation, and the
mental advantages derived from education, "fine
people" are perhaps rather better endowed, as a
class, than others. Their lavish means for obtaining
instruction, and their facilities for travelling, if they
are but moderately endowed by nature and moderately
inclined to profit by them, certainly enable them to
see, hear, and know more of the surface of things
than others. This is, no doubt, a merely superficial
superiority; but I suppose that there are not many
people, and certainly no class of people, high, low, or
of any degree, who go much below surfaces. . . . If
you knew how, long after I have passed it, the colour
of a tuft of heather, or the smell of a branch of honey-

suckle by the roadside, haunts my imagination, and
how many suggestions of beauty and sensations of
pleasure flow from this small spring of memory, even
after the lapse of weeks and months, you would
understand what I am going to say, which perhaps
may appear rather absurd without such a knowledge
of my impressions. I think I like fine places better
than "fine people;" but then one accepts, as it were,
the latter for the former, and the effect of the one, to a
certain degree, affects one's impressions of the other.
A great ball at Devonshire House, for instance, with
its splendour, its brilliancy, its beauty, and magnificence of all sorts, remains in one's mind with the
enchantment of a live chapter of the "Arabian
Nights;" and I think one's imagination is still more
impressed with the fine residences of "fine people" in
the country, where historical and poetical associations
combine with all the refinements of luxurious civilization, and all the most exquisitely cultivated beauties
of nature to produce an effect which, to a certain
degree, frames their possessors to great advantage,
and invests them with a charm which is really not
theirs; and if they are only tolerably in harmony with
the places where they live, they appear charming too.
I believe the pleasure and delight I take in the music,
the lights, the wreaths, and mirrors of a splendid ball-
room, and the love I have for the smooth lawns,
bright waters, and lordly oaks of a fine domain, would
disgracefully influence my impressions of the people I
met amongst them. Still, I humbly trust I do not
like any of my friends, fine or coarse, only for their
belongings, though my intercourse with the first

gratifies my love of luxury and excites what my Edinburgh friends call my ideality. I don't think, however, I ever could like anybody, of any kind whatever,
that I could not heartily respect, let their intellectual
gifts, elegance, or refinement of manners be what they
might. Good-bye, dearest H——.

Ever your affectionate
F. A. K.

Great Russell Street, October 3rd, 1831.

My dearest H——,
    I received your last letter on Thursday
morning, and as I read it exclaimed, "We shall be
able to go to her!" and passed it to Dall, who seemed
to think there was no reason why we should not, when
my father said he was afraid it could not be managed,
as the theatre, upon second arrangements, would require me before this month was over. It seems to me
that, instead of one disappointment, I have had twenty
about coming to you, dear H——, and the last has
fairly broken the poor camel's back. My father promised to see what could be done for me, and to get me
spared as long as possible ; but the final arrangement
is, that on the 24th I shall have to act Queen Katharine, for which, certainly, a week of daily rehearsals will
be barely sufficient preparation. This, you see, will
leave me hardly time enough to stay at Ardgillan to
warrant the fatigue and expense of the journey. I am
afraid it would be neither reasonable nor right to spend
nearly a week in travelling and the money it must
cost, to pass a fortnight with you. . . . Give my love
to your sister, and tell her how willingly I would have

accepted her hospitality had circumstances permitted
it; but "circumstances," of which we are so apt to
complain, may, perhaps, at some future time, allow me
to be once more her guest. The course of events is,
after all, far more impartial than, in moments of
disappointment, we are apt to admit, and quite as often
procures us unexpected and unthought-of pleasures
as defeats those we had proposed for ourselves.
Pazienza! Dear Dall, who I see, has produced her
invariable impression upon your mind, bids me thank
you for the kind things you say of her, at the same
time that she says, "though they are undeserved, she
is thankful for the affection that dictates them." She
is excellent. You bid me tell you of my father, and
how his health and spirits continue to struggle against
his exertions and anxieties: tolerably well, thank God!
I sometimes think they have the properties of that
palm tree which is said to grow under the pressure of
immense weights. He looks very well, and, except the
annoyances of his position in the theatre, has rather
less cause for depression than for some time past.
Though we have not yet obtained our "decree," we
understand that the Lord Chancellor says openly that
we shall get it, so that uncertainty of the issue no
longer aggravates the wearisome delays of this
unlucky appeal. . . . I need not tell you what my
feeling about acting Queen Katharine is; you, who
know how conscious I am of my own deficiencies for
such an undertaking, will easily conceive my distress
at having such a task assigned me. Dall, who
entirely agrees with me about it, wishes me to
remonstrate upon the subject, but that I will not do.

I am in that theatre to earn my living by serving its interests, and if I was desired to act Harlequin, for those two purposes, should feel bound to do so. But I cannot help thinking the management short-sighted. I think their real interest, as far as I am concerned, which they overlook for some immediate tangible advantage, is not to destroy my popularity by putting me into parts which I must play ill, and not to take from my future career characters which require physical as well as mental maturity, and which would be my natural resources when I no longer become Juliet and her youthful sisters of the drama. But of course they know their own affairs, and I am not the manager of the theatre. Those who have its direction, I suppose, make the best use they can of their instruments.

[My performance of Queen Katharine was not condemned as an absolute failure only because the public in general didn't care about it, and the friends and well-wishers of the theatre were determined not to consider it one. But as I myself remember it, it deserved to be called nothing else; it was a schoolgirl's performance, tame, feeble, and ineffective, entirely wanting in the weight and dignity indispensable for the part, and must sorely have tried the patience and forbearance of such of my spectators as were fortunate and unfortunate enough to remember my aunt; one of whom, her enthusiastic admirer, and my excellent friend, Mr. Harness, said that seeing me in that dress was like looking at Mrs. Siddons through the diminishing end of an opera-glass : I should think

my acting of the part must have borne much the
same proportion to hers. I was dressed for the trial
scene in imitation of the famous picture by Harlow,
and of course must have recalled, in the most provoking and absurd manner, the great actress whom I
resembled so little and so much. In truth, I could
hardly sustain the weight of velvet and ermine in
which I was robed, and to which my small girlish
figure was as little adapted as my dramatic powers
were to the matronly dignity of the character. I
cannot but think that if I might have dressed the
part as Queen Katharine really dressed herself, and
been allowed to look as like as I could to the little
dark, hard-favoured woman Holbein painted, it would
have been better than to challenge such a physical as
well as dramatic comparison by the imitation of my
aunt's costume in the part. Englishmen of her day
will never believe that Katharine of Arragon could
have looked otherwise than Mrs. Siddons did in
Shakespeare's play of "Henry VIII.;" but nothing
could in truth be more unlike the historical woman
than the tall, large, bare-armed, white-necked, Juno-
eyed, ermine-robed ideal of queenship of the English
stage. That quintessence of religious, conscientious
bigotry and royal Spanish pride is given, both in the
portraits of contemporary painters and in Shakespeare's delineation of her; the splendid magnificence
of my aunt's person and dress, as delineated in
Harlow's picture, has no affinity whatever to the real
woman's figure, or costume, or character.]

I

Great Russell Street, October 12th, 1831.

DEAREST H——,

I received my book and your letter very
safely about a week ago, and would have written to
say so sooner, but have been much occupied with one
thing and another that has prevented me. So you are
beaten, *vieilles perukes* that you are! not by one or
two, but by forty-one; and your bones are all the
likelier to ache, and I am not at all sorry. Think of
Brougham going down on his marrow-bones (there
can be none in them, though), and adjuring the Lords,
con quella voce! e quel viso! to pass the Bill, like
good boys, and remember the schoolmaster, who
surely, when he is at home, cannot be said to be
abroad. A good *coup de théâtre* is not an easy thing,
and requires a good deal of tact and skill. I cannot
help thinking there must have been something grotesque in this performance of Brougham's, as when
Liston turned tragedian and recited Collins's "Ode to
the Passions," in a green coat and top-boots. The
excitement, however, was tremendous; the House
thronged to suffocation; as many people crammed into
impossible space as the angels in the famous Needle-
point controversy. Lady Glengall declares that she sat
for four hours on an iron bar. I think this universal
political effervescence has got into my head. And
what will you do now? You cannot create forty-one
Peers; the whole Book of Genesis affords no precedent. I suppose Parliament will be prorogued,
ministers will go out, a "cloth of gold" and "cloth
of frieze" Government, with Brougham and Wellington
brought together into it, will be cobbled, and a new

Bill, which will set the teeth of the Lords so badly
on edge, will be concocted, which the people will accept
rather than nothing, if they are taken in the right
way. That, I suppose, is what you Whigs will do;
for an adverse majority of forty-one must be turned
somehow or other, as it can hardly be gone straight
at by folks who mean to keep on the box, or hold
the reins, or carry the coach to the end of the
journey. . . .

I do not know at all how I should like to live in
a palace; I am furiously fond of magnificence and
splendour, and not unreasonably, seeing that I was
born in a palace, with a sapphire ceiling hung with
golden lamps, and velvet floors all embroidered with
sweet-smelling, lovely-coloured flowers, and walls of
veined marble and precious, sparkling stones. I
almost doubt if any mere royal palace would be good
enough for me, or answer my turn. I should like all
the people in the world to be as beautiful as angels,
and go about crowned with glory and clothed with
light (dear me, how very different they are!); but
failing all that I should like in the way of enormously
beautiful things, I pick up and treasure like a baby all
the little broken bits of splendour and sumptuousness,
and thank Heaven that their number and gradations
are infinite, from the rainbow that the sun spans the
heavens with, to the fine, small jewel drawn from the
bowels of the earth to glitter on a lady's neck. . . .

My dearest H——, I wish I were with you with all
my heart, but, as if to diminish my regret by putting
the thing still further beyond the region of possibility,
I act next Monday the 17th, instead of the 24th.

(They say " a miss is as good as a mile ; " why does it always seem so much worse, then ?)   I begin with Belvidera, and have already begun my cares and woes and tribulations about lilac satins and silver tissues, etc., etc.   Young is engaged with us, and plays Pierre, and my father Giaffir, which will be very dreadful for me ; I do not know how I shall be able to bear all his wretchedness as well as my own.   To be a good politician one ought to have, as it were, only one eye for truth ; I do not at all mean to be single-eyed in the good sense of the word, but to be incapable of seeing more than one side of every question : one sees a part so much more strongly when one does not see the whole of a matter, and though a statesman may need a hundred eyes, I maintain that a party politician is the better for having only one.   Restricted vision is good for work, too ; people who see far and wide can seldom be very hopeful, I should think, and hope is the very essence of working courage.   The matter in hand should always, if possible, be the great matter to those who have to carry it through, and though broad brains may be the best for conceiving, narrow ones are, perhaps, the best for working with.

Thank you for your quotation from Sir Humphrey Davy ; it did me good, and even made me better for five minutes ; and your Irish letter, which interested me extremely.   " Walking the world."   What a sad and touching expression ; and how well it describes a broken and desponding spirit !   And yet what else are we all doing, in soul if not in body ?   Is not that solitary, wandering feeling the very essence of our existence here ?

You ask if the interests of the theatre and mine

are not identical? No, I think not. The management seems to me like our Governments for some time past, to be actuated by mere considerations of temporary expediency; that which serves a momentary purpose is all they consider. But it stands to reason that if they make me play parts in which I must fail, my London popularity must decrease, and with it my provincial profits; and that, of course, is a serious thing. In short, dear H——, where success means bread and butter, failure means dry bread, or none; and I hate the last, I believe, less than the first, though, as I never tried starvation, perhaps dry bread is nicer. . . .

The excitement about the Bill is rising instead of subsiding. The shops are all shut, and the people meeting in every direction; the windows of Apsley House have been smashed, and Wellington's statue (the Achilles in the Park) pelted and threatened to be pulled down. They say that Nottingham and Belvoir Castles are burnt down. All this is bad, and bodes, I fear, worse. Good-bye, dear.

Your affectionate

F. A. K.

Thursday, August 22nd.—I read some of "Cibber's Lives." I should like to read a well-written French life of Alin Chartier, Louis XI.'s ugly secretary, whose mouth Queen Margaret kissed while he was sleeping, ·" parce qu'elle avait dit de si belles choses." In the life, or rather the death, of Sackville, he notes his sitting up till eleven at night as a manifest waste of human existence. It is near two in the morning as I am now writing, but people's notions change as to

time as well as other things. We don't dine at
twelve any more. Macdonald, the sculptor, dined
with us; I like him for dear Scotland's sake, and the
blessed time I passed there.. After the gentlemen
came up into the drawing-room, Nourrit, the great
French tenor, sang delightfully for us; Adelaide sang
and played, and Nourrit made her try a charming
duet from the "Dame Blanche," which I accompanied,
and was frightened to death for self and sister. Macdonald wants to make a statue of me in "The
Grecian Daughter," at the moment of veiling the
face: he is right. An interval of some time elapsed,
in which I did not keep my journal regularly. I had
a long visit from my friend Miss S——. The lawsuit
about the theatre continued, the affairs of the concern
becoming more and more involved in difficulties every
day; and my father, worried almost to death with
anxiety, vexation, and hard work, had a serious
illness.

    Saturday, November 25th.—My father was not quite
so well this morning. I took Dr. Wilson home in
the carriage; he talked a great deal about this
horrible burking business (a series of atrocious murders committed by two wretches of the names of
Burk and Bishop, for the purpose of obtaining, for
the corpses of their victims, the price paid by the
Edinburgh surgeons for subjects for dissection; the
mode of death inflicted by these men came to be
designated by the name of the more hardened mur-
derer as burking).

    I called at Fozzard's for the boys, and set them
down at Angelo's (a famous school for fencing, boxing,

and single-stick, where my brothers took lessons in
those polite exercises). In the evening, at the theatre,
dear Charles Young played "The Stranger" for the
last time ; the house was very full, and I played very
ill. After the play Young was enthusiastically called
for. I have finished "Tennant's Tour in Greece,"
which I rather liked. I have been reading "Bonaparte's
Letters to Joséphine;" the vague and doubting spirit
which once or twice throws its wavering shadow
across his thoughts, startles one in contrast with the
habitual tone of the mind, which assuredly *ne doubtait
de rien*, especially of what his own power of will
could accomplish. The affection he expresses for his
wife is sometimes almost poetical from its intensity,
in spite of the grossness of his language. He seems
to have believed in nothing but volition, and that
volition is in itself, perhaps, a mere form of faith.
It's a dangerous worship, for the devil in that shape
does obey so long and so well before he claims his
due ; so much is achieved precisely by that belief in
what can be achieved ; the last round of the ladder,
somehow or other, however, always seems to break
down at last, and then I doubt if the people who fall
from it can all declare, as Holcroft did when he fell
from his horse, and, as his surgeon assured him, broke
his ribs, that he was positive he had not, because in
falling he had exerted the energy of will, and could
not therefore have broken his bones.

Sunday, 29th.—The great good fortune of a good
sermon at church. After church Mrs. Jameson, John
Mason, and Mr. Loudham called ; the latter said he
had good news about that fatal theatre of ours, for

that Mr. Harris seemed to be inclined to come into
some accommodation, and so perhaps this cancer of
a Chancery suit may stop eating our lives away. Oh
dear ! I am afraid this is too good news to be true.
I went to my father's room and sat by him for a long
time, and talked about the horse I had bought for
him ; and there he lies in his bed, and God knows
when he will even be able to walk again.

Monday, 30th.—I went to rehearsal. It seems that
the managers and proprietors (of course not my poor
father) had summoned a meeting of all the actors to
try and induce them to accept for the present a
reduced rate of salary till the theatre can be in some
measure relieved of its most pressing difficulties. I
knew nothing of this, and, finding them all very
solemnly assembled in the green room, asked them
cheerfully why they were all there, which must have
struck them strangely enough. I dare say they do
not know how little I know, or wish to know, about
this disastrous concern. On my retun home, I heard
that Dr. Watson had seen my father, and requested
that Dr. Wilson might be sent for. They fear inflammation of the lungs ; he has gone to the very limit
of his tether, for had he continued fagging a night or
two longer the effects might have been fatal. Poor,
poor father ! . . .

Lady Francis and Mrs. Sullivan called in the afternoon ; I was feeling miserable, and exhausted with my
rehearsal. In the evening I helped my mother to
move all the furniture, which I think is nothing in the
world but a restless indication of her anxiety about
my father ; it is the fourth time since she came back
from the country.

Tuesday, December 1st. . . . It seems that in the
arrangement, whatever it may be, which has taken
place between the actors and the managment, Mr.
Harley and Mr. Egerton are the only ones who have
declined the proposed accommodation. Young has
behaved like an angel, offering to play for nothing till
Christmas; how kind and liberal he is! Mr. Abbott,
Mr. Duraset, Mr. Ward, and all the others, have been
as considerate and generous as possible. But the
thing is doomed, and will go to the ground, in spite of
every effort that can be made to stave the ruin off.

I was greeted this morning, when I came down to
breakfast, with a question that surprised and amused
me very much. "Pray, Fanny," said John, "did you
ever thank Mr. Bacon (one of the editors of the *Times*)
for his book (the "Life of Francis I." which Mr. Bacon
had been kind enough to send me); for here is a very
abusive critique in to-day's *Times* of the play last
night." "Well," thought I, "that's a comical
sequitur, and a fine estimate of criticism;" but the
conclusion was droller still. I had not forgotten to
thank the friendly author for his book, nor had he
written the article in question; but it seems a young
gentleman, much in love with Miss Phillips (a promising and very handsome young actress at Drury Lane),
had found pulling me to pieces the easiest way of
showing his admiration for her. That is not a very
exalted style of criticism either, but it is just as well
that one should occasionally know what the praise
and blame one receives may be worth. It seems that
when it was determined that Miss Sheriff should
come out, Mr. Welsh, whose pupil she was, made a

great feast, and invited two and twenty gentlemen
connected with the press to a private hearing of her.
. . . In the evening, we all went to hear her, being
every way much interested in her success. John and
Henry went into the front of the house; my mother,
Dr. Moore (the Rev. Dr. Moore, a great friend of my
father and mother's), and myself, went up to our own
box. The house was crammed, the pit one black,
crowded mass. Poor child! I turned as cold as ice
as the symphony of "Fair Aurora" (the opera was
"Artaxerxes") began, and she came forward with Mr.
Wilson. The bravos, the clapping, the noise, the
great sound of popular excitement overpowering in
all its manifestations; and the contrast between the
sense of power conveyed by the acclamations of a
great concourse of people, and the weakness of the
individual object of that demonstration, gave me the
strangest sensation when I remembered my own
experience, which I had not seen. When I saw the
thousands of eyes of that crowded pitful of men, and
heard their stormy acclamations, and then looked at
the fragile, helpless, pretty young creature standing
before them trembling with terror, and all woman's
fear and shame in such an unnatural position, I more
than ever marvelled how I, or any woman, could ever
have ventured on so terrible a trial, or survived the
venture. It seemed to me as if the mere gaze of all
that multitude must melt the slight figure away like
a wreath of vapour in the sun, or shrivel it up like
a scrap of silver paper before a blazing fire. It made
poor Dr. Moore and myself both cry, but there was
a deal more sympathy in my tears than in his; for I

had known the dizzy terror of that moment, had felt
the ground slide from under my feet and the whole air
become a sea of fiery rings before my swimming eyes.
Besides my fellow-feeling for her actual agony, I had
one for what her after trials may be, and I hoped for
her that she might be able to see the truth of all
things in the midst of all things false; and then, if
she takes pleasure in her gilded toys, she will not
have too bitter a heartache when they are broken.
She sang well, and soon recovered from her fright,
which, even from the first, did not affect her voice.
She is rather pretty, but does not walk or move
gracefully; she was well dressed, all but her hair,
which was dressed in the present frizzy French
fashion, and looked ridiculous for Mandane. Her
singing was good, of a good style; I do not mean only
that she sang "Fly, soft ideas, fly," and "Monster,
away!" and "The Soldier Tired," brilliantly, because
they do not test the best singing, but the *soave
sostenuto* of her "If e'er the cruel tyrant love," and
"Let not rage thy bosom firing," were specimens of
the best and most difficult school of singing. They
were flowing, smooth, soft, and sweet, without trick
or device of mere florid ornamentation, and were as
intrinsically good in her execution as they are admirable in that peculiar style of composition. Her shake
is not genuine, and some of her rapid descending
scales want finish and accuracy; her use of her arms
and her gestures were very pretty and graceful, and
we were all greatly pleased with her. Braham was
magnificently great, in spite of his inches. What a
noble artist he is! and with what wonderful vigour

he acts through his singing ! being no actor at all the moment he stops singing. Wilson sang out of tune ; the music is not in his voice, and he was frightened. Miss Cawse was rather a dumpy Artaxerxes, which is an impertinent remark for me to make ; she has a beautiful contralto voice. The opera went off brilliantly, and after it the audience called for " God Save the King," which was performed. Paganini was in the box opposite to us ; what a cadaverous-looking creature he is ! Came home and saw my father, and gave him the report of Miss Sheriff's success. . . .

Friday, December 2nd. . . . I went to see Cecilia Siddons ; I thought her looking aged and thin, and Mrs. Wilkinson (Mrs. Siddons's companion for many years previous to her death) looking sad and ill too. They have both lost the one idea of their whole lives.

Saturday, 3rd. . . . It seems the doctors recommend my father's going to Brighton. I was urging him to do so this morning. . . . . After tea I looked on the map for Rhodez, the scene of that horrible Fualdes tragedy (a murder the commission of which involved some singular and terribly dramatic incidents). I read Daru's " History of Venice " till bedtime.

Sunday, December 4th. . . . My father, for the first time this fortnight, was able to dine with us. After dinner I read the whole trial of Bishop and Williams, and their confession. My mother is reading aloud to us Lord Edward Fitzgerald's Life.

Great Russell Street, Dec. 4th, 1831.

DEAR H——,

It is at the sensible hour of a quarter-past twelve at night that I begin this immense sheet of paper, and with the sensible purpose of filling it before I go to bed. . . . What an unsatisfactory invention letter-writing is, to be sure ; and yet there is none better for the purpose.   When you asked me so affectionately in your letter whether I was going to bed, I concluded naturally that you were writing to me instead of doing so yourself ; but I received the letter at half-past nine in the morning, when I was getting ready to ride.   This sort of epistolary cross questions and crooked answers is sometimes droll, but oftener sad : we weep with those who did weep, when they have dried their eyes ; and rejoice with those who did rejoice, but the corners of whose mouths are already drawn down for crying, while we fancy we are smiling sympathetically with them. . . . You ask me how the world goes with me, and I can only say round, as I suppose it does with everybody.   All goes on precisely as usual with me ; my life is exceedingly uniform, and it is seldom that anything occurs to disturb its monotonous routine.   My dear father, thank Heaven, is better, but still very weak, and I fear it will be yet some time before he recovers his strength. He came down to dinner to-day for the first time in this fortnight ; indeed, it is only since the day before yesterday that he has left his bed ; but I trust that this attack will serve him for a long time, and that with rest and quiet he will regain his strength.

I am really glad my aunt Kemble is better, though

I remember having some not unpleasant ideas as to how, if she were not, you would go to Leamington to nurse her, and so come on and stay with us in London; but I cannot wish it at the price of her prolonged indisposition, poor woman ! . . . I am sorry to say my father is pronounced worse to-day ; he has a bad side-ache, and they are applying mustard poultices to overcome it. There is some apprehension of a return of fever. This is a real and terrible anxiety, dear H——. The theatre, too, is going on very ill, and he is unable to give it any assistance ; and for the same reason I can do nothing for it, for all my plays require him, except Isabella and Fazio, and these are worn threadbare. It is all very gloomy ; but, however, time doth not stand still, and will some day come to the end of the journey with us. . . . You say Undine reminds you of me. . . . The feeling of an existence more closely allied to the elements of the material universe than even we acknowledge our dust-formed bodies to be, 'possesses me sometimes almost like a little bit of magnus ; bright colours, fleeting lights and shadows, flowers, and above all water, the pure, sparkling, harmonious, powerful element, excite in me a feeling of intimate fellowship, of love, almost greater than any human companionship does. Perhaps, after all, I am only an animated morsel of my palace, this wonderful, beautiful world. Do you not believe in numberless, invisible existences, filling up the vast intermediate distance between God and ourselves, in the lonely and lovely haunts of nature and her more awful and gloomy recesses ? It seems as if one must be sur-

rounded by them; I do not mean to the point of
merely suggesting the vague "suppose?" *that*, I
should think, must visit every mind; but rather like
a consciousness, a conviction, amounting almost to
certainty, only short of seeing and hearing. How
well I remember in that cedar hall at Oatlands, the
sort of invisible presence I used to feel pervading the
place. It was a large circle of huge cedar trees in a
remote part of the grounds; the paths that led to it
were wild and tangled; the fairest flower, the fox-
glove, grew in tall clumps among the foliage of the
thickets and shrubberies that divided the lawn into
undulating glades of turf all round it; a sheet of
water in which there was a rapid current—I am not
sure that it was not the river—ran close by, and the
whole place used to affect my imagination in the
weirdest way, as the habitation of invisible presences
of some strange supernatural order. As the evening
came on, I used frequently to go there by myself,
leaving our gentlemen at table, and my mother and
Lady Francis in the drawing-room. How I flew along
by the syringa bushes, brushing their white fragrant
blossoms down in showers as I ran, till I came to that
dark cedar hall, with its circle of giant trees, whose
wide-sweeping branches spread, as it were, a halo of
darkness all round it. Through the space at the top,
like the open dome of some great circular temple,
such as the Pantheon of Rome, the violet-coloured
sky and its starry worlds looked down. Sometimes
the pure radiant moon and one fair attendant star
would seem to pause above me in the dark frame-
work of the great tree-tops. That place seemed

peopled with spirits to me; and while I was there I had the intensest delight in the sort of all but conscious certainty that it was so. Curiously enough, I never remember feeling the slightest nervousness while I was there, but rather an immense excitement in the idea of such invisible companionship; but as soon as I had emerged from the magic circle of the huge black cedar trees, all my fair visions vanished, and, as though under a spell, I felt perfectly possessed with terror, and rushed home again like the wind, fancying I heard following footsteps all the way I went. The moon seemed to swing to and fro in the sky, and every twisted tree and fantastic shadow that lay in my path made me start aside like a shying horse. I could have fancied they made grimaces and gestures at me, like the rocks and roots in Retsch's etchings of the Brocken; and I used to reach the house with cheeks flaming with nervous excitement, and my heart thumping a great deal more with fear than with my wild run home; and then I walked with the utmost external composure of demure propriety into the drawing-room, as who should say, " Thy servant went no whither," to any inquiry that might be made as to my absence. . . .

It seems to me that you would be a poet but for your analysing, dissecting, inquiring, and doubting mental tendency. Your truth is not a matter of intuition, but of demonstration; and when you get beyond demonstrability, then nothing remains to you but doubt. . . . God bless you, dear !

I am yours ever affectionately,

F. A. K.

Monday, Dec. 5th. . . . My father is worse again to-day. Ohimé! His state is most precarious, and this relapse very alarming. It is dreadful to see him drag himself about, and hear his feeble voice. Oh, my dear, dear Father! Heaven preserve you to us!

Tuesday, 6th.—My father is much worse. How terrible this is! . . . Dall met me on the stairs this morning, and gave me a miserable account of him; he had just been bled, and that had somewhat relieved him. I went and sat with him while my mother drove out in the carriage. I stayed a long while with him, and he seemed a little better. . . . My father's two doctors have returned again, and paid him two visits daily. I read Daru all the evening.

Wednesday, 7th. . . . So I am to play Belvidera on Monday, and Bianca on Wednesday. That will be hard work; Bianca is terrible.

Thursday, 8th. . . . My dear father is beginning to gain strength once more, thank Heaven! I received a letter from Lady Francis about the play (a translation of the French piece of "Henri Trois," by Lord Francis, the production of which at Covent Garden is being postponed in consequence of my father's illness). Poor people! I am sorry for their disappointment. . . . I devised and tried on a new dress for Bianca; it will be very splendid, but I am afraid I shall look like a metal woman, a golden image. [The dress in question was entirely made of gold tissue; and one evening a man in the pit exclaimed to a friend of mine sitting by him, " Oh! doesn't she look like a splendid gold

pheasant?" the possibility of which comparison had
not occurred to me, not being a sportsman.]

Friday, 9th. . . . I went with my mother to the
theatre to hear "Fra Diavolo," with which, and Miss
Sheriff's singing in it, we were delighted.

Saturday, 10th. . . . We had a talk about the
fashion of southern countries of serenading, which I
am very glad is not an English fashion. Music, as
long as I am awake, is a pure and perfect delight to
me, but to be wakened out of my sleep by music is to
wake in a spasm of nervous terror, shaking from
head to foot, and sick at my stomach, with indescribable fear and dismay; certainly no less agreeable
effect could possibly be contemplated by the gallantry
of a serenading admirer, so I am glad our admirers
do not serenade us English girls. This picturesque
practice prevails all through the United States, where
the dry brilliancy of the climate and skies is favourable
to the paying and receiving this melodious homage,
and where musical bands, sometimes numbering fifty,
are marshalled by personal or political admirers,
under the balconies of reigning beauties or would-be-
reigning public men. My total ignorance of this
prevailing practice in the United States led to a very
prosaic demonstration of gratitude on my part towards
my first serenaders; for I opened my window and
rewarded them with a dollar, which one of the
recipients informed me he should always keep, to my
no small confusion, not knowing the nature of my
gratuitous indulgence, and that, like my Lady Green-
sleeves in the old English ballad, "My music still
to play and sing" would be, while I remained in

America, a disinterested demonstration of the devotion of my friends. . . . My poor mother is in the deepest distress about my father. Inflammation of the lungs is dreaded, and he is spitting blood. I felt as if I were turning to stone as I heard it. I came up to my own room and cried most bitterly for a long time. In the afternoon I was allowed to go in and see my father; but I was so overcome that, as I stooped to kiss his hand, I was almost suffocated with suppressed sobs. I did control myself, however, sufficiently to be able to sit by him for a while with tolerable composure. Cecilia and Mrs. Wilkinson called, and were very kind and affectionate to me. They brought news that Harry Siddons had arrived in India and been sent off to Delhi. My brother Henry, poor child, came and lay on the sofa in my room, and we cried together almost through the whole afternoon, in spite of our efforts to comfort each other. My heart dies away when I think of my dear father. . . . I got a very kind and affectionate letter from Lady Francis; she wants us very much to go again to Oatlands. After all, perhaps it would not be so sad there as I think, though it must appear changed enough in some respects, if not in all. Everything is winter now, within and without me; and when I was last there it was summer, in my heart and over all the earth. My cedar palace is there still, and to that I should bring more change than I should find. Poor Undine! how often I think of that true story. When I went to the theatre my heart really sickened at my work; my eyes smarted, and my voice was broken, with my whole day's crying. The house seemed good; I played ill, and felt very ill.　Lord M—— was in the stage-box, which annoyed me.　I hate to have my society acquaintance close to me while I am acting.　The play was "Venice Preserved."　After I came home I saw my father, who is a little better; but now Henry is quite unwell, and I am in a high fever—I suppose with all this wretchedness and exertion.

Thursday, 13*th.*—My father has passed a quieter night, thank God.　I went to Fozzard's riding school with John, and tried a hot little hunter that they want to persuade Lady Chesterfield to ride—a very pretty creature, but quite too eager for the school.　While I was riding Lady Grey came in, very much frightened, upon her horse, which was rather fresh.　She took Gazelle, which I was riding, and I rode her horse tame for her.　It is very odd that, riding as well as she does, she should be so miserably nervous on horseback. . . .　I drove to Mrs. Mayo's, who impressed and affected me very much.　Those magnificent eyes of hers are becoming dim; she is growing blind, with eyes like dark suns.　I could not help expressing the deep concern I felt for such a calamity.　She replied that doubtless it was a trial, but that she saw many others afflicted with dispensations so much heavier than her own, that she was content.　To grow blind contentedly is to be very brave and good, and I admired and loved her even more than I did before.　When I came home, I went and sat with my father.　He has decided that we shall not go to Oatlands, and I am hardly sorry for it.

Friday, 14*th.*—Went over my part for to-night. . . .　Victoire came with me to the theatre instead of Dall,

whose whole time is taken up attending on my
father. The house was bad, and I thought I acted
very ill, though Victoire and John, who was in the
front, said I did not. Henry Greville was in the
boxes, and to my surprise went from them to the pit,
though I ought not to have been surprised, for, for
such a fine gentleman, he is a very sensible man.
Colonel and Lady C. Cavendish were in the orchestra,
and how I did wish them further. I do so wonder, in
the middle of my stage despair, what business my
drawing-room acquaintances have sitting staring at
it. My dress was beautiful. As for the audience, I
do not know what ailed them, but they seemed to
have agreed together only to applaud at the end of
the scenes, so that I got no resting interruptions, and
was half dead with fatigue at the end of the play. I
read Daru's "Venice" between the scenes, and saw
my father for a few minutes after I came home.

Thursday, 15*th.*—Had a delightful long letter from
H——, who is a poet without the jingle. . . . Another
physician is to be called in for my father. Oh, my
dear father! Mr. Bartley was with him about this
horrible theatre business. . . . My mother went in
the evening with John to hear Miss Sheriff in Polly.
It is her first night in " The Beggar's Opera," and my
father wished to know how it went. I stayed at home
with poor Henry, and after tea sat with my father till
bedtime.

Friday, 16*th.*—Went to the theatre at eleven, and
rehearsed Isabella in the saloon, the stage · being
occupied with a rehearsal of the pantomime. When
my rehearsal was over, the carriage not being come,.

I went down to see what they were doing. There was poor Farleigh, nose and all (a worthy, amiable man, and excellent comic character, with a huge excrescence of a nose), *qui se déménait* like one frantic; huge Mr. Stansbury, with a fiddle in his hand, dancing, singing, prompting, and swearing; the whole *corps de ballet* attitudinizing in muddy shoes and poke bonnets, and the columbine, in dirty stockings and a mob-cap, ogling the harlequin in a striped shirt and dusty trousers. What a wrong side to the show the audience will see!

My father is better, thank God. After dinner sat with poor Henry till time to go to the theatre. Played Isabella. House bad. I played well; I always do to an empty house (this was my invariable experience both in my acting and reading performances, and I came to the conclusion that as my spirits were not affected by a small audience, they, on the contrary, were exhilarated by the effect upon my lungs and voice of a comparatively cool and free atmosphere). I read Daru between my scenes; I find it immensely interesting. . . . I read Niccolini's "Giovanni di Procida," but did not like it very much; I thought it dull and heavy, and not up to the mark of such a very fine subject.

Saturday, 17*th*. . . . My father, thank God, appears much better. . . . I have christened the pretty mare I have bought "Donna Sol," in honour of my part in "Hernani." In the evening I read Daru, and wrote a few lines of "The Star of Seville;" but I hate it, and the whole thing is as dead as ditch-water.

Sunday, 18*th*.—To church. . . . After I came home

I went and sat with my father. Poor fellow! he is
really better; thank God inexpressibly!

Great Russell Street, December 18th.

Dear H——,
    I have had time to write neither long nor
short letters for the last week; Mr. Young's engagement being at an end, I have been called back to my
work, and have had to rehearse, and to act, and to be
much too busy to write to you until to-day, when I
have caught up all my arrears.

My father, thank God, is once more recovering,
but we have twice been alarmed at such sudden re-
lapses that we hardly dare venture to hope he is really
convalescent. Inflammation on the lungs has, it seems,
been going on for a considerable time, and though
they think now that it has entirely subsided, yet, as
the least exertion or exposure may bring it on again,
we are watching him like the apples of our eyes.
He has not yet left his bed, to which he has now been
confined more than a month. . . . The exertion I
have been obliged to make when leaving him to go and
act, was so full of misery and dread lest I should find
him worse, perhaps dead, on my return, that no words
can describe what I have suffered at that dreadful
theatre. Thank God, however, he is now certainly
better, out of present danger, and I trust and pray
will soon be beyond any danger of a relapse. Anything like Dall's incessant and unwearied care and
tenderness you cannot imagine. Night and day she
has watched and waited on him, and I think she must
have sunk under all the fatigue she has undergone

but for the untiring goodness and kindness of heart that has supported her under it all. She is invaluable to us all, and every day adds to her claims upon our love and gratitude. . . .

In the passage you quote from Godwin, he seems to think a friend of more use in reproving what is evil in us than I believe is really the case. Do you think our faults and follies can ever be more effectually sifted, analyzed, and condemned by another than by our own conscience ? I do not think if one could put one's heart into one's friends' hand that they could detect one defect or evil quality that had not been marked and acknowledged in the depths of one's own consciousness. Do you suppose people shrink more from the censure of others than from self-condemnation ? I find it difficult to think so. . . . You appear to me always to wish to submit your faith to a process which invariably breaks your apparatus and leaves you very much dissatisfied, with your faith still a simple element in you, in spite of your endeavours to analyze or decompose it. Are not, after all, our convictions our only steadfastly grounded faith ? I do not mean conviction wrought out in the loom of logical argument, where one's understanding must have shuttled backwards and forwards through every thread a thousand times before the woof is completed, but the spiritual convictions, the intuitions of our souls, that lie upon their surface like direct reflections from heaven, distinct and beautiful enough for reverent contemplation, but a curious search into whose nature would, at any rate temporarily, blur and dissipate and destroy. . . .

The sense of power which man cannot control is

one thing that makes the sea such a delightful object
of contemplation; the huge white main, and deep,
tremendous voice of the vast creature over which
man's daring and his knowledge give him but such
imperfect mastery, suggest images of strength which
are full of sublime fascination as one stands on the
shore, looking at the vasty deep, and remembers how
precarious and uncertain is man's dominion over it,
and how God alone rules and governs it. It is impossible not to rejoice in the great sense of its huge
power and freedom, even though their manifestations
towards men are so often terrible and destructive.
. . . Oh yes, indeed, I, like Wallenstein, have faith in
the "strong hours," and hold their influence the more
efficacious that we seldom think of resisting it; or, if
we do, are seldom successful in the attempt. . . .

The theatre is going on very ill, but negotiations
are pending between the partners, which it is hoped
may eventually terminate in some arrangement with
the creditors about the property. I have been acting
Bianca again; I certainly am not jealous, and
cannot imagine being so, any more of my husband
than of my friend. I doubt if I have the power of
loving which produces jealousy, in spite of which that
part tries me dreadfully. I can conceive no torment
comparable to that passion which, however, I think is
foreign to my own nature. I am reading Daru's
"History of Venice," and am rather disappointed in
the entertainment I expected to derive from it. It is
a pretty long undertaking, too. . . . Remember me to
all your people; and since you will have it that I am
twin-sister to a fountain, remember me to my cousin,

the dear little spring in the dell, which I love the more that it sometimes reflects your face and figure, as well as the fairies who dance round it by night. Do you hear that poor Lord Grey is said to be haunted by a vision of Lord Castlereagh's head? It sounds like a temptation of the devil to scare him into cutting his throat. Lord Brougham and the Duke of Wellington seem to me the only two men likely to keep their heads in these times of infinite political perturbation; but the one is made of steel, and the other of india-rubber.

Yours, dearest, always,

F. A. K.

Monday, 19*th.*—Went to Fozzard's, and had a pleasant, gossiping ride with Lady Grey and Miss Cavendish. While I was still riding, the Duchess of Kent and our little queen that is to be came down into the school; I was presented to them at their desire, and thought Princess Victoria a very unaffected, bright-looking girl. Fozzard made me gallop round; I think he is rather proud of showing me off. . . . My father is not so well again to-day. How dreadful these alternations are! I read Daru all the afternoon, and then sang in my own room to amuse Henry, till dinner-time. Colonel Bailey sent me the mare's saddle and bridle, and after dinner the boys put them on a chair for me, and gave me an absurd make-believe ride.

Wednesday, 21*st.*—Dear Mr. Harness called, and I received him. He tells me that at the theatre they want to do his tragedy ("The Wife of Antwerp," was, I

think, the name of the piece) without my father; but
this seems to me really sheer madness. The play is a
pretty, interesting, well-written piece, and, well propped
and sustained, may perhaps succeed for a few nights,
but as to throwing the whole weight, or rather weakness of it, upon my shoulders, or any one pair of
shoulders, it is folly to think of it. It is not a powerful sort of monologue like "Fazio," where the interest
centres in one person and one passion, and therefore
if that character is well sustained the rest can shift
for itself. It is no such matter; it is a play of incident
and not of character, and must be played by people
and not one person. What terrible bad management!
But, poor people! what can they do, with my father
lying disabled there? If it was not for their complete
disregard for their own interest, I should be inclined
to quarrel with them for the way in which they are
ruining mine; and I sincerely hope, for the sake of
everybody concerned, that Mr. Harness will resist this
senseless proposition.

I went with John in the afternoon to Angerstein's
Gallery (M. Angerstein's fine collection of pictures
was not then incorporated in the National Gallery, of
which it subsequently became so important a portion);
there are some new pictures there. Unluckily, we had
only an hour to stay, but I brought away a great deal
with me for so short a time. Among the additions
was a very singular old painting, "The Holy Family,"
by one of the earliest masters, whose name I forget,
not being familiar with it. I looked long at the
glorious Titian, the "Bacchus and Ariadne," which
always reminds me of—

"Whence come ye, jolly Satyrs, whence come ye?
Like to a moving vintage down they came."

One of the most famous pictures here is "Our
Saviour disputing with the Doctors," by Leonardo
da Vinci. I hardly ever receive pleasure from his
pictures; there is a mannerism in all that I have
seen that is positively disagreeable to me. How the
later artists lost the simple secret of earnest vigour of
their predecessors, while gaining in everything that
was not that! Grace, finish, refinement, accuracy of
drawing, richness of colouring, all that merely tended
towards perfection and execution, while the simplicity
and single-heartedness of conception died away more
and more. All art seems by degrees to outgrow its
strength, and certainly in painting the archaic cradle
touches one's imagination as neither the graceful
youth nor mature manhood do. "Le mieux c'est
l'ennemi du bien" in nothing more than the progress
of art after a certain period of its development, and
when its mere mechanism is best understood, and
applied in the most masterly manner. The spirit has
tarried behind, and we have to return to seek it among
the earlier days, when the genius of man was like a
giant, rude, naked, and savage, but vigorous and free,
—unadorned indeed, but also untrammelled. Only a
certain proportion of excellence is allowed to our race,
but that is granted; and let us stretch it, expand
it, roll and beat it out as we will, it is still but
the same square inch made thin to cover a greater
surface. For one good we still must yield another;
we have no gain that is not loss, no acquisition but

surrender, " exchange " which may perhaps be " no
robbery," though quantity does seem a poor substitute
for quality in matters of beauty. I wish I had lived
in the times when the ore lay in the ingot (and had
been one of the few who owned a nugget), instead of
in these times of universal gold-leaf, glitter without
weight, and shining shallowness of mere surface.
Vigour is better than refinement, and to create better
than to improve, and to conceive better than to combine. I wonder if the world, or rather the human
mind, will ever really grow decrepit, and the fountain
of beauty in men's souls run dry to the dregs ; or will
the manifestations only change, and the eternal spirit
reveal itself in other ways ? . . .

On our way home I had a long and interesting talk
with John about the different forms of religious faith
into which the gradual development of the human
mind has successively expanded ; each, of course,
being the result of that very development, acting on
the original necessity to believe in and worship and
obey something higher and better than itself, im-
planted in our nature. It seems strange that he
has a leaning to Roman Catholicism, which I have
not. Our Protestant profession appears to me the
purest creed—form—that Christianity has yet arrived
at ; but, I suppose, a less spiritual one, or perhaps I
should say external accompaniments, affecting more
palpably the senses and imagination, are wholesome
and necessary to the cultivation and preservation of
the religious sentiment in some minds. Catholicism
was the faith of the chivalrous times, of the poetical
times, of times when the creative faculty of man

poured forth in since unknown abundance masterpieces of every kind of beauty, as manifestations of
the pious and devout enthusiasm. Protestantism is
undoubtedly the faith of these times; a denying faith,
a rejecting creed, a questioning belief, its evil seems
essentially to coincide with the worst tendency of the
present age, but its good seems to me positive and un-
conditional, independent of time or circumstance; the
best, in that kind, that the believing necessity in our
nature has yet attained. Rightly understood and
lived up to, the only service of God which is intellectual freedom, as all His service, lived up to, under
what creed soever, is moral freedom. And it is in
some sort in spite of myself that I say this, for my
fancy delights in all the devout and poetical legendary
conceptions which the stern hand of reason has
stripped from our altars.

I found a letter at home from Emily Fitzhugh;
she writes me word she has been revising my aunt
Siddons's letters; thence an endless discussion as to
the nature of genius, what it is. I suppose really
nothing but the creative power, and so it remains a
question if the greatest actor can properly be said to
possess it. Again, how far does the masterly filling
out of an inferior conception by a superior execution
of it, such as really great actors frequently present,
fall short of creative power, properly so called? Is it
a thing positive, of individual inherent quality, or
comparative, and composed of mere respective quantity? Can its manifestation be partial, and restricted
to one faculty, or must it be a pervading influence,
permeating the whole mind? Certainly Mrs. Siddons

was what we call a great dramatic genius, and off the
stage gave not the slightest indication of unusual
intellectual capacity of any sort. Kean, the only
actor whose performances have ever realized to me
my idea of the effect tragic acting ought to produce,
acted part of his parts rather than ever a whole
character, and a work of genius should at least show
unity of conception. My father, whose fulfilling of a
particular range of characters is as nearly as possible
perfect, wants depth and power, and power seems to
me the core, the very marrow, so to speak, of genius;
and if it is not genius that gave incomparable majesty
and terror to my aunt's Lady Macbeth, and to Kean's
Othello incomparable pathos and passion, and to my
father's Benedict incomparable spirit and grace, what
is it? Mere talent carried beyond a certain point?
If so, where does the one begin and the other end? Or
is genius a precious, inconvertible, intellectual metal,
of which some people have a grain and a half, and
some only half a grain. . . . There is dreadful news
from Spain, and I fear it is too true. Torrijos has
made another attempt. Oh, how thankful we must
be that John is returned to us!

Great Russell Street, Monday, December 23rd.

DEAR MRS. JAMESON,

I owe you many excuses for not having
sooner acknowledged your letter, but you may have
seen by the papers that we have been bringing out a
new piece, and that is always, while it goes on, an
engrossing of time and attention paramount to all
other claims. It is a play of Lord Francis Leveson's,

and I know you will be glad to hear that it has been successful and is likely to prove serviceable to the theatre. Another reason, too, for my silence is, that I have been working very hard at "The Star of Seville," which, I am thankful to say, has at length reached its completion. I have sent it to the theatre upon approbation, in the usual routine of business; and am waiting very patiently the decision of the management on its fitness or unfitness for their purposes.

I know not whether your party at Teddesley are good thermometers, by which to judge of the state of political feeling here in London, but at this moment the rumour is rife that the Ministry dare not make the new batch of Peers, cannot carry the Bill, and must resign. To whom? is the next question, and it seems a difficult one to answer. One hardly sees, looking round the political ranks, who are to be the men to come forward and take up this tangled skein effectually. I write with rather a sympathetic lean-ing towards the Tory side of this Reform question, and do not know whether in so doing I am affronting you or not. In any case, I imagine, there can be but one opinion as to the difficulty, and even danger, of the present position of public affairs and public temper with regard to them.

Do you not soon think of returning to Town? or are you so well pleased with your present abode as to prolong your visit? London is particularly full, I think, for the time of year, and people are meeting in smaller numbers and a more sociable and agreeable way than they do later in the season. I was at two

parties last week, each time, I am ashamed to say,
after acting. I can't say that I find society pleasant;
it reminds me a good deal of a tiresome game, somewhat out of date in its original form, called "Conversation Cards," the insipid flippancy of whose
questions and answers seems to me to survive in
these meetings, miscalled occasionally *conversaziones*.
Dancing appears to me rational, and indeed highly
intellectual, in comparison with such talk; and that I
am as fond of as ever, but that has not begun yet, and
I find these *soirées causantes* drearily unedifying.

Talking of stupid parties, your beautiful little
picture of me and my various costumes helped away
two hours of such intolerably dull people here the
other night; I assure you we all voted you devout
thanks on the occasion. . . . We are all tolerably
well; my father is gradually recovering his strength,
and though after such an attack as his has been the
progress must of necessity be slow, we are inclined to
hope, from that very circumstance, that it will be the
more sure. . . . If you do not return soon, perhaps I
shall hear from you again; pray recollect that it will
give me great pleasure to do so, and that I am very
sincerely yours,

F. A. K.

I dressed my Juliet the last time I acted it, exactly
after your little sketch of her. . . .

Thursday.—Worked at "The Star of Seville." In
the evening the play was "Isabella;" the house very
bad. I played very well. The Rajah Ramahun Roy
was in the Duke of Devonshire's box, and went into
fits of crying, poor man!

Friday, 23rd.—It is all too true; John has had a letter from Spain; they have all been taken and shot. I felt frozen when I heard the terrible news. Poor Torrijos ! And yet I suppose it is better so: he would only have lived to bitter disappointment, and the despairing conviction that the spirit he appealed to did not animate one human being in his deplorable and degenerate land. A young Englishman, of the name of Boyd, John's sometime friend and companion, was taken and shot with the rest : it choked me to think of his parents, his brothers and sisters. Surely God has been most merciful to us in sparing us such an anguish, and bringing our wanderer home before this day of doom. How I thought of Richard Trench and his people ! John did not seem to me to be violently affected, though his first exclamation was one of sharp and bitter pain: I suppose he must, long ere this, have felt that there could be no other end to this utterly hopeless attempt. . . . In the afternoon I called on Mrs. Norton, who is always to me astonishingly beautiful. The baby was asleep, and so I could not see it, but Spencer has grown into a very fine child.

Monday, 26th.—Went to see how the pantomime did. I did not think it very amusing, but there was an enchanting little girl (Miss Poole) who did Tom Thumb, and whose attitudes in her armour were most of them copied from the antique, and really beautiful. Poor dear, bright little thing !

My father was in bed when we returned; I went and saw him for a minute, to tell him how the pantomime had succeeded; it ended with some wonder-

ful tight-rope dancing by an exceedingly steady,
graceful man; but it turned me perfectly sick, and I
hate all those sort of things.

Thursday, 29th.—After dinner worked at "The
Star of Seville." I really wonder I have the
patience to go on with it, it is such heavy trash.
After tea my father begged me to sing to him. I
am always horribly frightened at singing before my
mother; I cannot bear to distress her accurate ear
with my unsteady intonation, and the more I think of
it, the colder my hands grow and the hotter my face,
the huskier my voice and the flatter my notes; I
bungle over accompaniments that I have at my
fingers' ends, and forget words I know as well as my
alphabet; in short, I feel like a wretch, and I sing
like a wretch, and I make wretched all my hearers. My
mother's own nervous terror when she had to sing on
the stage, as a young woman, was excessive, as she
has often told me; and her mother repeatedly but
vainly endeavoured to bribe her with the promise of a
guinea if she would sing as well in public any of the
songs that she sang perfectly well at home. I sang
for some time, and by degrees got more courage, till
at last I managed to sing tolerably in tune. My
mother says I have more voice than A——. I am
sorry to hear her voice has grown thin—that sweet,
melodious voice I did so love to listen to; but perhaps
it will recover its tone.

Wednesday, 28th.—My dear, dear father came down
to breakfast, looking horribly thin and pale, poor
fellow! but, thank God, he was able to come once
more among us. I am to act Euphrasia on Monday;

how I do hate it! Monday week my father talks of
resuming his work again with Mercutio. Dear me!
how happy I shall be! once more speaking the love
poetry of Juliet after all these "meaner beauties of
the night" that I have been executing ever since he
has been ill. Juliet did very right to die; she would
have become Bianca when once she was Mrs. Romeo
Montague. . . . I wrote to Lady Francis about
"Katharine of Cleves" (Lord Francis' translation of
"Henri Trois"), who is once more beginning to lift
up her head. My father thinks it may be done on
Wednesday week. . . . It is now determined that
Henry should go into the army, and my mother wants
me to besiege Sir John through Lady Macdonald (the
general's general) about a commission for him. In
the evening, not having to be anybody tragical or
heroical, I indulged in my own character, and had a
regular game of romps with the boys; my pensive
public would not have believed its eyes if it could
have seen me with my hair all dishevelled, not because
of my woes, but because of riotous fun, jumping over
chairs and sofas, and dodging behind curtains and
under tables to escape from my pursuers. "Is that
Miss Kemble?" as poor Mr. Bacon involuntarily
exclaimed the first time he saw me.

Great Russell Street, December 29, 1831.

MY DEAREST H——,
        You shall not entreat in vain, neither shall
you have a short answer because you have an immediate one. . . . I should not have answered you so
instantaneously, but that my last account of my dear

father was so bad that I cannot delay telling you how
much better he is, and how grateful we all are for his
restoration to health. He is released from his bed,
of which he must be heartily sick, and comes down to
breakfast at the usual time : of course he is still weak
and low, and wretchedly thin, but we trust a little
time will bring back good spirits and good looks,
though after such a terrible attack I fear it will
be long before his constitution recovers its former
strength, if indeed it ever does. He talks of resuming his labours at the theatre next Monday week.
Oh ! my dear H——, what a dreadful season of
anxiety this has been ! but, thank God, it is past.

I had intended that this letter should go to you to-
day, but you will forgive the delay of a day in my
finishing it when I tell you that I have some hope of
its producing a commission for Henry. Sir John Macdonald, at whose house you dined in the summer with
my mother, is now adjutant-general, and I know not
what besides ; and after my mother and myself had
expended all our eloquence in winding up my father's
mind to resolve upon the army as Henry's profession,
she thought the next best thing I could do would be
to attack Lady Macdonald and secure the general's
interest. They happened to call this afternoon, and
your letter, my dear H——, has been left unfinished
till past post-time, while I was soliciting this favour,
which I have every hope we shall obtain. Lady
Macdonald is extremely kind and good-natured, and I
am sure will exert herself to serve us, and if this can
be accomplished I shall be haunted by one anxiety
the less.

Henry is too young and too handsome to be doing nothing but lounging about the streets of London, and even if he should be ordered to the Indies, it is something to feel that he is no longer aimless and objectless in life—a mere squanderer of time, without interest, stake, or duty, in this existence. I am sure this news will pacify you, and atone for the day's delay in this letter reaching you.

[My youngest brother Henry had a passionate desire to be a sailor, and never exhibited the slightest inclination for any other career. Admiral Lake, who was a very kind friend of my father's and mother's, knowing this to be the lad's bent, offered, on one occasion, to take charge of him, and have him trained for his profession under his own supervision. Such, however, was my mother's horror of the sea, and dread of losing her darling, if she surrendered him to be carried from her to Nova Scotia, whither I think Admiral Lake was bound when he offered to take my brother with him, that she induced my father to decline this most friendly and advantageous offer. Henry never after that exhibited the slightest prefer- ence for any other profession, and always said, " They may put me at a plough-tail if they like." He went through Westminster School, after a previous training at Bury St. Edmunds, not otherwise than creditably ; but a very modest estimate of his own capacity made him beg not to be sent to Cambridge, where he said he was sure he should only waste money, and do himself and us no credit. (The bitter disappointment of my brother John's failure there had made a deep impression upon him.) Finally it was decided that

he should go into the army, and the friendly interest
of Sir John Macdonald and the liberal price Mr.
Murray gave me for my play of " Francis I." enabled
me to get him a commission ; it was the time when
they were still purchaseable. My poor mother, unable
to refuse her consent to this second favourable opportunity of starting him in life, acquiesced in his military,
though she had thwarted his naval, career, and was
well content to see her boy-ensign sent over with his
troops to Ireland.   But from Ireland his regiment
was ordered to the West Indies, and after his departure thither she never again saw him in her life.]

I think it would be a wise thing if I were to go to
America and work till I have made 10,000l., then return
to England and go the round of the provinces, and act
for a few nights' leave-taking in London.   Prudence
would then, perhaps, find less difficulty in adjusting
my plans for the future. That is what I think would be
well for me to do, supposing all things remain as they
are and God preserves my health and strength.   It
will not do to verify all Poitier's lugubrious congratu--
lation to his children in the Vaudeville on their
marriage :—

> " Ji ! Ji ! mariez-vous,
> Mettez-vous dans la misère !
> Ji ! Ji ! mariez-vous,
> Mettez-vous la corde au cou."

. . . Jealousy, surely, is a disposition to suspect and
take umbrage where there is no cause for suspicion or
offence, which, to say the least of it, is very unreasonable; but that a woman should break her heart because
her husband does love another woman better than her,

seems to me natural enough, and with regard to Bianca, her provocations certainly warranted a very rational amount of misery; and though, had she not been a woman of violent passions and a jealous temperament, she probably would not have taken the means she did of resenting Fazio's treatment of her, it appears to me that nothing but divine assistance and the strongest religious principle could preserve one under such circumstances from despair, madness, suicide, perhaps; hardly, however, the murder of one's husband. But assassinating other people seems a much more common mode of relieving their feelings among Italians than destroying themselves, which is rather a northern way of meeting, I should say of avoiding, difficulties.

I have had a holiday this week, and every now and then have written a word or two of "La Estrella;" it will never be done, and when it is it will be the horridest trash that ever was done; but I will let you have the pleasure of reading it, I promise you. On Monday I play that favourite detestation of mine, Euphrasia; the Monday after that my father hopes to be able for Mercutio, and I return to Juliet. By-the-by, you say Bianca is my best part, and I think my Juliet is better; I am not sure that there is not some kindred in the characters. We are going to bring out a play of Lord Francis', translated from the French, a sort of melodrama in blank verse, in which I have to act a part that I cannot do the least in the world, but of course that doesn't signify.

["Katharine of Cleves," translated from the French play of "Henri Trois et sa Cour," and made the

subject of one of Mr. Barham's inimitably comical
poems in the "Ingoldsby Legends." Mdlle. Mars
acted the part of the heroine in Paris, and it was one
of several semi-tragical characters, in which, at the
end of her great theatrical career, she reaped fresh
laurels in an entirely new field, and showed the world
that she might have been one of the best serious, not
to say tragic, actresses of the French stage, as well as
its one unrivalled female comedian.]

We have spent a wretched Christmas, as you may
suppose; a house with its head sick all but to death,
and all its members smitten with the direst anxiety, is
not the place for a merry one. God bless you, my
dear, and send you years of peace of mind and health
of body! this is, I suppose, what we mean when we
wish for happiness here, either for ourselves or others.
Give my love and kindest good wishes to your people.

Have you seen in the papers that poor Torrijos and
his little band, consisting of sixty men, several of
whom John knew well, have been lured into the interior
of Spain, and there taken prisoners and shot? This
news has shocked us all dreadfully, especially poor
John. You may imagine how grateful we are that he
is now among us, instead of having fallen a victim to
his chimerical enthusiasm. I hardly know how to
deplore the event for Torrijos himself: death has
spared him the bitter diappointment of at last being
convinced that the people he would have made free
are willing slaves, and that the time when Spain is to
lift herself up from the dust has not yet come.

I went the other day with John to the Angerstein
Gallery. . . . The delight I find in a fine painting is

one of the greatest and most enduring pleasures I have; my mind retains the impression so long and so very vividly. . . . Good-bye, my dearest H——.

Ever affectionately yours,

F. A. K.

Saturday, 31*st.*—After breakfast went to the theatre to rehearse "The Grecian Daughter," and Mr. Ward, for whom the rehearsal was principally given, never came till it was over. Pleasant creature! . . .

The day seemed beautifully fine, and my father and mother took a drive, while Henry and I rode, that my father might see the horse I had bought for him; but it was bitterly cold, and I could not make my mare trot, so she cantered and I froze. Mr. Power was there, on that lovely horse of his. I think the Park will become bad company, it is so full of the player folk. Frederick Byng called, and I like him, so I went and sat with him and my father and mother in the library till time to dress for dinner. After dinner wrote "The Star of Seville." I have got into conceit with it again, and so poor, dear, unfortunate Dall coming in while I was working at it, I seized hold of her, like the Ancient Mariner of the miserable "Wedding Guest," and compelled her, in spite of her outcries, to sit down, and then, though she very wisely went fast asleep, I read it to her till tea-time. . . .

My mother wished to sit up and see the New Year in, and so we played quadrille till they sat down to supper, which had been ordered for the vigil, and I went fast asleep. At twelve o'clock kisses and good wishes went round, and we were all very merry, in spite of which

I once or twice felt a sudden rush of hot tears into my eyes. All the hours of last year are gone, standing at the bar of Heaven, our witnesses or accusers: the evil done, the good left undone, the opportunities vouchsafed and neglected, the warnings given and unheeded, the talents lent and unworthily or not employed, they are gone from us for ever! for ever! and we make merry over the flight of Time! O Time! our dearest friend! how is it that we part so carelessly from you, who never can return to us? . . . A New Year. . . .

A NEW YEAR, 1832.   .

January 1st, Sunday.—When I came down my father wished me a happy New Year, and I am sure we were both thinking of the same thing, and neither of us felt happy. . . .

Thursday, 5th. . . . Wrote all the afternoon. Mr. Byng dined with us and stayed till one o'clock, having reduced my mother to silence, and my father to sleep, John to snuff, and Henry and I to playing (*sotto voce*) "What's my thought like?" to keep ourselves from tumbling off the perch.

Monday, 9th.—Rehearsed "Romeo and Juliet" with all my heart. Oh, light, life, truth, and lovely poetry! I sat on the cold stage, that I might hear them even mumble over their parts as they do. My father seemed to me very weak, and not by any means fit for his work to-night. After dinner went over my part again, and went to the theatre at half-past five. My new dress was very handsome, though rather burly, in

spite of which Dall said it made me look taller,
so its rather burliness didn't.matter. John Mason
played Romeo for the first time ; he was beautifully
dressed, and looked very well ; he acted tolerably well,
too. He has a good deal of energy and spirit, but
wants feeling and refinement; his voice, unfortunately,
is very unpleasant, wiry, harsh, and monotonous ; of
the last defect he may cure by practice. I came to
the side scene just as my father was going on, to hear
his reception ; it was very great, a perfect thunder of
applause ; it made the tears start into my eyes. Poor
father ! They received me with infinite demonstra-
tions of kindness too. I thought I acted very well; I
am sure I played the balcony scene well. When the
blood keeps rushing up into one's cheeks and neck
while one is speaking, I wonder if that ought to be
called acting. To be sure, Hamlet's player's face
turned pale for Hecuba ; so Shakespeare thought acting might make one change colour.

I cannot get over the *sensibleness* of Henry Greville,
who was in the pit again to-night. Upon my word !
he deserves to see good acting. After the play dear
William and Mary Harness came home to supper with
us, and we all got into a long discussion about Shakespeare's character, John maintaining that his views
of life were gloomy and that he must himself have
been an unhappy man. I don't believe a bit of it ; no
one, I suppose, ever thinks this world, and the life we
live in it, absolutely pleasant or good, but the poet's
ken, which is as an angel's compared with that of
other men, must see more good and beauty, as well as
more evil and ugliness, than his short-sighted fellows,

and the better elements predominating over the worse
(as they do, else the world would fall asunder). The
man who takes so wide a view as Shakespeare, whatever
his judgment of parts, must, upon the whole, pro-
nounce the whole good rather than bad, and rejoice
accordingly. I was too tired and sleepy to talk, or
even to listen, much.

Wednesday, 11*th*. . . . Lady Charlotte Greville and
General Alaba called. I am always grateful to him
for the beautiful copy of Schlegel's " Dramatic
Lectures " which he gave me. Lady Charlotte was
all curiosity and anxiety about Lord Francis' play. I
am afraid the newspapers may not be much inclined
to be good-natured about it. I hope he does not care
for what may be said of it. In the evening the boys
went to the theatre, and I stayed at home, industri-
ously copying " The Star of Seville " till bedtime.

Thursday, 12*th.*—To the theatre to rehearsal, after
which I drove to Hayter's (the painter), taking him
my bracelets to copy, and permission to apply to the
theatre wardrobe for any drapery that may suit his
purpose. I saw a likeness of Mrs. Norton he is just
finishing; very like her indeed, but not her handsomest look. I think it had a slight, curious resem-
blance to some of the things that have been done of
me. I saw a very clever picture of all the Fitzclarences,
either by himself or his brother, George Hayter. The
women are very prettily grouped, and look picturesque
enough; the modern man's dress is an abominable
object, of art or nature, and Lord Munster's costume,
holding, as he does, the very middle of the canvas, is
monstrous (which I don't mean for a rudeness, but a

pun). The Right Reverend Father in God (A. F.) is
laughably like. They have insisted on having a portrait
of their mother introduced in the room in which they
are sitting, which seems to me better feeling than taste.
Their royal father is absent. I worked at " The Star
of Seville " till I went to the theatre ; as I get nearer
the end, I get as eager as a race-horse when in sight
of the goal. . . . The piece was "The School for
Scandal ; " the house was very full. I did not play
well ; I spoke too fast, and perceived it, and could not
make myself speak slower—an unpleasant sort of
nightmare sensation ; besides, I was flat, and dull,
and pointless—in short, bad was the sum total. How
well Ward plays Joseph Surface ! The audience were
delightful ; I never heard such pleasant shouts of
laughter. . . . My father says perhaps they will bring
out " The Star of Seville," which notion sometimes
brings back my old girlish desire for " fame." Every
now and then I feel quite proud at the idea of acting
in a play of my own at two and twenty, and then I
look again at my " good works," this precious play,
and it seems to be no better than "filthy rags." But
perhaps I may do better hereafter. Hereafter ! Oh
dear ! how many things are better than doing even
the best in this kind ! how many things must be better
than real fame ! but if one has none of those, fame
might, perhaps, be pleasant. No actor's fame, or rather
celebrity, or rather notoriety, would satisfy me ; that
is the shadow of a cloud, the echo of a sound, the
memory of a dream, nothing come of nothing. The
finest actor is but a good translator of another man's
work ; he does somebody else's thought into action,

but he creates nothing, and that seems to me the test
of genius, after all.

Friday.—At eleven to the theatre to rehearse
" Katharine of Cleves." . . . We all went to the theatre
to see "Rob Roy," and I was sorry that I did, for it
gave me such a home-sick longing for Edinburgh, and
the lovely sea-shore out by Cramond, and the sunny
coast of Fife.   How all my delightful, girlish, solitary ·
rambles came back to me !   Why do such pleasant
times ever pass ? or why do they ever come ?   The
Scotch airs set me crying with all the recollections
they awakened.   In spite, moreover, of my knowing
every plank and pulley, and scene-shifter and car-
penter behind those scenes, here was I crying at this
Scotch melodrama, feeling my heart puff out my
chest for " Rob Roy," though Mr. Ward is, alas ! my
acquaintance, and I know when he leaves the stage
he goes and laughs and takes snuff in the green room.
How I did cry at the Coronach and Helen Macgregor,
though I know Mrs. Lovell is thinking of her baby,
and the chorus-singers of their suppers.   How I did
long to see Loch Lomond and its broad, deep, calm
waters once more, and those lovely green hills, and
the fir forests so fragrant in the sun, and that dark
mountain well, Loch Long, with its rocky cliffs along
whose dizzy edge I used to dream I was running in a
whirlwind ; the little bays where the sun touched the
water as it soaked into cushions of thick, starry moss,
and the great tufts of purple heather all vibrating
with tawny bees !   Beautiful wilderness ! how glad I
am I have once seen it, and can never forget it ; nor
the broad, crisping Clyde, with its blossoming bean-

fields, its jagged rocks and precipices, its grey cliffs
and waving woods, and the mountain streams of
clear, bright, fairy water, rushing and rejoicing down
between the hills to fling themselves into its bosom;
and Dumbarton Castle, with its snowy roses of Stuart
memory! How glad I am that I have seen it all, if I
should never see it again! And "Rob Roy" brought
all this and ever so much more to my mind. If I had
been a mountaineer, how I should have loved my land!
I wish I had some blood-right to love Scotland as I
do. Unfortunately, all these associations did not
reconcile me to the cockney-Scotch of our Covent
Garden actors, and Mackay's Baillie, Nichol Jarvie,
was not the least tender of my reminiscences. [It
was at a public dinner in Edinburgh, at which
Walter Scott and Mackay were guests, that, in refer-
ring to the admirable impersonation of the Baillie,
Scott's habitual caution with regard to the authorship
of the Waverley Novels for a moment lost its balance,
and in his warm commendation of the great comedian's
performances a sentence escaped him which appeared
conclusive to many of those present, if they were still
in doubt upon the subject, that he was their writer.]
Miss Inveraretie was a cruel Diana, but who would
not be? . . .

Saturday, 14th.—I rode at two with my father.
Passed Tyrone Power; what a clever, pleasant man
he is! Count d'Orsay joined us; he was riding a
most beautiful mare; and then James Macdonald,
cum multus aliis, and I was quite dead, and almost
cross, with cold. . . . After dinner I came up to my
room, and set to work like a little galley-slave, and

by tea-time I had finished my play. "Oh, joy for ever! my task is done!" I came down rather tipsy, and proclaimed my achievement. After tea I began copying the last act, but my father desired me to read it to them; so, at about half-past nine, I began. My mother cried much; what a nice woman she is! My father, Dall, and John agreed that it was beautiful, though I believe the two first excellent judges were fast asleep during the latter part of the reading, which was perhaps why they liked it so much. At the end my mother said to me, "I am proud of you, my dear;" and so I have my reward. After a little congratulatory conversation, I came to bed at two o'clock, and slept before my head touched the pillow. So now that is finished, and I am glad it is finished. Is it as good as a second piece of work ought to be? I cannot tell. I think so differently of it at different times that I cannot trust my own judgment. I will begin something else as soon as possible. I wonder why nowadays we make all our tragedies foreign? Romantic, historical, knightly England had people and manners once picturesque and poetical enough to serve her play-writers' turn, though Shakespeare always took his stories, though not his histories, from abroad; but people live tragedies and comedies everywhere and all time. I think by-and-by I will write an English tragedy. [I little thought then that I should write a play whose miserable story was of my own day, and call it "An English Tragedy."]

Sunday, 15th. . . . In the afternoon hosts of people called; among others Lady Dacre, who stayed a long time, and wants us to go to her on Thursday. Copied

" The Star of Seville " all the evening. At ten dear
Mr. Harness came in, and stayed till twelve.

Monday, 16*th*.—Rehearsed "Katharine of Cleves"
at eleven, but as Lord Francis did not come till twelve
we had to begin it again, and kept at it until two.
The actors seem frightened about it. Mr. Warde
quakes about the pinching (an incident in the play
taken, I suppose, from Ruthven's proceeding towards
Mary Stewart at Lochleven). I am only afraid I
cannot do anything with my part; it is a sort of
melodramatic, pantomimic part that I have no
capacity for. The fact is, that neither in the first
nor last scenes are my legs long enough to do justice
to this lady. The Douglas woman who barred the
door with her arm to save King James's life must have
been a strapping lass, as well as a heroine in spirit.
I am not tall enough for such feats of arms. Copied
my play till time to go to the theatre. My aunt
Victoire came to my dressing-room just as I was
going on, and persuaded dear Dall, who has never
once seen me act, to go into the front of the house.
She came back very soon in a state of great excitement and distress, saying she could not bear it. How
odd that seems! Dear old Dall! she cannot bear
seeing me make-believe miserable. The house was
very good, and I played fairly well.

Monday, 17*th*.—Went to my mother's room before
she was down, with Henry. It is her birthday, and I
carried her the black velvet dress I have got for her,
with which she seemed much pleased. Went to
rehearsal at twelve. Lord and Lady Francis were
there, and we acted the whole play, of course, to please

51

them, so that I was half dead at the end of the
rehearsal. They want us to go to Lady Charlotte's
(Greville) to-morrow. My father said we would if we
were all well and *in spirits* (*i.e.*, if the play was not
damped). . . . I wonder how my dear old Newhaven
fish-wife does. "Eh! gude gracious, ma'am, it's yer
ain sel come back again!" Poor body! I believe I
love the very east wind that blows over the streets of
Edinburgh. . . . After dinner Mrs. Jameson's beautiful
toy-likeness of me helped off the time delightfully till
the gentlemen came up, and then helped it off delightfully till everybody went away. What a misfortune
it is to have a broken nose, like poor dear Thackeray!
He would have been positively handsome, and is positively ugly in consequence of it. John and his friend
Venables broke the bridge of Thackeray's nose when
they were schoolboys playing together. What a mis-
hap to befall a young lad just beginning life! [I
suppose my friend Thackeray's injury was one that
did not admit a surgical remedy, but my father, late
in life, fell down while skating, and broke the bridge
of his nose, and Liston, the eminent surgeon, urged
him extremely to let him raise it—"build it again,"
as he used to say. My father, however, declined the
operation, and not only remained with his handsome
nose disfigured, but suffered a much greater inconvenience, which Liston had predicted—very aggravated
deafness in old age, from the stopping of the passages
in the nose, which helped to transmit sound to the
brain.] After all, I suppose, it does not much signify
to a man whether he is ugly or not. Wilkes, who
was pre-eminently so, but brilliantly agreeable, used

always to say that he was only half an hour behind-
hand with the handsomest man in England.

Wednesday, 18*th*.—Went to the theatre to rehearse
" Katharine of Cleves ; " we were kept at it till half-
past two. Drove home through the park. The day
was beautiful, but my poor father could not get
released from that hateful theatre, and went without
his ride. . . . I had not felt at all nervous about to-
night till the carriage came to the door, and then I
turned quite faint and sick with fright. At the theatre
found Madame le Beau (the forewoman of the great
fashionable French milliner, Madame Dévy, by
whom all my dresses were made) waiting for me. All
was in darkness in my dressing-room ; neither Mrs.
Mitchell nor Jane were come (my two servants, or
dressers, as they are called at the theatre). Presently
in scuttled the former, puffing, and whimpering
apologies, and presently the room was filled with the
pleasant incense of eight candles that she lighted, and
blew out and re-lighted, and wondered that we didn't
enjoy the operation. Then Jane bounced breathless
in, and made our discomfort perfect. I sat speechless,
terrified, and disconsolate. My fright was increasing
every instant, and by the time I was dressed I shook
like an aspen leaf from head to foot, and was as
sick as no heart could desire. My dresses were most
beautiful, and fitted me to perfection. The house was
very fine. My poor dear father, who was as perfect
in his part as possible this morning, did not speak
three words without prompting ; he was so nervous
and anxious about the success of the piece that his
own part was driven literally out of his head. I never

saw anything so curious. To be sure, his illness has
shattered him very much, and all the worry he has
had this week has not mended matters. However,
the play went admirably, and was entirely successful,
to assist which result I thought I should have broken
a blood-vessel in the last scene, the exertion was so
tremendous. My voice was weak with nervousness
and excitement, and at last I could hardly utter a
word audibly. I almost broke my arm, too, in good
earnest, with those horrible iron stanchions. However,
it did be over at last, and "all's well that ends well."
I was so tired that I could scarcely stand; my mother
came down from her box and seemed much pleased
with me. She went to my father's room to see if
I might not go home instead of to Lady Charlotte's,
but he seemed to think it would please them if we
made the effort of going for a few minutes; and so I
dressed and set off, and there we found a regular
"swarry," instead of something to eat and drink, and
a chair to sit upon in peace and quiet. There was a
room full of all the fine folks in London; very few chairs,
no peace and quiet, and heaps of acquaintance to talk
to. . . . All the London world that is in London.
Lord and Lady Francis took their success very com-
posedly. I don't think they would have cared much
if the play had failed. Henry Greville seemed to be
much more interested for them than they for themselves, and discussed it all for a long time with me.
I like him very much. . . . At long last I got home,
and had some supper, but what with fatigue and
nervousness, and it—i.e., the supper—so late, I had a
most wretched night, and kept dreaming I was out in

my part and jumping up in bed, and all sorts of
agonies.   What a life!   I don't steal my money, I'm
sure.

Thursday, 19th. . . . Henry and I rode in the park,
and though the day was detestable, it did me good.
As we were walking the horses round by Kensington
Gardens, Lord John Russell, peering out of volu-
minous wrappers, joined us.   Certainly that small,
sharp-visaged gentleman does not give much outward
and visible sign of the inward and spiritual power
he possesses and wields over this realm of England
just now.   His bodily presence might almost be described as St. Paul's.   This turner inside out and upside
down of our body, social and political, this hero of
reform, one of the ablest men in England—I suppose
in Europe—he rode with us for a long time, and
I thought how H—— would have envied me this
conversation with her idol. . . . In the evening, at
the theatre, though I had gone over my part before
going there, for the first time in my play-house experience I was *out* on the stage.   I stopped short in
the middle of one of my speeches, thinking I had
finished it, whereas I had not given Mr. Warde the cue
he was to reply to.   How disgraceful! . . . After the
play, my mother called for us in the carriage, and we
went to Lady Dacre's, and had a pleasant party
enough. . . . C—— G—— was there, with her
mother (the clever and accomplished authoress of
several so-called fashionable novels, which had great
popularity in their day).   Miss G——, now Lady
E—— T——, used to be called by us " la Dame
Blanche," on account of the dazzling fairness of her

complexion. She was very brilliant and amusing, and I remember her saying to one of her admirers one evening, when her snowy neck and shoulders were shining in all the unveiled beauty of full dress, "Oh, go away, P——, you *tan* me." (The gentleman had a shock head of fiery red hair.)

Friday. . . . I am horribly fagged, and after dinner fell fast asleep in my chair. At the theatre, in the evening, the house was remarkably good for a "second night," and the play went off very well. . . . My voice was much better to-night, though it cracked once most awfully in the last scene, from fatigue. . . . I think Lord Francis, or the management, or somebody ought to pay me for the bruises and thumps I get in this new play. One arm is black and blue (besides being broken every night) with bolting the door, and the other grazed to the bone with falling in fits upon the floor on my elbows. This sort of tragic acting is a service of some danger, and I object to it much more than to the stabbing and poisoning of the "Legitimate Drama;" in fact, "I do not mind death, but I cannot bear pinching."

Saturday. . . . Rode in the park with my father. Lord John Russell rode with us for some time, and was very pleasant. He made us laugh by telling us that Sir Robert Inglis (most bigoted of Tory anti-reformers) having fallen asleep on the ministerial benches at the time of the division the other night, they counted him on their side. What good fun! I never saw a man look so wretchedly worn and harassed as Lord John does. They say the ministry must go out, that they dare not make these new peers, and that the Bill will stick fast by the way instead of passing. What frightful trouble there will be ! . . .

Sunday, 22nd. . . . After church looked over the critiques in the Sunday papers on "Katharine of Cleves." Some of them were too good-natured, some too ill-natured. The *Spectator* was exceedingly amusing.

By far the best account and criticism of this piece is Mr. Barham's metrical report of it in the "Ingoldsby Legends." Lord Francis himself used to quote with delight, "She didn't mind death, but she couldn't bear pinching." . . .

Great Russell Street, January 22nd, 1832.

Thank you, my dearest H——, for your last delightful letter, which I should have answered before, but for the production of a new piece at Covent Garden, which has taken up all my time for the last week in rehearsals, and trying on dresses and the innumerable and invariable etceteras of a new play and part. It has been highly successful, and I think is likely to bring money to our treasury, which is *the* consummation most devoutly to be wished. It is nothing more than an interesting melodrama, with the advantage of being written in gentlemanly (noblemanly?) blank verse instead of turgid prose, and being acted by the principal instead of the secondary members of the company. This will suffice to make you appreciate my satisfaction, when I am complimented upon my acting in it, and you will sympathize with the shout of laughter my father and myself indulged in in the park the other day, when Lord John

Russell, who was riding with us, told us that a young
lady of his acquaintance had assured him that
" Katharine of Cleves " (the name of the' piece) was
vastly more interesting than anything Shakespeare
had ever written.

The report is that there is to be no new creation of
peers, and that the Bill will not pass.   Certainly
poor Lord John looks worried to death.   He and
Lord Grey have almost the whole weight and re-
sponsibility of this most momentous question upon
their shoulders, and it must be no trifle to carry.
As for the judicious young lady's judgment about
" Katharine of Cleves," it is just this sort of thing
that makes me *rub the hands of my mind* with satisfaction that I have never cared for my profession as
my family has done.   I think if I had, such folly, or
rather stupidity, would have exasperated me too
much.   Besides, I should have been much less useful to
the theatre, for I should have lived in an everlasting
wrangle with authors, actors, and managers on behalf
of the mythological bodies supposed to preside over
tragedy and comedy, and I should have killed myself
(or perhaps been killed), and that quickly, with ineffectual protests against half the performances
before the lamps, which are enough to make the
angels weep and laugh—in short, go into hysterics, if
they ever come to the play. . . .

Do you know you have almost increased my very
sufficient tendency to superstition by your presenti-
ment when you last left us that you should never
return to this house.   There is some talk now of our
leaving it.   My mother yearns for her favourite

suburban haunts, the scene of her courtship, and the spot where most of her happy youthful associations abide, and has half persuaded my father to let this house and take one in a particular row of " cottages of gentility " called Craven Hill. It only consists of twelve houses, in *five* of which my mother has, at different periods of her life, resided. This is all vague at present; I will let you know if it assumes a more definite shape. Some time will elapse before it is decided on, and more before it is done; and in any case, somehow or other, you must be once more under this roof with us before we leave it. . . .

I quite agree with you that such books as Mr. Hope's (on the nature and immortality of the soul, the precise title of which I have forgotten) "may be useless," and sometimes, indeed, worse. If a person has nothing better to do than count the sea sands or fill the old bottomless tub of the Danaides, they may be excused for devoting their time and wits to such riddles, perhaps. But when the mind has positive, practical work to perform, and time keeps bringing *all the time* specific duties, or when, as in your case, a predisposition to vague speculation is the intellectual besetting sin, I think *addition* to such subjects to be avoided. I suppose all human beings have, in some shape or degree, the desire for that knowledge which is still the growth of the forbidden tree of Paradise, and the lust for which, inevitably thrusts us against the bars of the material life in which we are consigned; but to give up one's time to writing and reading elaborate theories of a past and future which we may conceive to exist, but

of the existence of which it is impossible we should
achieve *any* proof, much less any detailed knowledge,
appears to me an unprofitable and unsatisfactory
misuse of time and talent. . . .

You are mistaken in supposing me familiar with
the early history of Poland. I am ashamed to say
I know nothing about it, and my zeal for the cause
of its people is an ignorant sentiment*alism*—partly,
perhaps, mere innate combativeness that longs to
strike on the weaker side, and partly, too, resentful
indignation at the cold-blooded neutrality observed
by all the powers of Europe while that handful of
men were making so brave a stand against the
Russian giant.

That reminds me that Prince Zartoryski, who is in
this country just now, came to the play the other
night, and was so struck with my father that he sent
'round to him to say that he desired the honour of his
acquaintance, and begged he would do him the favour
of dining with him on some appointed day, which
seemed to me a very pretty piece of impulsive enthusiasm. I believe Prince Zartoryski is a royal
personage, and so above conventionalities. . . .

My father is pretty well, though very far from
having entirely regained his strength, but he is
making gradual progress in that direction. . . .

Always affectionately yours,

FANNY.

Tuesday, 24th. . . . Read over "The Star of Seville,"
as Mr. Bartley (our worthy stage manager) has cut
it, with a view to its possible performance. He has

cut it with a vengeance—what one may call to the
quick. However, I suppose they know their own
business (though, by-the-by, I am not always so sure
of that). At any rate, I shall make no resistance,
but be silent while I am sheared. . . .

I rode in the park with John. My mare was ill,
and Mew (the stable-keeper) had sent me one of his
horses, a great awkward brute, who, after jolting me
well up Oxford Street, no sooner entered the park
than he bolted down the drive as fast as legs could
carry him, John following afar off. In Rotten Row we
were joined by young T——. . . . When I thought the
devil was a little worked out of my horse, I raised him
to a canter again, whereupon scamper the second—I
like a flash of lightning, they after me as well as
they could. John would not force my father's horse,
but Mr. T——, whose horse was a thorough-bred
hunter, managed to keep up with me, but lamed his
horse in so doing. We then walked soberly round
the park and saw our friends and acquaintances, and,
turning down the drive, I determined once more to
try my horse's disposition, whereupon off he went
again like a shot, leaving John far behind. I flitted
down Rotten Row like Faust on the demon horse, and
as I drew up and turned about I heard, "Well, that
woman does ride well," which was all, whoever said
it, knew of the matter; whereas, in my mad career,
I had passed Fozzard, who shook his head lamentably
at John, exclaiming, "Oh, Miss Fanny! Miss Fanny!"
After this last satisfactory experiment I made no
more, and we cut short our ride on account of my
unmanageable steed. . . .

We had a dinner party at home, and in the evening
additional guests, among them Thackeray, who is very
clever and delightful. We had music and singing and
pleasant, bright talk, and they departed and left us in
great good humour.

  Wednesday, 25th.—Read the "Prometheus Un-
bound." How gorgeous it is! I do not think Shelley
is read or appreciated now as enthusiastically as he
was, even in my recollection, some few years ago. I
went over my part, and at half-past five to the theatre.
The play was "Katharine of Cleves," the house very
good; and, to please Henry Greville, I resumed the
gold wreath I had discarded and restored the lines I
had omitted. After the play came home and supped,
and at eleven went to Lady F——'s. . . . A very fine
party; "everybody"—that is in town—was there, and
Mrs. Norton looking more magnificent than "everybody." Old Lady S—— like nothing in the world
but the mummy carried round at the Egyptian
feasts, with her parchment neck and shoulders bare,
and her throat all drawn into strings and cords, hung
with a dozen rows of perfect precious stones glittering
in the glare of the lights with the constant shaking
of her palsied head. [This lady continued to frequent
the gayest assemblies in London when she had
become so old and infirm that, though still persisting
daily in her favourite exercise on horseback, she used
to be tied into her saddle in such a manner as to
prevent her falling out of it. She had been one of
the finest riders in England, but used often, at the
time when I knew her, to go to sleep while walking
the horse round the park, her groom who rode near

her being obliged to call to her "My lady! My lady!"
to make the poor old woman open her eyes and see
where she was going. At upwards of eighty she died
an unnatural death—writing by candle light on a
winter's evening. It is supposed that her cap must
have taken fire, for she was burnt to death, and
had for her funeral pile part of the noble historical
house of Hatfield, which was destroyed by the same
accident.]

Lord Lansdowne desired to be introduced to me,
and talked to me a long time. I thought him very
good-natured and a charming talker. Mrs. Bradshaw
(Maria Tree) was there, looking beautiful. Our
hostess's daughter, Miss F——, is very pretty, but
just misses being a beauty; in that case a miss is
a great deal worse than a mile. Just as the rooms
were beginning to thin, and we were going away,
Lord O—— sat down to the piano. I had heard
a great deal about his singing, and was rather disappointed; he has a sweet voice and a sweet face,
but Henry Greville's bright, sparkling countenance
and expressive singing are worth a hundred such
mere musical sentimentalities. [Mr. Henry Greville
was one of the best amateur singers of the London
society of his day. He was the intimate personal
friend of Macio, whom I remember he brought
to our house, when first he arrived in London, as
M. de Candia, before the beginning of his public
career, and when, in the very first bloom of youth,
his exquisite voice and beautiful face produced in
society an effect which only briefly forestalled the
admiration of all Europe when he determined to

adopt the profession which made him famous as the
incomparable tenor of the Italian stage for so many
years.]   Then, too, those lads sing songs, the words
of which give one the throat-ache with strangled
crying, and when they have done you hear the
women all round mincing, "Charming!—how nice!
—sweet!—what a dear!—darling creature!"

Thursday, 26th.—Murray was most kind and good-
natured and liberal about all the arrangements for
publishing "Francis I." and "The Star of Seville."
He will take them both, and defer the publication
of the first as long as the managers of Covent Garden
wish him to do so.   [As there was some talk just
then of bringing out "The Star of Seville" at the
theatre, it was thought better not to forestall its
effect by the publication of "Francis I."]

At the theatre the play was "The School for
Scandal."   A—— F—— was there, with young
Sheridan; I hope the latter approved of my method
of speaking the speeches of his witty great-grand-
father.   I played well, though the audience was dull
and didn't help me.   Mary and William Harness
supped with us. . . .

Friday, 27th.—A long discussion after breakfast
about the necessity of one's husband being clever.
Ma foi je n'en vois pas la nécessité.   People don't
want to be entertaining each other all day long; *very*
clever men don't grow on every bush, and *middling*
clever men don't amount to anything.   I think I
should like to have married Sir Humphrey Davy.
A well-assorted marriage, as the French say, seems
to me like a well-arranged duet for four hands; the

treble, the woman, has all the brilliant and melodious part, but the whole government of the piece, the harmony, is with the bass, which really leads and sustains the whole composition and keeps it steady, and without which the treble for the most part *runs to tune* merely, and wants depth, dignity, and real musical importance.

In the afternoon went to Lady Dacre's. . . . She read me the first act of a little piece she has been writing; while listening to her I was struck as I never had been before with the great beauty of her countenance, and its very varied and striking expression. . . . At home spent my time in reading Shelley. How wonderful and beautiful the "Prometheus" is! The unguessed heavens and earth and sea are so many storehouses from which Shelley brings gorgeous heaps of treasure and piles them up in words like jewels. I read "The Sensitive Plant" and "Rosalind and Helen." As for the latter— powerful enough, certainly—it gives me bodily aches to read such poetry.

What extraordinary proceedings have been going on in the House of Commons! Mr. Percival getting up and quoting the Bible, and Mr. Hunt getting up and answering him by quoting the Bible too. It seems we are to have a general fast—on account of the general national misconduct, I suppose; serve us right.

Sunday, 29*th*.—Went into my mother's room before going to church. Henry Greville has sent her Victor Hugo's new book, "Notre Dame de Paris," but she appears half undetermined whether she will go on

reading it or not, it is so painfully exciting. I took
Mrs. Montague up in the carriage on my way to
church, and after service drove her home, and went
up to see Mrs. Procter, and found baby (Adelaide
Procter) at dinner. That child looks like a poet's
child, and a poet. It has something "doomed"
(what the Germans call "fatal") in its appearance—
such a preternaturally thoughtful, mournful expression
for a little child, such a marked brow over the heavy
blue eyes, such a transparent skin, such pale-golden
hair. John says the little creature is an elf-child. I
think it is the prophecy of a poet. [And so, indeed, it
was, as all who know Adelaide Procter's writings will
agree—a poet who died too early for the world,
though not before she had achieved a poet's fame,
and proved herself her father's worthy daughter.] . . .
In the afternoon, I found my mother deep in her
French novel, from which she read me two very
striking passages—the description of Esmeralda,
which was like a fine painting, and extremely beautiful, and the sketch of Quasimodo's life, ending with
his riding on the great bell of the cathedral. Very
powerful and very insane—a sort of mental nightmare, giving one as much the idea of disorder of
intellect as such an image occurring to one in a
dream would of a disordered stomach. Harmony,
order, the beauty of goodness and the justice of God,
are alike ignored in such works. How sad it is for
the future as well as for the present !

Monday, 30*th*.—King Charles's martyrdom gives me
a holiday to-night. Excellent martyr ! Victor Hugo
has set my mother raving. She didn't sleep all

night, and says the book is bad in its tendency and shocking in its details; nevertheless, she goes on reading it. . . .

Tuesday, January 31st. . . . Went to Turnerelli's. He is making a bust of me, that will perhaps be like— the man in the moon. Dall was kind enough to read to me Mrs. Jameson's "Christina" while I sat. I like it extremely. After I came home, read Shirley's play of "The Two Sisters." I didn't like it much. It is neither very interesting, very witty, nor very poetical, and might almost be a modern work for its general want of power and character. The women appear to me a little exaggerated—the one is mad and the other silly. At the theatre in the evening the house was very good indeed—the play, "Katharine of Cleves;" but poor Mr. Warde was so ill he could hardly stand.

Wednesday, February 1st. . . . Drove out with Henry in the new carriage. It is very handsome, but by no means as convenient or capacious as our old rumble. Oh, these vanities! How we sacrifice every- thing to them!

Thursday, 2nd. . . . Rode out with my father. The whole world was abroad in the sunshine, like so many flies. My mother was walking with John and Henry, and Henry Greville. I should like to tell him two words of my mind on the subject of lending "Notre Dame de Paris" about to women. At any rate, we vulgar females are not as much accustomed to mental dram-drinking as his fine-lady friends, and don't stand that sort of thing so well. . . . In the evening we went to the theatre to see "The Haunted Tower." Youth and first impressions are wonderful magicians.

52

(I forget whether the music of this piece was by Storace or Michael Kelly.) This was an opera which I had heard my father and mother talk of for ever. I went full of expectation accordingly, and was entirely disappointed. The meagreness and triteness of the music and piece astonished me. After the full orchestral accompaniments, the richly harmonized concerted pieces and exquisite melodies lavished on us in our modern operas, these simple airs and their choruses and mean finales produce an effect from their poverty of absolute musical starvation.

Great Russell Street, January 31st, 1832.

MY DEAREST H—— G——,

You are coming to England, and you will certainly not do so again without coming to us. My father and mother, you know, speak by me when I assure you that a visit from you would give us all the greatest pleasure. . . . Do not come late in the season to us, because at present we do not know whether June or July may take us out of town. . . . With my scheme of going to America, I think I can look the future courageously in the face. It is something to hold one's fortune in one's own hands; if the worst comes to the worst it is but another year's drudgery, and the whereabouts really matters little. . . . We hear that the cholera is in Edinburgh. I cannot help thinking with the deepest anxiety of those I love there, and I imagine with sorrow that beautiful, noble city, those breezy hills, those fresh, sea-weedy shores and coasts breathed upon by that dire pestilence. The city of the winds, where the

purifying currents of keen air sweep through every
thoroughfare and eddy round every corner—perched
up so high upon her rocky throne, she seems to sit in
a freer, finer atmosphere than all the world beside!
(I appear, in my enthusiastic love for Edinburgh, to
have forgotten those Immonderraze, the wynds and
closes of the old town.) I hope the report may
not prove true, though from a letter I have received
from my cousin Sally (Siddons) the plague is cer·
tainly within six miles of them. She writes very
rationally about it, and I can scarce forbear super-
stitiously believing that God's mercy will especially
protect those who are among His most devoted and
dutiful children. . . .

You speak of my love of nature almost as if it
were a quality for which I deserve commendation.
It is a blessing for which I am most grateful. You
who live unenclosed by paved streets and brick walls,
who have earth, sea, and sky à discrétion spread round
you in all their majestic beauty, cannot imagine how
vividly my memory recalls and my mind dwells upon
mere strips of green sward, with the shadows of trees
lying upon them. The colours of a patch of purple
heather, broken banks by roadsides through which .
sunshine streamed—often mere effects of light and
shade—return to me again and again like tunes, and
to shut my eyes and look at them is a perfect delight
to me. I suppose one is in some way the better
as well as the happier for one's sympathy with the
fair things of this fair world, which are types of
things yet fairer, and emanations from the great
Source of all goodness, loveliness, and sublimity.

Whether in the moral or material universe, images
and ideas of beauty must always be in themselves
good. Beauty is one manifestation and form of
truth, and the transition seems to me almost inevitable from the contemplation of things that are
lovely to one's *senses* to those which are *lovable* by
one's spirits' higher and finer powers of apprehension.
The mind is kept sunny and calm, and free from ill
vapours, by the influence of beautiful things; and
surely God loves beauty, for from the greatest to the
smallest it pervades all His works; and poetry,
painting, and sculpture are not as beautiful as the
things they reproduce, because of the imperfect
nature of their creator—man; though *his* works are
only good in proportion as he puts his soul—*i.e.* the
Spirit of God—inspiration into them.

Your affectionate

F. A. K.

Great Russell Street, February 17, 1832.

MY DEAREST H——,

"Francis I." will come out on the 1st of
March, so your starting on the 25th will do quite well
for that; but it is right I should tell you what
may possibly deter you from coming. A report prevails that the cholera is approaching London, and
though I cannot say that I feel nervous upon the subject, perhaps, under these circumstances, you had
rather or better not come.

There have been many assertions and contradictions
about it, of course, and I know nothing but that such
a rumour is prevalent, and if this should cause you

or (what is more likely) yours an instant's hesitation, you must give up your visit. I know our disappointment will be mutual and equal, and I am sure you will not inflict it either upon yourself or me without adequate reason, so I will say no more about it.

The reason for bringing out "Francis I." now is that Milman has undertaken to review it in the next *Quarterly*, and Murray wishes the production of the play at the theatre to be simultaneous with the publication of the *Review*.

My wrath and annoyance upon the subject have subsided, and I have now taken refuge with restored equanimity in my "cannot help it." Certainly I said and did all I could to hinder it.

I do not feel at all nervous about the fate of the play—no English public will damn an attempt of that description, however much it may deserve it; and paradoxical as it may sound, a London audience, composed as it for the most part is of pretty rough, coarse, and hard particles, makes up a most soft-hearted and good-natured whole, and invariably in the instance of a new actor or a new piece—whatever partial private ill will may wish to do—the majority of the spectators is inclined to patience and indulgence. I do not mean that I shall not turn exceedingly sick when I come to set my foot upon the stage that night; but it will only be with a slight increase of the alarm which I undergo with every new part. My poor mother will be the person to be pitied; I wish she would take an opiate and go to bed, instead of to the theatre that night. . . .

I was at a party last night where I met Lord Hill

(then commander of the forces), who had himself
presented to me, and who renewed in person the promise he had sent me through Sir John Macdonald
(who was adjutant-general), to exert and interest
himself to the utmost of his power about Henry's
commission.

John has finished his Anglo-Saxon book, and
Murray has undertaken to publish it for him, offering
at the same time to share with him whatever profits
may accrue from it. The work is of a nature which
cannot give either a quick or considerable return; but
the offer, like all Mr. Murray's dealings with me, is
very kind and liberal, for a publisher is not easily
found any more than readers for such matter. (The
book was the Anglo-Saxon Poem of Beowulf.) He
asked me to let him publish "Francis I.," as it is
to be acted, without the fifth act, but this I would not
consent to. I have rather an affection for my last
scene in the Certoso at Pavia, with the monks singing
the "De Profundis" while the battle was going on, and
the king being brought in a prisoner and making the
response to the psalm—which is all historically
true. . . .

I must bid you good-bye, dear, as I am going to the
Angerstein Gallery with the Fitzhughs. . . .

                    Yours ever affectionately,
                                   F. A. K.

Saturday, 4th.—I was obliged to send an excuse to
Turnerelli. I could not sit to him this morning, as
it is now determined that "Francis I." is to be
brought out, and received official notice that it was

to be read in the green room to-day. We went to the
theatre at eleven, and all the actors were there. I felt
very uncomfortable and awkward; but, after all, writing
a play is not a sin, so I plucked up my courage and
sat down with the rest. My father read it beautifully,
but even cut as it is, it is of an *unendurable* length.
They were all very kind and civil, and applauded it
very much; but I do not love the sound of clapping
of hands, and did not feel on this occasion as if I had
done the sort of thing that deserves it. . . .

At half-past five went to the theatre; it was the
first night of the opera, and rained besides, both
which circumstances thinned our house; but I suspect
" Katharine of Cleves " has nearly lived her life.
Driving to the theatre, my father told me that they
had entirely altered the cast of "Francis I." from
what I had appointed, and determined to finish the
play with the fourth act. I felt myself get very red,
but I didn't speak, though I cannot but think an
author has a right to say whether he or she will have
certain alterations made in their work. My position
is a difficult one, for did I not feel bound to comply
with my father's wishes I would have no hand in this
experiment. I would forfeit fifty—nay, a hundred—
pounds willingly rather than act in this play, which
I am convinced ought not to be acted at all. Any
other person might do this, but with me it is a
question of home duty, instead of a mere matter of
business between author, actress, and manager.
They couldn't act the play without me, and but for
my father I should from the first have refused to act
in it at all. I do not think that they manage wisely;

it is a mere snatch at a bit of profit by a way
of catch-penny venture, to secure which they are
running the risk of injuring me more ways than
one, and through me their own interests. It seems
to me short-sighted policy, but I cannot help myself.
After the play came home to supper, and at eleven
went to Lady Dacre's. Sidney Smith, Rogers. Conversation sharp. Lots of people that I knew, in spite
of which, in consequence, I suppose, of my own state
of spirits, I did not enjoy myself. Mrs. Norton was
there; she sang "My Arab Steed," and "Yes, Aunt,"
and "Joe Hardy;" the latter I do not think very good.
They made me sing; I was horribly frightened.
Julian Young was there; his manner and appearance
are not very good, but his voice is beautiful and
he sang very well.

Sunday, 5th. . . . When I came back from church
I found Campbell with my mother, scraping up information about Mrs. Siddons for his and her "life."
I left him with her, and when I came back he was
gone, and in his place, as if he had turned into her,
sat Mrs. Fitzgerald in a green velvet gown trimmed
with sables, which excited my admiration and envy.
I should like to have been living in the days and
countries where persons, as a mark of favour, took
off their dress and threw it on your shoulders. How
pleasant it would have been! . . .

Just before going to bed I spoke of writing a preface
to "Francis I.," which brought on a discussion with
my mother on the subject of that ill-fated piece,
in the middle of which my father came in, and I
summoned up courage to say something of what

I felt about it, and how disagreeable it was to me to act in it, feeling as I did. I do not think I can make them understand that I do not care a straw whether the piece dies and is damned the first night, or is cut up alive the next morning, but that I do care that, in spite of my protestations, it should be acted at all, and should be cut and cast in a manner that I totally disapprove of.

Monday, 6th. . . . On our way to the theatre my father told me that the whole cast of "Francis I." is again turned topsy-turvy. Patience of me! I felt very cross, so I held my tongue. Mr. and Miss Harness came home to supper with us, and had a long talk about "Francis I.," my annoyance about which culminated, I am ashamed to say, in a fit of crying.

Tuesday, 7th.—So "Francis I." is in the bills, I see. . . .

Wednesday, 8th. . . . At eleven "The Provoked Husband" was rehearsed in the saloon, and Mr. Meadows brought Carlo to see me. [Carlo was a splendid Newfoundland dog, which my friend, Mr. Drinkwater Meadows, used to bring to the theatre to see me. His solemnity, when he was desired to keep still while the rehearsal was going on, was magnificent, considering the stuff he must have thought it.] . . . After dinner went to the theatre. The house was bad; the play, "The Provoked Husband." I played ill in spite of my pink gauzé gown, which is inestimable and as fresh as ever. After supper dressed and off to Mrs. G——'s, and had a very nice ball. . . .

Friday, 10th. . . . I wrote to H—— to beg her

to come to me directly; I wish her so much to be
here when my play comes out. Went to the theatre
at a quarter to six. The house was bad; the play,
"Katharine of Cleves." I acted pretty well, *though*
my dresses are getting shockingly dirty, and in one
of the scenes my wreath fell backwards, and I was
obliged to take it off in the middle of all my epistolary
agony; and what was still worse, after my husband had
locked me in one room and my wreath in another,
it somehow found its way back upon my head for
the last scene. At the end of the play, which has
now been acted ten nights, some people began hissing
the pinching incident. It was always considered the
dangerous passage of the piece, but a reasonable
public should know that a play must be damned
on its first night, or not at all.

Saturday, 11*th*. . . . A long walk with my mother,
and a long talk about Shakespeare, especially about
the beauty of his songs. . . .

Tuesday, 14*th*. . . . Read the family my prologue.
My mother did not like it at all; my father said it
would do very well. John asked why there need be
any prologue to the play, which is precisely what
I do not understand. However, I was told to write
one and I did, and they may use it or not just as
they please. I am determined to say not another
word about the whole vexatious business, and so
peace be with them. . . . In the evening a charming
little dinner-party at Mr. Harness's. The G——s,
Arthur K——, Procter (Barry Cornwall), who is
delightful, Sir William Millman, and ourselves. . . .
Dear Mr. Harness has spoken to Murray about

John's book, and has settled it all for him. On my
return home, I told John of the book being accepted,
at which he was greatly pleased. [The book in
question was my brother's history of the Anglo-
Saxons, of which Lord Macaulay once spoke to me
in terms of the highest enthusiasm, deploring that
John had not followed up that line of literature to
a much greater extent.]

Wednesday, 15th. . . . My father went to the opening dinner of the Garrick Club. . . . After tea I read
Daru, and copied fair a speech I had been writing for
an imaginary member of the House of Peers, on the
Reform Bill. John Mason called, and they sat down
to a rubber, and I came to my own room and read
" King Lear." . . .

Thursday, 16th. . . . While I was at the Fitzhughs' Miss Sturges Bourne came in, and she and
Emily had a very interesting conversation about
books for the poor. Among other things, Emily said
that Lady Macdonald had written up to her from
the country, to say that she wanted some more
books of sentiment, for that by the way in which
these were thumbed it was evident that they alone
would "go down." Upon inquiry, I found that
these "sentimental" books were religious tracts,
highly flavoured with terror or pathos, and in one
way or another calculated to convey the strongest
excitement upon the last subject with which excitement ought to have anything to do. Pious stimulants, devout drams, this is trying to do good, but
I think mistaking the way. . . .

In the evening we went to Lady Farquhar's; this

was a finer party, as it is called, than the last, but
not so pleasant. All the world was there. Mrs.
Norton the magnificent, and that lovely sister of
hers, Mrs. Blackwood (afterwards Lady Dufferin),
crowned like Bacchantes with grapes, and looking
as beautiful as dreams. Heaps of acquaintance and
some friends. . . .

Sunday, 19*th*. . . . In the evening I read Daru.
What fun that riotous old Pope Julius is! Poor
Gaston de Foix! It was young to leave life and
such well-begun fame. The extracts from Bayard's
life enchant me. I am glad to get among my old
acquaintance again. Mr. Harness came in rather
late and said all manner of kind things about "The
Star of Seville," but I was thinking about his play
all the while; it does not seem to me that the management is treating him well. If it does not suit the
interests of the theatre to bring it out now, he surely
should be told so, and not kept in a state of suspense,
which cannot be delightful to any author, however
little of an egotist he may be.

Monday, 20*th*.—Went to Kensington Gravel Pits to
see Lady Calcott, and sat with her a long time. That
dying woman, sitting in the warm spring sunlight,
surrounded with early blowing hyacinths, the youngest
born of the year, was a touching object. She is a
charming person, so full of talent and of goodness.
She talked with her usual cheerfulness and vivacity.
Presently Sir Augustus came down from the painting-
room to see me. . . . I could hardly prevent myself
from crying, and I am afraid I looked very sad. As
I was going away and stooped to kiss her, she sweetly

and solemnly bade "God bless me," and I thought her prayer was nearer to heaven than that of most people. . . .

Tuesday, 21st. . . . After tea dropped John at Mr. Murray's in Albemarle Street, and went on to the theatre to see the new opera; our version of "Robert the Devil." The house was very full. Henry Greville was there, with the Mitfords and Mrs. Bradshaw. What an extraordinary piece, to be sure! I could not help looking at the full house and wondering how so many decent Englishmen and women could sit through such a spectacle. . . . The impression made upon me by the subject of Meyerbeer's celebrated opera appears to have entirely superseded that of the undoubtedly fine music; but I never was able to enjoy the latter because of the former, and the only shape in which I ever enjoyed "Robert the Devil," was in M. Levassor's irresistibly ludicrous account of it in the character of a young Paris *badaud*, who had just come from seeing it at the theatre. His version of its horrors was laughable in the extreme, especially when, coming to the episode of the resurrection of the nuns, he contrived to give the most comical effect of a whole crowd—gibbering, glissading women greeting one another with the rapid music of the original scene, to which he adapted the words—

> "Quoi c'est moi c'est toi,
> Oui c'est toi c'est moi;
> Comme nous voila bien dégommés."

Mendelssohn's opinion of the subjects chosen for

operas in his day (even such a story as that of the
Sonnambula) was scornful in the extreme.

Friday, 24th. . . . Dined with the Fitzhughs, and
after dinner proceeded to the Adelphi, where we went
to see "Victorine," which I liked very much. Mrs.
Yates acted admirably the whole of it, but more particularly that part where she is old and in distress
and degradation. There was a dreary look of uncom-
plaining misery about her, an appearance as of
habitual want and sorrow and suffering, a heavy,
slow, subdued, broken deportment, and a way of
speaking that was excellent and was what struck
me most in her performance, for the end is sure to
be so effective that she shares half her merit there
with the situation. Reeve is funny beyond anything;
his face is the most humorous mask I ever saw in my
life. I think him much more comical than Liston.
The carriage was not come at the end of the first
piece, so we had to wait through part of "Robert the
Devil" (given at last, such was its popularity, at every
theatre in London). Of course, after our own grand
diablerie, it did not strike me except as being wonderfully well done, considering the size and means of
their little stage. [Yates made a most capital fiend :
I should not like a bit to be Mrs. Yates after seeing
him look that part so perfectly.]

Great Russell Street, Feb. 24th, 1832.

DEAREST H——,

I have this moment received your letter, and
though rather disappointed myself, I am glad you are
to see Dorothy as well as we, so that your visit south-

ward is to be two pleasures instead of one. The representation of " Francis I." is delayed until next Wednesday, 7th March ; not on account of cholera, but of scenery and other like theatrical causes of postponement. . . .

I am greatly worried and annoyed about my play. The more I see and hear of it the stronger my perception grows of its defects, which, I think, are rendered even more glaring by the curtailments and alterations necessary for its representation; and the whole thing distresses me as much as such a thing can. I send you the cast of the principal characters for the instruction of my Ardgillan friends, by whose interest about it I am much gratified.   My father is to be De Bourbon ; John Mason, the king ; Mr. Warde, the monk ; Mr. Bennett, Laval.   These are the principal men's parts.   I act the queen-mother ; Miss Taylor, Margaret de Valois ; and Miss Tree, François de Foix.

I am reading Cooper's novel of " The Borderers." It is striking and powerful, and some of it I think very beautiful, especially all that regards poor Ruth, which, I remember, is what struck you so much. I like the book extremely.   There is a soft sobriety of colour over it all that pleases me, and reminds me of your constant association of religion and the simple labours of an agricultural life.   It is wonderful how striking the description of this neutral-tinted existence is, in which life, love, death, and even this wild warfare with the savage tribes, by which these people were surrounded, appear divested of all their natural and usual excitements.   Religion alone (and this, of course, was inevitable) is the one imaginative

and enthusiastic element in their existence, and that
alone becomes the source of vehement feeling and
passionate excitement which ought least to admit of
fanciful interpretations and exaggerated and morbid
sentiment. But the picture is admirably well drawn,
and I cannot help sometimes wishing I had lived in
those days, and been one of that little colony of sternly
simple and fervently devout Christian souls. But I
should have been a furious fanatic; I should have
"seen visions and dreamed dreams," and fancied
myself a prophetess to a certainty.

   That luckless concern, in which you are a luckless
shareholder (Covent Garden), is going to the dogs
faster and faster every day; and, in spite of the
Garrick Club and all its noble regenerators of the
drama, I think the end of it, and that no distant one,
will be utter ruin. They have been bringing out a
new grand opera, called "Robert the Devil," which
they hope to derive much profit from, as it is beyond
all precedent absurd and horrible (and, as I think,
disgusting); but I am almost afraid that it has none
of these good qualities in a sufficient degree to make
it pay its own enormous cost. I have seen it once,
and came home with such a pain in my side and con-
fused chaos in my head that I do not think I shall
ever wish to see it again. Write me a line to say
when I may look for you.

                     Ever affectionately yours,
                                     F. A. K.

   Saturday, 25th. . . . Finished Fennimore Cooper's
interesting and pathetic novel, "The Borderers." . . .

I came down into the drawing-room with a headache, a sideache, a heartache, and swollen red eyes, and my mother greeted me with the news that the theatre was finally ruined, that at Easter it must close, that we must all go different ways, and I probably to America. I was sobered from my imaginary sorrow directly; for it is astonishing what a different effect real and fictitious distress have upon one. I could not answer my mother, but I went to the window and looked up and down the streets that were getting empty and dark and silent, and my heart sank as I thought of leaving my home, my England. . . . After dinner Madame le Beau came to try on my Louisa of Savoy's dress; it is as ugly and unbecoming, but as correct, as possible. . . .

Wednesday, *23rd.*—At eleven went to the theatre to rehearse "Francis I." The actors had most of them been civil enough to learn their parts, and were tolerably perfect. Mr. Bennett will play his very well indeed, if he does not increase in energy when he comes to act. Miss Tree, too, I think, will do her part very nicely. John Mason is rather vulgar and 'prentice-like for Francis, that mirror of chivalry. After rehearsal I went to Dévy, to consult about my dress. I have got a picture of the very woman, Louisa of Savoy, queen-mother of France, and, short of absolute hideousness, I will make myself as like her as I can. . . .

Arthur Hallam dined with us. I am not sure that I do not like him the best of all John's friends. Besides being so clever, he is so gentle, charming, and winning. At half-past ten went to Mrs. Norton's.

My father, who had received a summons from the
Court of Chancery, did not come. . . . It was a very
fine, and rather dull, party. . . . Mrs. Norton looks
as if she were made of precious stones, diamonds,
emeralds, rubies, sapphires; she is radiant with
beauty. And so, in a different way, is that vision of
a sister of hers (Georgiana Sheridan, Lady St. Maur,
Duchess of Somerset, and Queen of Beauty), with her
waxen, round, white arms, and eyes streaming with
soft brilliancy, like fountains by moonlight. To look
at two such creatures for an hour is enough to make
the world brighter for several hours.

Thursday, 24th.—At eleven went to rehearsal. While
we were rehearsing Mr. Bartley came and told me
that the play, " Francis I.," would not be done for
a fortnight, and afterwards my father told me he did
not think it was right, or fitting, or doing me justice
to bring out my play without some little attention
to scenery, decorations, etc. I entreated him to go
to no expense for it, for I am sure it will not repay
them. Moreover, they have given their scenery, and
finery, and dressing, and decoration, and spectacle
in such profusion to " Robert the Devil " that I am
sure they cannot afford a heavy outlay upon anything
else just now. However, I could not prevail, and
probably the real reason for putting off " Francis I."
is the expediency of running the new opera as long
as it will draw before bringing out anything else,
which, of course, is good policy. . . .

Wednesday, 29th.—H—— has gone to York. What
a disappointment! After all, it's only one more
added to the budget. Yet why do I say that? One

scores one's losses, and takes no reckoning of one's gains, which is neither right nor fair to one's life. . . .

I rode with Henry, and after I got home told my father that his horse was quite well, and would be fit for his use on Saturday. He replied sadly that his horse must be sold, for that from the first, though he had not liked to vex me by saying so, it was an expense he could not conscientiously afford. I had expected this, and certainly, when from day to day a man may be obliged to declare himself insolvent, keeping a horse does seem rather absurd. He then went on to speak about the ruin that is falling upon us; and dismal enough it is to stand under the crumbling fabric we have spent having and living, body, substance, and all but soul, to prop, and see that it must inevitably fall and crush us presently. Yet from my earliest childhood I remember this has been hanging over us. I have heard it foretold, I have known it expected, and there is no reason why it should now take any of us by surprise, or strike us with sudden dismay. Thank God, our means of existence lie within ourselves; while health and strength are vouchsafed to us there is no need to despond. It is very hard and sad to be come so far on in life, or rather so far into age, as my father is, without any hope of support for himself and my mother but toil, and that of the severest kind; but God is merciful. He has hitherto cared for us, as He cares for all His creatures, and He will not forsake us if we do not forsake Him or ourselves. . . . My father and I need scarcely remain without engagements, either in London or the provinces. . . . If our

salaries are smaller, so must our expenses be. The
house must go, the carriage must go, the horses must
go, and yet we may be sufficiently comfortable and
very happy—unless, indeed, we have to go to
America, and that will be dreadful. . . . We are yet
all stout and strong, and we are yet altogether. It is
pitiful to see how my father still clings to that theatre.
Is it because the art he loves, once had its noblest
dwelling there? Is it because his own name and
the names of his brother and sister are graven, as it
were, on its very stones? Does he think he could not
act in a smaller theatre? What can, in spite of his
interest, make him so loth to leave that ponderous
ruin? Even to-day, after summing up all the sorrow
and care and toil, and waste of life and fortune which
that concern has cost his brother, himself, and all
of us, he exclaimed, "Oh, if I had but £10,000, I
could set it all right again, even now!" My mother
and I actually stared at this infatuation. If I had
twenty, or a hundred thousand pounds, not one far-
thing would I give to the redeeming of that fatal
millstone, which cannot be raised, but will infallibly
drag everything tied to it down to the level of its own
destruction. The past is past, and for the future we
must think and act as speedily as we may. If our
salaries are half what they are now we need not
starve; and, as long as God keeps us in health of
body and mind, nothing need signify, provided we are
not obliged to separate and go off to that dreadful
America. . . .

    Thursday, March 1st. . . . After dinner I read
over again Knowles's play, "The Hunchback," and

like it better than ever. What would I not give to
have written that play! He cannot agree with Drury
Lane about it, and has brought it back to us, and
means to act Master Walter himself. I am so very
glad. It will be the most striking dramatic exhibition that has been seen since Kean's *début*. I wish
" Francis I." was done, and done with, and that we
were rehearsing " The Hunchback."

Great Russell Street, March 1st, 1832.

. . . . As for any disappointment of mine about
anything, dear H——, though some things are by no
means light to me, I soon make up my mind to whatever must be, and I think those who do not endure
well what cannot be avoided are only less foolish
than those who endure what they can avoid.
" Francis I." will not, I think, interfere with your
visit to us. Murray wishes it to be postponed till after
the publication of the *Quarterly*, which will come
out about the 11th or 12th. Lockhart, and not
Milman, has reviewed it very favourably, I hear, and
Murray expects to sell one edition immediately upon
the publication of the article in the *Quarterly*. So
that you can stay at Fulford some time yet; and
should the play be given before you wish to leave it, I
shall not expect you in person, but feel sure that you
are with me in spirit; and the next day I will write
you word of the result.

Dearest H——, I am just now much burdened with
anxiety. I will tell you more of this when we meet.
Thank God, though not of a sanguine, I am not of a
desponding nature; and though I never look forward

with any great satisfaction to the future, I seldom find
it difficult to accept the present with tolerable equanimity. . . . I spent the evening on Wednesday with
Mrs. Jameson. She is just returned to town, and
came immediately, thinking you were here, to engage
us for the next evening; and as you did not come I
went, and spent three hours very pleasantly with her.
She knows so much, and I am so very ignorant, that
her conversation is delightfully instructive as well as
amusing, full of interest and information. Poor
woman! she left Tedsley and a very agreeable party
to come up to town upon a false alarm of "Francis
I.'s" coming out. I think I have told you of the
work upon Shakespeare she is engaged with; she
has been teaching herself to etch, and has
executed some charming designs, with which she
means to illustrate it. I have not an idea what our
plans for this summer are to be; whether America, or
the provinces, or the King's Bench; but I suppose we
shall see a little more clearly into the future by the
time you come to us; and if we do not, abundantly
"sufficient for the day is the evil thereof" with us
just now. . . . I have been reading nothing but
Daru's "History of Venice" lately. How could you
tell me to read that sad story, "The Borderers"! I
half killed myself with crying over it, and did not
recover from the effect it had upon me for several
days. . . .

Dearest H——, I am writing nonsense, and with an
effort, for I am very low; and so I will leave off.

Your affectionate

F. A. K.

Friday, March 2nd.—I read Shirley's " Gentleman
of Venice," and did not like it much. . . . While I
was riding in the park with John, Mr. Willett came up
to us, and told me, as great good news, that they were
out of Chancery, and had obtained an order to have
their money out of court. I thought this indeed good
news, and we cantered up the drive in hopes of
meeting my mother in the carriage ; but she had gone
home. On reaching home, I ran to look for her, but
thought she would like better to hear the news from
my father.

I told Dall of it, however ; and she, who had just
seen my father, said that he considered what had
happened a most unfortunate thing for him ; and so
my bright, new joy fell to the ground, and was broken
all to pieces.   Upon further explanation, however, it
seems that it is an advantage to the other proprietors,
though not to him ; no part of the recovered money
returning to him, because he had borrowed his share
of it from Mr. Willett ; and the only difference is that
he will not have to pay the interest on it any more, and
so far it is a small advantage to him. But it is a
great one to them, poor men ! and therefore we ought
to be glad, and not look only at our own share of the
business, though naturally that is the most interesting
to us. I sometimes doubt, after all, if we have really
by any means a clear and comprehensive view of the
whole state of that concern, receiving our impressions
from my father, who naturally looks at it only from
the side of his own personal stake in it. . . . After
dinner John read me a letter he had just received
from Richard Trench—a most beautiful letter. What

a fine fellow he is, and what a noble set of young men
these friends of my brother's are! After tea read
Arthur Hallam's essay on the philosophical writings
of Cicero. It is very excellent; I should like to have
marked some of the passages, they are so admirably
clear and true; but he has only lent it to me. His
Latin and Greek quotations were rather a trial, but I
have no doubt his English is as good as anything he
quotes. Surely England twenty years hence should
be in a higher state of moral and intellectual development than it is now: these young heads seem to me
admirably good and strong, and some score years
hence these fine spirits will be influencing the national
mind and soul of England; and it pleases me much to
think so. [Alas! as far as dear Arthur Hallam was
concerned, my prophetic confidence was vain.] After
finishing Hallam's essay, I took up " King Lear," and
read the end of that, "and my poor fool is hanged!"
O Lord, what an agony! In reading " Lear," one of
Mr. Harness's criticisms on my " Star of Seville "
recurred to me. In the scene where Estrella deplores
her brother's death, I have used frequent repetition of
the same words and exclamations. I wrote upon
impulse, without deliberation, and simply as my conception of sorrow prompted me, such words as grew
from my heart and not my understanding. But in
reading " King Lear," the iteration in the expression
of deep grief confirms me in the opinion that it is
natural to all men, and not peculiar to myself, for
Shakespeare has done it. In the scene where Glos-
ter tells Cornwall and Regan of Edgar's supposed
wickedness, the wretched old father uses frequent

repetition, as, " Oh, madam, my old heart is cracked;
it's cracked!"   " Oh, lady, lady, shame would have it
hid!"   "I know not, madam : 'tis too bad, too bad!"
and in the last scene, that most piteous and terrible
close that story ever had, the poor old king, in his
moanings over Cordelia, repeats his words over and
over again.   I defend my conception, not my execution of it; and true and touching as these repetitions
of Shakespeare's are, mine may be "damnable
iteration," and nothing else.   Heart-broken sorrow
has but few words ; utter bereavement is not eloquent;
and David, when the darling of his soul was dead, did
but cry, "O Absalom, my son, my son! would
God I had died for thee, my son !" A vastly different
expression of a vastly different grief from that which
poured itself out in the sad and noble dirge, "The
beauty of Israel is slain upon thy high places : how
are the mighty fallen !"

Saturday, 3rd.—Henry has obtained his commission ; one great piece of good fortune amid all the
bad, for which God be thanked.   [The liberal price
given me by Mr. Murray for my play of " Francis
I." enabled me to purchase my brother's commission, which, however, the money would not have
obtained without the extremely kind interest exerted
in his favour by Lord Hill, then commander, and Sir
John Macdonald, adjutant-general of the forces.]

Sunday, 4th. . . . My father is in deplorable
spirits, and seems bowed down with care.   I believe
all that befalls us is right.   I know we must bear it;
all I pray for is health, strength, and courage, to bear
it well.   In the evening the Harnesses drank tea
with us.

Monday, 5th.—Got ready things for the theatre, and went over my part. . . . In the afternoon, I hoped to hear the result of the meeting that had been held by the creditors of the theatre; but my father had been obliged to leave it before anything was settled, and did not know what had been the termination of the consultation. At the theatre the house was not good, neither was my acting. My father acted admirably, to my amazement; for he has been in a most wretched state of depression for the last week, and to-day at dinner his face looked drawn and haggard and absolutely lead-coloured.

Tuesday, 6th.—After breakfast went with Henry and my father to Cox and Greenwood's, the great army agents, to pay for his commission. Oh, what a good job, to be sure! Then to the Horse Guards, to thank dear Sir John Macdonald; then to Stable Yard, to call upon Lord Fitzroy Somerset; and then home, much happier than I had been for a long time. . . . Madame le Beau brought my dress for Louisa of Savoy; it is very handsome, but I look hideous, and as grim as Queen Death in it. However, it is a precise copy of the woman's own picture, and I must comfort myself with that. In the evening we went to a pleasant party at the Basil Montagues', where for an hour I recovered my love of dancing, which has rather forsaken me of late. The Rajah Ramohun Roy had himself introduced to me, and we presently began a delightful nonsense conversation, which lasted a considerable time, and amused me extremely. His appearance is very striking; his picturesque dress and colour make him, of course, a remarkable object in

a London ball-room ; his countenance, besides being
very intellectual, has an expression of great sweetness
and benignity ; and his remarks and conversation are
in the highest degree interesting, when one remembers
what mental energy and moral force and determination he must have exerted to break through all the
trammels which have opposed his becoming what he
is.   I was turning away from him for a few moments,
to speak to Mr. Montague, who had begun a very
interesting discourse on the analysis of the causes of
laughter, when the Rajah recalled my attention to
himself by saying, " I am going to quote the Bible to
you : you remember that passage, ' The poor ye have
always with you, but Me ye have not always.'   Now,
Mr. Montague you have always with you, but me you
have not always."   So we resumed our conversation
together, and kept up a brief interchange of persiflage
which made us both laugh very much, and in which
he showed a very ready use of English language for a
stranger.

Mrs. Procter talked to me a great deal about her
little Adelaide, who must be a most wonderful creature.
The profound and unanswerable questions put to us
by these "children of light " confound us with the
sense of our own spiritual and mental darkness.   I
often think of Tieck's lovely and deep-meaning story
of " The Elves."   How little we know of the hidden
mysterious springs from which these crystal cups are
filled, or of the unseen companions that may have
strayed with their fellow to the threshold of this earth,
and walk with it while it yet retains its purity and
innocence ; but, as it journeys on, turn back and for-

sake it, and return to their home, leaving their sister-soul to wander through the world with sin and sorrow for companions.

Wednesday, 7th.—I sent " The Merchant of Venice " to Ramohun Roy, who, in our conversation last night, expressed a great desire to read it. . . .

Thursday, 8th. . . . In the evening acted Beatrice. The house was very good, which I was delighted to see. The Harnesses supped with us. While we were at supper, the *Quarterly Review* came from Murray's, and I read the article on "Francis I." aloud to them. It is very "handsome," and I should think must satisfy my most unreasonable friends. It more than satisfied me, for it made me out a great deal cleverer than ever I thought I was, or ever, I am afraid, shall be.

Friday, 9th.—Rehearsed "Francis I." When I came home found a charming letter and some Indian books, from that most amiable of all the wise men of the East, Ramohun Roy. Mrs. Jameson and Mr. Harness called.

Saturday, 10th.—Rehearsed "Francis I." Tried on my dresses for "The Hunchback;" they will be beautiful. The rehearsal was over long before the carriage came for me; so I went into my father's room and read the newspaper, while he and Mr. Bartley discussed the cast of Knowles's play. It seems my father will not act in it. I am sorry for that; it is hardly fair to Knowles, for no one else can do it. My poor father seemed too bewildered to give any answer, or even heed, to anything, and Mr. Bartley went away. My father continued to

walk up and down the room for nearly half an hour,
without uttering a syllable; and at last flung himself
into a chair, and leaned his head and arms on the
table. I was horribly frightened, and turned as cold
as stone, and for some minutes could not muster
up courage enough to speak to him. At last I got up
and went to him, and, on my touching his arm, he
started up and exclaimed, "Good God, what will
become of us all!" I tried to comfort him, and
spoke for a long time, but much, I fear, as a blind
man speaks of colours. I do not know, and I do not
believe any one knows, the real state of terrible
involvement in which this miserable concern is
wrapped. What I dread most of all is that my
father's health will break down. To-day, while he
was talking to me, I saw him suddenly put his hand
to his side in a way that sent a pang through my
heart. He seems utterly prostrated in spirit, and I
fear he will brood himself ill. God help us all! I
came home with a heavy heart, and got ready my
things for the theatre, and went over my part.
Emily called. . . . She brought me my aunt Siddons's
sketches of Constance and Lady Macbeth. They are
simply written, and though not analytically deep or
powerful, are true, clear, and good, as far as their
extent reaches. She thinks Constance more motherly
than queenly, and I do not altogether agree with her.
I do not think the scene after Arthur is taken
prisoner alone establishes my aunt's position; the
mother's sorrow there sweeps every other consideration away. It is before that that I think her
love for her child is in some measure mixed with the

feeling of the sovereign for his heir ; a love of power, in fact, embodied in the boy who was to continue the dominion of a race of princes. He was her royal child, and that I do not think she ever forgot till he was, in her imagination, her dead child. She says she could endure his being thrust from all his rights if he had been a less gracious creature, and goes on—

"But thou art fair, dear boy ! and at thy birth
Nature and fortune joined to make thee great ;"

and then bursts forth into her furious vituperation of those whose treachery has frustrated his natural claim to greatness. The woman, too, who in the utmost bitterness of disappointment, in the utter helplessness and desolation of betrayal, and the prostration of anguish and despair, calls on the earth, not for a shelter, not for a grave, or for a resting-place, but for a throne, is surely royally ambitious, a queen more than anything else. Mrs. Siddons's conception of Lady Macbeth is very beautiful, and I was particularly struck by her imagination of her outward woman : the deep blue eyes, the fair hair and fair skin of the northern woman (though, by-the-by, Lady Macbeth is a Highlander—I suppose a Celt ; and they are a dark race) ; the frail feminine form and delicate character of beauty, which, united to that undaunted mettle which her husband pays homage to in her, constituted a complex spell, at once soft and strong, sweet and powerful, and seemed to me a very original idea. My aunt makes a curious suggestion, supported only by her own con- viction, for which, however, she demonstrates no grounds, that in the banquet scene Lady Macbeth

sees Banquo's ghost at the same time Macbeth does.
It is very presumptuous in me to differ from her who
has made such a wonderful study of this part, but it
seems to me that this would make Lady Macbeth all
but superhuman; and in the scene with her husband
that precedes the banquet Macbeth's words to her
give me to understand that she is entirely innocent of
the knowledge even of his crime.

Monday, 12th.—Went to the theatre to rehearse
" Francis I." Miss Tree and Mr. Bennett will act
their parts admirably, I think. . . . When I got
home got ready my things for the theatre, and went
over my part. The play was " Much Ado about
Nothing," and I played as ill as usual. The house
was pretty good.

[Here occurs an interruption of some weeks in my
journal.]

My friend, Miss S——, came and paid me a long
visit, during which my play of " Francis I." and
Knowles's play of " The Hunchback " were produced,
and it was finally settled that Covent Garden should
be let to the French manager and entrepreneur,
Laporte, and that my father and myself should
leave England, and go for two years to America.

[The success of " Francis I." was one of entirely
indulgent forbearance on the part of the public.
An historical play, written by a girl of seventeen,
and acted in it by the authoress at one and twenty,
was, not unnaturally, a subject of some curiosity;
and, as such, it filled the house for a few nights. Its
entire want of real merit, of course, made it impossible that it should do anything more ; and, after

a few representations, it made way for Knowles's delightful play, which had a success as great and genuine as it was well deserved, and will not fail to be a lasting favourite, alike with audiences and actors.]

Thursday, June 14th.—A long break in my journal, and what a dismal beginning to it again! At five o'clock H—— started for Ireland. . . . Poor dear Dall cried bitterly at parting from her (my aunt was to accompany me to America, and it was uncertain whether we should see Miss S—— again before we sailed). . . . When I returned, after seeing her off, I went disconsolately to my own room. As I could not sleep, I took up the first book at hand, but it was " Tristram Shandy," and too horribly discordant with my frame of mind; besides, I don't like it at any time; it seems to me much more coarse even than witty and humorous.

Friday, 15th. . . . Almost at our very door met old Lady Cork, who was coming to see us. We stopped our carriages, and had a bawling conversation through the windows respecting my plans, past, present, and to come, highly edifying, doubtless, to the whole neighbourhood, and which ended by her ladyship shrieking out to me that I was "a super- natural creature " in a tone which must have made the mummies and other strange sojourners in the adjacent British Museum jump again. . . . In the evening, at the theatre, the play was " The Hunch- back," for Knowles's benefit, and the house was not good, which I do think is a shame. I played well, though Miss Taylor disconcerted me by coming so near me in her second scene that I gave her a real

· slap in the face, which I was very sorry for, though
she deserved it. After the play, Mr. Harness, Mrs.
Clarke, and Miss James supped with us; and after
supper, I dressed for a ball at the G——s', . . . and
much I wondered what call I had to be at a ball,
except that the givers of this festival are kind and
good friends of ours, and are fond of me, and I of
them. But I was not very merry at their ball for
all that. We came home at half-past two, which
is called "very early." Mr. Bacon was there (editor
of the *Times*, who married my cousin, Fanny Twiss),
but I had no chance to speak to him, which I was
sorry for, as I like his looks, and I liked his books:
the first are good, and the latter are clever. I cried
all the way home, which is a cheerful way of returning from a ball.

Saturday, 16th. . . . Mrs. Clarke, Miss James, the
Messrs. M——, and Alfred Tennyson dined with us.
I am always a little disappointed with the exterior of
our poet when I look at him, in spite of his eyes,
which are very fine; but his head and face, striking
and dignified as they are, are almost too ponderous
and massive for beauty in so young a man; and
every now and then there is a slightly sarcastic expression about his mouth that almost frightens me,
in spite of his shy manner and habitual silence.
But, after all, it is delightful to see and be with
any one that one admires and loves for what he has
done, as I do him. Mr. Harness came in the evening.
He is excellent, and I am very fond of him. They
all went away about twelve.

Monday, 18th. . . . At the theatre, in the evening,
54

the house was good, and I played pretty fairly. . . .
At supper my father read us his examination before
the committee of the House of Commons about this
minor theatre business. Of course, though every
word he says upon the subject is gospel truth, it will
only pass for the partial testimony of a person deeply
interested in his own monopoly.

Thursday, 21st.—Called on Mrs. Norton, . . . and
on Lady Dacre, to bid her good-bye. At the theatre,
in the evening, the house was good, and I played very
well. How sorry I shall be to go away! The actors,
too, all seem so sorry to have us go, and it will be so
hard to see none of the accustomed faces, to hear none
of the familiar voices, while discharging the tasks that
are often so irksome to me. John Mason came home
after the play and supped with us.

Friday, 22nd. . . . In the afternoon I called upon
the Sotherbys, to bid them good-bye; afterwards to
the Goldsmiths', on the same cheerless errand.
Stopped at dear Miss Cottin's to thank her for the
beautiful bracelet she had sent me as a farewell
present; and then on to Lady Callcott's, with whom I
spent a few solemn moments—solemnity not without
sweetness—and I scarcely felt sorrowful when she said,
" I shall never see you again." She is going to what
we call heaven, nearer to God (that is, in her own
consciousness, nearer to God). . . .

In the evening to the theatre. I only played pretty
well, except the last scene, which was better than the
rest. At the end of the play Mr. Bartley made the
audience a speech, mentioning our departure, and be-
speaking their goodwill for the new management.

The audience called for Knowles, and then clamoured
for us till we were obliged to go out. They rose to receive us, and waved their hats and handkerchiefs, and
shouted farewell to us. It made my heart ache to
leave my kind, good, indulgent audience ; my friends,
as I feel them to be ; my countrymen, my English
folk ; my " very worthy and approved good masters ;"
and as I thought of the strangers for whom I am now
to work in that distant strange country to which we
are going, the tears rushed into my eyes, and I hardly
knew what I was doing. I scarcely think I even made
the conventional courtesy of leavetaking to them, but
I snatched my little nosegay of flowers from my sash,
and threw it into the pit with handfuls of kisses, as a
farewell token of my affection and gratitude. And so
my father, who was very much affected, led me off,
while the house rang with the cheering of the audience.
When we came off my courage gave way utterly, and I
cried most bitterly. As my father was taking me to my
dressing-room Laporte ran after us, to be introduced
to me, to whom I wished success very dolorously from
the midst of my tears. He said he ought to cry at our
going away more than any one ; and perhaps he is
right, but we should be better worth his while when we
come back, if ever that day comes. I saw numbers of
people whom I knew standing behind the scenes to
take leave of us. . . .

I took an affectionate farewell of poor dear old Rye,
(the property-man), and Louis, his boy, gave me two
beautiful nosegays. It was all wretched, and yet it
was a pleasure to feel that those who surrounded and
were dependent on us cared for us. I know all the

servants and workpeople of the theatre were fond of
me, and it was sad to say good-bye to all these kind,
civil, cordial, humble friends ; from my good, pretty
little maid, who stood sobbing by my dressing-room
door, to the grim, wrinkled visage of honest old
Rye. . . .

[That was the last time I ever acted in the Covent
Garden my uncle John built ; where he and my aunt
took leave of the stage, and I made my first entrance
upon it. It was soon after altered and enlarged, and
turned into an opera-house ; eventually it was burnt
down, and so nothing remains of it.]

The Harnesses, and their friend, Mr. F——, supped
with us. Mr. Harness talked all sorts of things to try
and cheer me ; he laboured hard to prove to me that
the world was good and happy, but only succeeded in
convincing me that he was the one, and deserved
to be the other.

Friday, 29th.—On board the Scotch steamer for
Edinburgh. . . . We passed Berwick and Dunbar,
and the Douglases' ancient hold Tantallon, and the
lines from "Marmion" came to my lips. Poor Walter
Scott ! he will never sail by this lovely coast again,
every bold headland and silver creek of which lives in
his song or story. He has given of his own immortality to the earth which must ere long receive the
whole of his mortality. . . .

Saturday, 30th. — Went to rehearsal. . . . After
dinner Mary Anne, my maid, knowing my foible,
came in with her arms full of two of the most beautiful children I ever saw in my life. . . . [These
beautiful children were the daughters of the Duc de

Grammont, and were sharing with their parents the
exile of the King of France, Charles X., who had
found in his banishment a royal residence as ruined
as his fortunes, in the old Scottish palace of Holy-
rood.   Ida de Grammont, the eldest of my angels,
fulfilled the promise of her beautiful childhood as
the lovely Duchesse de Guyche.]   We spent a pleasant
evening at Mrs. Harry Siddons's.   Mr Combe and
Macdonald (the sculptor) were there. . . .

Sunday, July 1st. . . . We dined at Mr. Combe's,
and had a very pleasant dinner, but unluckily, owing
to a stupid servant's mistake, my old friend, Mr.
McLaren, who had been invited to meet me, did not
come.   After dinner, there was a tremendous discussion about Shakespeare, but I do not think these
men knew anything about him.   I talked myself into
a fever, and ended, with great modesty and propriety,
by disabling all their judgments, at which piece of
impertinence they naturally laughed very heartily.

Edinburgh, July 1st, 1832.

DEAREST H——,
            We left London on Wednesday at eight
o'clock. The parting between my mother and Dall (who
never met again ; my dear aunt died in America, in the
second year of our stay there), and myself and my
dear little sister, was most bitter. . . . John came
down to Greenwich with us, but would not come on
board the steamboat.   He stood on the shore and I
at the ship's side, looking at what I knew was him,
though my eyes could distinguish none of his features
from the distance.   My poor mother stood crying by

my side, and bade me send him away. I gave him
one signal, which he returned, and then ran up
the beach, and was gone!—gone for two years,
perhaps more; perhaps gone from me for ever in this
world ! . . .

We shall be in Liverpool on Monday morning, the
16th of July, and go to Radley's Hotel, where I hope
we shall find you on our arrival. My father is pretty
well, in spite of all the late anxieties and annoyances
he has had to wade through. In the course of the
day preceding our departure from London two arrests
were served upon him by creditors of the theatre, who,
I suppose, think when he is gone the whole concern
must collapse and fall to pieces, and I began to think
some means would be devised to prevent our leaving
England after all. Our parting on Wednesday
morning, was, as I told you, most miserable. . . .
My poor mother was braver than I had expected ; but
her parting from us, poor thing, is yet to come. . . .

I found a letter from Emily Fitzhugh here, en-
closing one as an introduction to a lady in New York,
who had once been her friend. . . . Edinburgh is
lovely and dear, and peace and quiet and repose
are always found by me near my dear Mrs. Harry
Siddons ; but my heart is, oh, so sad ! . . . Pray
answer this directly. The time is at hand when the
quickest "directly" in our correspondence will be
three months.—Ever your affectionate

F. A. K.

Monday, 2nd.—My father and I went to the theatre
to rehearse " Romeo and Juliet." In the evening the

house was very fair, considering how much the hot
weather is against us; but of all the comfortless
people to act to, commend me to an Edinburgh audience. Their undemonstrativeness, too, is something
more than mere critical difficulty to be pleased; there
is a want of kindliness in the cold, discourteous way
in which they allow a stranger to appear before them
without ever affording him the slightest token of their
readiness to accept the efforts made to please them.
I felt quite sorry this evening for poor Mr. Didear, to
whom not the faintest sign of encouragement was
vouchsafed on his first coming on. This is being cold
to an unamiable degree, and seems to me both a want
of good feeling and good breeding. I acted as well
as they would let me. As for poor John Mason, con-
cluding, I suppose, from their frozen silence that he
was flat and ineffective, he ranted and roared, and
pulled me about in the last scene, till I thought I
should have come to pieces in his hands, as the housemaids say of what they break. I was dreadfully
exhausted at the end of the play; there is nothing so
killing as an ineffectual appeal to sympathy, and, as
the Italians know, " ben servire e non gradire " is one
of the " tre cose da morire." . . .

Tuesday, 3rd.—Went to the theatre to rehearse.
. . . In the evening the house was good, and the
play went off very well. I acted well, in spite of my
new dresses, which stuck out all round me portentously, and almost filled the little stage. J—— L——
was like a great pink bird, hopping about hither and
thither, and stopping to speak,. as if it had been well
tamed and taught. The audience actually laughed and

applauded, and I should think must have gone home
very much surprised and exhausted with the unwonted
exertion.

Wednesday, 4th.—Went to the theatre to rehearse
" Francis I." After I got home, my mother told me
she had determined to leave us on Saturday, and go
back to London with Sally Siddons; and I am most
thankful for this resolution. . . . How sad it will be
in that strange land beyond the sea, among those
strange people, to whom we are nothing but strangers !
But this is foolish weakness; it must be; and what a
world of strength lies in those two little words ! . . .
At the theatre the house was very good, and I played
very well. . . ,

Thursday, 5th.—After breakfast went to rehearse
" The Gamester." . . . In the evening the house
was not good. My father acted magnificently; I
never played this part well, and am now gone off in
it, and play it worse than not well; besides, I cannot
bully that great, big man, Mr. Didear; it is mani-
festly absurd.

Friday, 6th.—To the theatre to rehearse " Francis
I." On my return found Mr. Liston and his little
girl waiting to ride with me. . . . [This was the
beginning of my acquaintance with the celebrated
surgeon Liston, who afterwards became an intimate
friend of ours, and to whose great professional skill
my father was repeatedly indebted for relief under a
most painful malady. He was a son of Sir Robert
Liston, and cousin of the celebrated comedian,
between whom and himself, however, there certainly
was no family likeness, Liston, the surgeon, being

one of the handsomest persons I ever saw. The last
time I saw him has left a melancholy impression on
my mind of his fine face and noble figure. He had
been attending me professionally, but I had ceased to
require his care, and had not seen him for some time,
when one morning walking, according to my custom
in summer, before seven o'clock, as I came to the
bridge over the Serpentine in Kensington Gardens, a
horseman crossing the bridge stopped by the iron
railing, and, jumping off his horse, came towards me.
It was Liston, who inquired kindly after my health,
and, upon my not answering quite satisfactorily, he
said, "Ah! well, you are better than I am." I
laughed incredulously, as I looked at a magnificent
figure leaning against the great black horse he rode,
and looking like a model of manly vigour and beauty.
But in less than a week from that day Liston died
of aneurism; and I suppose that when I met him
he was well aware of the death which had got him
literally by the throat.]

Saturday, 7th.—Miserable day of parting! of tearing
away and wrenching asunder! . . . At eleven we
were obliged to go to rehearsal, and when we returned
found my mother busy with her packing. . . . When
she was gone, I sat down beside my father with a book
in my hand, not reading, but listening to his stifled
sobbing; and every now and then, in spite of my
determination not to do it, looking up to see how far
the ship had moved. (Our windows looked over the
Forth.) But the white column of steam was rising
steadily from close under Newhaven, and for upwards
of half an hour continued to do so. I had resolved not

to raise my eyes again from my book, when a sudden
exclamation from my father made me spring up, and
I saw the steamer had left the shore, and was moving
fast towards Inchkeith, the dark smoky wake that
lingered behind it showing how far it had already
gone from us, and warning us how soon it would be
beyond the ken of our aching eyes. . . . The carriage was announced, and with a heavy heart and
aching head, I drove to the theatre. . . . The play
was "Francis I.," for the first time. The house was
very fine ; I acted abominably, but that was not much
to be wondered at. However, I always have acted
this part of my own vilely ; the language is not
natural—mere stilted declamation from first to last,
most fatiguing to the chest, and impossible for me to
do anything with, as it excites no emotion in me
whatever. . . .

Edinburgh, July 8, 1832.

My dearest H——,

I had just left my father at the window that
overlooks the Forth, watching my poor mother's ship
sailing away to England, when I received your letter ;
and it is impossible to imagine a sorer, sadder heart
than that with which I greeted it. . . . Thank you
for the pains you are taking about your picture for
me ; crammed with occupation as my time is here, I
would have done the same for you, but that I think in
Lawrence's print you have the best and likest thing
thing you can have of me. . . . I cannot tell you at
what hour we shall reach Liverpool, but it will be
very early on Monday morning. . . . I am glad you

have not deferred sitting for your picture till you came
to Liverpool, for it would have encroached much upon
our time together. I remember when I returned from
abroad, a school-girl, I thought I had forgotten my
mother's face. This copy of yours will save me from
that nonsensical morbid feeling, and you will surely
not forget mine. . . . You bid me, if anything
should go ill with me, summon you across the Atlantic. Alas! dear H——, you forget that before a
letter from that other world can reach this, more than
a month must have elapsed, and the writer may no
longer be in either. You say you hope I may return
a renewed being; and I have no doubt my health will
be benefited, and my spirits revived by change of
external objects; but oh, how dreary it all is now!
You bid me cheer my father when my mother shall
have left us, without knowing that she is already
gone. I make every exertion that duty and affection
can prompt; but, you know, it is my nature rather to
absorb the sorrow of others than to assist them in
throwing it off; and when one's own heart is all but
frozen, one knows not where to find warmth to
impart to those who are shivering with misery beside
one. . . . I have left myself scarcely any room to
tell you of my present life. I work very hard, rehearsing every morning and acting every night, and
spending the intervening time in long farewell rides
round this most beautiful and beloved Edinburgh.
Mr. Combe says I am wearing myself out, body and
mind; but I am already looking better, and less thin,
than when I left London; and besides, I shall presently
have a longer rest—holiday I cannot call it—on board

ship than I have had for the last three years. We
acted " Francis I." here last night, for the first time ;
and I am sure that, mingled with the applause, I
heard very distinct hissing ; whether addressed to the
acting, which was some of it execrable, or to the play
itself, which I think quite deserving of such a demonstration, I know not. . . . You know my opinion of
the piece ; and as, with the exception of the two parts
of De Bourbon and the Friar, and not excepting my
own, it really was vilely acted, hissing did not appear
to me an unnatural proceeding, though perhaps,
under the circumstances, not altogether a courteous
one on the part of the modern Athenians. I tell you
this, because what else have I to tell you, but that I
am your ever affectionate

F. A. K.

Tuesday, 10*th*.—At half-past twelve rode out with
Liston and his daughter, Mr. Murray, and Allen
(since Sir William, the celebrated artist, friend, and
painter, of Walter Scott and his family). . . . In
the evening, at the theatre, the house was very
full, and I acted very well, though I was so tired that
I could hardly stand, and every bone in my body
ached with my hard morning's ride. While I was
sitting in the green room, Mr. Wilson came in, and it
warmed my heart to see a Covent Garden face. He
tells me Laporte is giving concerts in the poor old
playhouse: well, good luck attend him, poor man
(though I know it won't, for "there's nae luck about
that house, there's nae luck at a'"). Walter Scott has
reached Edinburgh, and starts for Abbotsford to-

morrow; I am glad he has come back to die in his
own country, in his own home, surrounded by the
familiar objects his eyes have loved to look upon, and
by the hearts of his countrymen, and the prayers, the
blessings, the gratitude, and the love they owe him.
All Europe will mourn his death; and for years to
come every man born on this soil will be proud, for
his sake, to call himself a Scotchman.

Wednesday, 11th. . . . At half-past twelve met
Mr. Murray, Mr. Allen, and Mr. Byrne. . . . As we
started for our ride, and were "cavalcading" leisurely
along York Place, that most enchanting old sweetheart
of mine, Baron Hume, came out of a house. I rode
towards him, and he met me with his usual hearty,
kind cordiality, and a world of old-fashioned stately
courtesy, ending our conference by devoutly kissing
the tip of my little finger, to the infinite edification of
my party, upon whose minds I duly impressed the
vast superiority of this respectful style of gallantry to
the flippant, easy familiarity of the present day.
These old beaux beat the young ones hollow in the
theory of courtship, and it is only a pity that their
time for practice is over. Commend me to this
bowing and finger-kissing! it is at any rate more
dignified than the nodding, bobbing, and hand-
shaking of the present fashion. The be-Madaming,
too, has in it something singularly pleasing to my
taste; there's a hoop, and six yards of brocade, in
each of its two syllables. . . . At the theatre the
play was "Francis I." I acted well, and the play
went off very well. Mr. Allen came and sat in
the green room, telling me all about Constantinople

and the Crimea, and the beautiful countries he has
seen, and where his memory and his wishes are for
ever wandering; a rather sad comment upon the
perfect vision of content his charming home at
Laurieston had suggested to me.

Thursday, 12th. . . . At the theatre the play was
" The Hunchback." The house was very good, and I
acted very well. Dear Mr. Allen came into the green
room, and had a long gossip with me.

Friday, 13th. . . . Went with Mr. Combe to the
Phrenological Museum, and spent two hours listening
to some very interesting details on the anatomy of the
brain, which certainly tended to make the science
more credible to my ignorance, though the general
theory has never appeared to me as impossible and
extravagant as some people think it. The insuperable
point where I stick fast is a doubt of the practically
beneficial result which its general acceptance would
produce. I think they overrate the reforming power
of their system, though Mr. Combe's account of the
numbers who attend his lectures, and of the improvement of their bodily and mental conditions which he
has himself witnessed, must, of course, make me feel
diffident of my own judgment in the matter. Their
own experience can alone test the utility of their
system, and whether it does or does not answer their
expectations. I thought of Hamlet as I sat on the
ground, with my arms and lap full of skulls. It is
curious enough to grasp the empty, worthless,
unsightly case in which once dwelt the thinking
faculty of a man. One of the best specimens of the
human skull, it seems, is Raphael's; a cast of whose

head I held lovingly in my hands, wishing it had been
the very house where once abode that spirit of im-
mortal beauty. [The phrenological authorities were
mistaken, it seems, in attributing this skull to Raphael.
I believe that it has been ascertained to be that of his
friend, the engraver, Marc Antonio.] At the theatre
the play was "The Hunchback;" the house very good,
and I played very well.

Saturday, 14th.—My last day in Edinburgh for two
years; and who can tell for how many more? At
eleven o'clock, Mr. Murray, Mr. Allen, Mr. Byrne, and
myself sallied forth on horseback towards the Pentlands, having obtained half an hour's grace off
dinner-time, in order to get to Habbies How. We
went out by the Links, and up steep rises over a white
and dusty road, with a flaring stone dyke on each side,
and neither tree nor bush to shelter us from the
scorching sunlight till we came to Woodhouseleigh,
the haunted walk of a white spectre, who, it seems,
was fond of the shade, for her favourite promenade
was an avenue overarched with the green arms of
noble old elm trees; and we blessed the welcome
shelter of the Ghost's Haunt. . . . A cloud fell over
all our spirits as we rode away from this enchanting
spot, and Mr. Murray, pointing to the sprig of heather
I had put in my habit, said they would establish an
Order of Knighthood, of which the badge should be a
heather spray, and they three the members, and I the
patroness; that they would meet and drink my health
on the 14th of July, and on my birthday, every year
till I returned; and a solemn agreement was made by
all parties that whenever I did return and summoned

my worthies, we should again adjourn together to the
glen in the Pentlands. When we reached home, Mr.
Allen, who cannot endure a formal parting, shook
hands with me and bade me good-bye as I dismounted,
as if we were to ride again to-morrow. [And I never
saw him again. Peace be with him! He was a most
amiable and charming companion, and during these
days of friendly intimacy, his conversation interested
and instructed me, and his poetical feeling of Nature,
and placid, unruffled serenity, added much to the
pleasure of those delightful rides.] . . . At the theatre
the play was "The Provoked Husband," for my
benefit; the house was very fine, and I played pretty
well. After it was over, the audience shouted and
clamoured for my father, who came and said a few
words of our sorrow to leave their beautiful city. . . .
Mrs. Harry, Lizzie, and I were in my dressing-room,
crying in sad silence, and vainly endeavouring to
control our emotion. Presently my father came
hurriedly in, and folding them both in his arms, just
uttered in a broken voice, "Good-bye! God bless
you!" and I, embracing my dear friends for the last
time, followed him out of the room. It is not the
time only that must elapse before I can see her again,
it is the terrible distance, the slowness and uncertainty
of communication; it is that dreadful America.

Thursday, 19th, Liverpool. . . . At eleven went to
the theatre for rehearsal; it was very slovenly. I
wonder what the performance will be? In the
evening to the theatre; the play was "Francis I.,"
and the house was very good, which was almost
to be wondered at in this plague-stricken city.

[The cholera was raging in Liverpool.] I was frightened, as I always am at a new part, even in my own play, though glad enough to resign that odious dignity, the queen-mother. [The part of Louisa of Savoy had been given to me when first the piece was brought out at Covent Garden ; I was now playing the younger heroine, Françoise de Foix.] I played pretty well, though there is nothing to be done with the part. She is perfectly uninteresting and ineffective ; but it is better for the cast of the play that I should act her instead of Louisa. And when one can have such a specimen of a queen as we had to-night, it would be a thousand pities the audience should be put off with my inferior views of royalty. Such bouncing, frowning, growling, and snarling might have challenged a whole zoological garden full of wild beasts to surpass. It's a comfort to see that it is possible to play that part worse than I did.

Friday, 20th.—Went to rehearsal. . . . Received a letter from Lizzie, giving me an account of my dear old Newhaven fish-wife, poor body ! to whom I had sent a farewell present by her. I received also a long copy of anonymous verses, in which I was rather pathetically remonstrated with for seeking fame and fortune out of my own country. The author is slightly mistaken ; neither the love of money nor notoriety would carry me away from England, but the love of my father constrains me. . . . The American Consul and Mr. Arnold called. After dinner I read Combe's "Constitution of Man," which interested me very much, though it fails to convince me that phrenology can alone bestow this insight into human

55

nature. At the theatre "The School for Scandal;"
I played pretty well, though the actors were all dreadfully imperfect, and some of them so nervous and
quick, and some so nervous and slow, that it was
hardly possible to keep pace with them.

Saturday, 21*st*.—From Liverpool to Manchester.
After all, this Liverpool, with all its important wealth
and industry, is a dismal-looking place, a swarming
world of dingy red houses and dirty streets. . . .
How well I remember the opening of this railway.
. . . They have placed a marble tablet in the side of
the road to commemorate the spot where poor
Huskisson fell; I remembered it by the pools of dark-
green water that, as we passed them then, made a
dismal impression on me; they looked like stony basins
of verdigris. How glad I was to see Chatmoss—that
villainous, treacherous, ugly, useless bog—trenched
and ditched in process of draining and reclaiming,
with the fair, holy, healthy grain waving in bright
green patches over the brown peaty soil! Next to
moral conversion, and the reclaiming to their noble
uses the perverted powers of human nature, there is
nothing does one's heart so much good as the sight of
waste and barren land reclaimed to the uses and
wants of man; to see vegetation clothe the idle space,
and the cursed and profitless soil teaming with the
means of life and bringing forth abundant produce to
requite the toil that fertilized it; to see the wilderness
crowned with bounteous increase, and the blessing of
God rising from the earth to reward the labour of His
creatures. It forcibly reminds one of all that is left
undone, and might be done, with that far more

precious waste land, those multitudes of our ignorant
poor, whose minds and spirits are as dark, as profitless, as barren, as dreary, and as dangerous, as this
wild bog was formerly, and who were never ordained
to live and die like so many human morasses. . . .
In the evening to the theatre, which was crammed
from the floor to the ceiling; they are a pleasant
audience, too, and make a delightful quantity of sympathetic noise.   I did not play well, which was a pity
and a shame, because they really deserved that one
should do so; but my coadjutors were too much
for me. . . .

Sunday, 22nd, Liverpool.—I did not think there was
such another day in store for me as this.   I thought
all was past and over, and had forgotten the last drop
in the bitter cup. . . . The day was bitter cold, and
we were obliged to have a fire.

Liverpool, July 22nd.

MY DEAR MRS. JAMESON,

   I fear you are either anxious or vexed, or
perhaps both, about the arrival of your books, and my
non-acknowledgment of them.   They reached me in
all safety, and but for the many occupations which
swallow up my time would have been duly receipted
ere this.   Thank you very much for them, for they
are very elegant outside, and the dedication page, with
which I should have been most ungracious to find any
fault.   The little sketch on that leaf differs from the
design you had described to me some time ago, and I
felt the full meaning of the difference.   I read through
your preface all in a breath; there are many parts of

it which have often been matters of discussion between
us, and I believe you know how cordially I coincide
with most of the views expressed in it. The only
point in your preliminary chapter on which I do not
agree with you is the passage in which you say that
humour is, of necessity and in its very essence,
vulgar. I differ entirely with you here. I think
humour is very often closely allied to poetry; not only
a large element in highly poetic minds, which surely
refutes your position, but kindred to the highest and
deepest order of imagination, and frequently eminently
fanciful and graceful in its peculiar manifestations.
However, I cannot now make leisure to write about
this, but while I read it I scored the passage as one
from which I dissented. That, however, of course
does not establish its fallacy; but I think, had I
time, I could convince you of it. I acted Juliet on
Wednesday, and read your analysis of it before doing
so. Oh, could you but have seen and heard my
Romeo! . . . I am sure it is just as well that an
actress on the English stage at the present day should
not have too distinct a vision of the beings Shakespeare intended to realize; for she might be induced,
like the unfortunate heroine of the song, to "hang
herself in her garters." To be sure, there is always
my expedient to resort to, of acting to a wooden vase;
you know I had one put upon my balcony, in "Romeo
and Juliet," at Covent Garden, to assist Mr. Abbott in
drawing forth the expression of my sentiments. I
have been reading over Portia to-day; she is still
my dream of ladies, my pearl of womanhood. . . .
I must close this letter, for I have many more to

write to-night, and it is already late.   Once more,
thank you very much for your book, and believe me,
Ever yours very truly,
F. A. K.

August 1st.—Sailed for America.

The book referred to in this letter was Mrs.
Jameson's " Analysis of Shakespeare's Female Characters," which she very kindly dedicated to me.   The
etching in the title-page was changed from the one
she at first intended to have put in it, and represented
a female figure in an attitude of despondency, sitting
by the sea, and watching a ship sailing towards the
setting sun ; a design which I know she meant to have
reference to my departure.   I believe she subsequently
changed it again to the one she had first executed, and
which was of a less personal significance. . . . I
exchanged no more letters with my friend Miss S——,
who joined me at Liverpool, and remained with me
till I sailed for America. . . . "A trip," as it is now
called, to Europe or America, is one of the commonest
of experiences, involving, apparently, so little danger,
difficulty, or delay, that the feelings with which I
made my first voyage across the Atlantic must seem
almost incomprehensible to the pleasure-seeking or
business-absorbed crowds who throng the great
watery highway between the two continents.

But when I first went to America, steam had not
shortened the passage of that formidable barrier
between world and world.   A month, and not a week,
was the shortest and most favourable voyage that

could be looked for. Few men, and hardly any
women, undertook it as a mere matter of pleasure or
curiosity; and though affairs of importance, of course,
drew people from one shore to the other, and the
stream of emigration had already set steadily west-
ward, American and European tourists had not
begun to cross each other by thousands on the high
seas in search of health or amusement.

I was leaving my mother, my brothers and sister,
my friends and my country, for two years, and could
only hear from them at monthly intervals. I was
going to work very hard, in a distasteful vocation,
among strangers, from whom I had no right to expect
the invariable kindness and indulgence my own people
had favoured me with. My spirits were depressed by
my father's troubled fortunes, and I had just received
the first sharp, smarting strokes in the battle of life;
those gashes from which poor " unbruised youth," in
its infinite self-compassion, fancies its very life-blood
must all pour away; little imagining under what
gangrened, festering wounds brave life will still hold
on its way, and urge to the hopeless end its warfare
with unconquerable sorrow. There is nothing more
pathetic than the terrified impatience of youth under
its first experience of grief, and its vehement appeal
of " Behold, and see if any sorrow be like unto my
sorrow ! " to the patient adepts in suffering such as it
has not yet begun to conceive of. Orlando's adjuration
to the exiled duke in " As You Like It," and the wise
Prince's reply, seems to me one of the most exquisite
illustrations of the comparative griefs of youth and
age.

Off Sandy Hook, Monday, Sept. 5th.

MY DEAREST H——,

We are within three hours' sail of New York, having greeted the first corner of Long Island (the first land we saw) yesterday morning; but we are becalmèd, and the sun shines so bright, and the air is so warm and breathless, that we seem to have every chance of lying here for the next—Heaven knows how long! In point of time, you see, our voyage has been very prosperous, and I am surprised that we have made such good progress, for the weather has been squally, with constant head-winds. I do not think we have had, in all, six days of fair wind, so that we have no reason whatever to complain of our advance, having come thus far in thirty-two days. You bade me write to you by ships passing us, but though we have encountered several bound eastward, we only hailed them without lying to; notwithstanding which, about a fortnight ago, on hearing that a vessel was about to pass us, I wrote you a scrawl, which none but you could have made out (so the fishes won't profit much by it), and a kind fellow-passenger undertook to throw it from our ship to the other as it passed us. She came alongside very rapidly, and though he flung with great force and good aim, the distance was too great, and my poor little missive fell into the black sea within twenty feet of its destination. I could not help crying to think that those words from my heart, that would have gladdened yours, should go down into that cold, inky water. . . . I pray to God that we may return to England, but I am possessed with a dread that I never shall. . . .

I have been called away from this letter by one of those little incidents which Heaven in its mercy sends to break the monotony of a sea-voyage. Ever since daybreak this morning an English brig has been standing at a considerable distance behind us. About an hour ago we went on deck to watch the approach of a boat which they were sending off in our direction. The distance was about five miles, and the men had a hard pull in the broiling heat. When they came on board, you should have seen how we all clustered about them. The ship was a merchantman from Bristol, bound to New York ; she had been out eleven weeks, her provisions were beginning to run short, and the crew was on allowance. Our captain, who is a gentleman, furnished them with flour, tea, sugar, porter, cold tongue, ham, eggs, etc., etc. The men remained about half an hour on board, and as they were re-manning their boat we saw a whole cargo of eatables carried to it from our steerage passengers. You know that these are always poor people, who are often barely supplied themselves with necessaries for their voyage. The poor are almost invariably kind and compassionate to one another, and Gaffer Gray is half right when he says—

> "The poor man alone,
> When he hears the poor moan,
> Of his morsel one morsel will give."

They (the men from the brig) gave us news from Halifax, where they had put in. The cholera had been in Boston, Philadelphia, Baltimore, and New York ; the latter town was almost deserted, and the people

flying in numbers from the others. This was rather
bad news to us, who were going thither to find
audiences (if possible not few, whether fit or not),
but it was awful to such as were going back to their
homes and families. I looked at the anxious faces
gathered round our informer, and thought how the
poor hearts were flying, in terrible anticipation of the
worst, to the nests where they had left their dear ones,
and eagerly counting every precious head in the homes
over which so black a cloud of doom had gathered in
their absence. . . . My father, though a bad sailor,
and suffering occasionally a good deal, has, upon the
whole, borne the voyage well. Poor dear Dall has
been the greatest wretch on board ; she has been
perfectly miserable the whole time. It has made me
very unhappy, for she has come away from those she
loves very dearly on my account, and I cannot but
feel sad to see that most excellent creature now, in
what should be the quiet time of her life, leaving home
and all its accustomed ways, habits, and comforts,
and dear A——, who is her darling, to come wandering to the ends of the earth after me. . . . These
distant and prolonged separations seem like foretastes
of death. . . . We have seen an American sun, and
an American moon, and American stars, and we think
they " get up these things better than we do." We
have had several fresh squalls, and one heavy gale ;
we have shipped sundry seas ; we have had rat-
hunting and harpooning of porpoises ; we have caught
several hake and dog-fish.

New York, America, Wednesday, Sept. 5th, 1832.

Here we really are, and perhaps you, whó are not
here, will believe it more readily than I who am, and
to whom it seems an impossible kind of dream from
which I must surely presently wake. We made New
York harbour Monday night at sunset, and cast
anchor at twelve o'clock off Staten Island, where we
lay till yesterday morning at half-past nine, when a
steamboat came alongside to take the passengers to
shore. A thick fog covered the shores, and the rain
poured in torrents ; but had the weather been more
favourable, I should have seen nothing of our approach
to the city, for I was crying bitterly. The town, as
we drove through it from the landing, struck me as
foreign in its appearance—continental, I mean ; trees
are mixed very prettily with the houses, which are
painted of various colours, and have green blinds
on the outside, giving an idea of coolness and
shade. . . .

The sunshine is glorious, and the air soft and
temperate ; our hotel is pleasantly situated, and our
rooms are gay and large. The town, as I see it from
our windows, reminds me a little of Paris. Yesterday
evening the trees and lighted shop-windows and
brilliant moonlight were like a suggestion of the
Boulevards ; it is very gay, and rather like a fair.

The cholera has been very bad, but it is subsiding,
and the people are returning to town. We shall begin
our work in about ten days. I have not told you half
I could say, but foolscap will contain no more. God
bless you, dear !

Affectionately yours,

F. A. K.

The foreboding with which I left my own country
was justified by the event. My dear aunt died, and I
married, in America; and neither of us ever had a
home again in England.

New York, Sept. 16th, 1832.

My dearest H——,

What shall I say to you? First of all, pray
don't forget me, don't be altered when I see you
again, don't die before I come back, don't die if I
never come back. . . . You cannot imagine how
strange the comparisons people here are perpetually
making between this wonderful sapling of theirs and
our old oak seem to me. . . . My father, thank
God, is wonderfully improved in health, looks, and
spirits; the fine, clear, warm (hot it should be called)
atmosphere agrees with him, and the release from the
cares and anxieties of that troublesome estate of his in
St. Giles' will, I am sure, be of the greatest service to
him. He begins his work to-morrow night with
Hamlet, and on Tuesday I act Bianca. It is thought
expedient that we should act singly the two first
nights, and then make a " constellation." Dall is in
despair because I am to be discovered instead of
coming on (a thing actors deprecate, because they do
not receive their salvo of entrance applause), and also
because I am not seen at first in what she thinks a
becoming dress. For my part, I am rather glad of this
decision, for besides Bianca's being one of my best
parts, the play, as the faculty have mangled it, is such
a complete monologue that I am less at the mercy
of my coadjutors than in any other piece I play
in. . . .

Dall is very well, very hot, and very mosquito-bitten. The heat seems to me almost intolerable, though it is here considered mild autumn weather: the mornings and evenings are, it is true, generally freshened with a cool delicious air, which is at this moment blowing all my pens and paper away, and compensating us for our mid-day's broiling. I do nothing but drink iced lemonade, and eat peaches and sliced melon, in spite of the cholera.

Baths are a much cheaper and commoner luxury (necessary) in the hotels here than with us; a great satisfaction to me, who hope in heaven, if I ever get there, to have plenty of water to wash in, and, of course, it will all be soft rain-water there. What a blessing! On board ship we were not stinted in that respect, but had as much water as we desired for external as well as internal purposes.

There are no water-pipes or cisterns in this city such as we have, but men go about as they do in Paris, with huge water-butts, supplying each house daily; for although a broad river (so called) runs on each side of this water-walled city, the one—the East River—is merely an arm of the sea; and the Hudson receives the salt tide-water, and is rendered brackish and unfit for washing or cooking purposes far beyond the city. There are fine springs, and a full fresh-water stream, at a distance of some miles; but the municipality is not very rich, and is economical and careful of the public money, and many improvements which might have been expected to have been effected here long ago are halting in their advance, leaving New York ill paved, ill lighted, and indifferently supplied with a good many necessaries and luxuries of modern civilization.

[This was fifty-six years ago. Times are altered since this letter was written. New York is neither ill paved nor ill lighted; the municipality is rich, but neither economical, careful, nor honest, in dealing with the public moneys. The rapid spread of superficial civilization and accumulation of easily-got wealth, together with incessant communication with Europe, have made of the great cities of the New World, centres of an imperfect but extreme luxury, vying with, and in some respects going beyond, all that London or Paris presents for the indulgence of tastes pampered by the oldest civilization of Europe.

One day, after the Croton water had been brought into New York, I was sitting with the venerable Chancellor Kent at the window of his house in Union Square, and, pointing to the fountain that sprang up in the midst of the enclosure, he said, "When I was a boy, much more than half a century ago, I used to go to the Croton water, and paddle, and fish, and bathe, and swim, and loiter my time away in the summer days. I cannot go out there any more for any of these pleasant purposes, but the Croton water has come here to me." What a ballad Schiller or Goethe would have made of that! That morning visit to Chancellor Kent has left that pretty picture in my mind, and the recollection of his last words as he shook hands with me : "Ay, madam, the secret of life is always to have excitement enough, and never too much." But he did not give me the secret of that secret.]

There are, on an average, half a dozen fires in
various parts of the town every night—I mean houses
on fire. The sons of all the gentlemen here are
volunteer engineers and firemen, and great is the
delight they take in tearing up and down the streets,
accompanied by red lights, speaking trumpets, and
a rushing, roaring escort of running amateur ex-
tinguishers, who make night hideous with their bawling and bellowing. This evening as I was observing
that we had had no fire to-day, Dall said the weather
was so hot, she thought they must have left off fires
for the season.

Speaking of carriages and the devices on the panels
of them here, which appear to be rather fancy pieces
than heraldic bearings, my father said, "I wonder
what they do for arms." "Use legs," said Dall
immediately, not at all bethinking herself how ancient
a device on the shield of the Island of Man the three
legs were, or knowing how much more ancient, on the
coins of Crotona, I think, or some other of the Magna
Grecian colonies.

The hours which prevail here are those of our shop-
keeping population ; they rise and go to business very
early, dine at three, which indeed is considered late,
take tea at five, and supper at nine, which seems to
us very primitive. . . . The women here are, generally speaking, very pretty little creatures, with a
great deal of freshness and brilliancy ; they dress in
the extreme of the French fashion, and, I suppose
from some unfavourable influence of the climate, they
lose their beauty prematurely—they become full-
blown very early, and their bloom is extremely

evanescent; they fade almost suddenly. . . . There
seems to be a great deal of consumption here.   The
climate is as capricious as ours, with this additional
disadvantage, that the extremes of heat and cold are
much more intense, and the transitions much more
violent, the temperature varying occasionally as much
as thirty degrees in the twenty-four hours.   I have
just left off writing for five minutes to watch the lightning, which is dancing in a fiery ring all round the
horizon—summer lightning, no thunder, although the
flashes are strong and vivid. . . .

We have had such a tremendous storm—really
gorgeous, grand, and awful; lightning that stretched
from side to side of the sky, making a blaze like daylight for several seconds at a time.   The mere reflection
of it on the ground was more than the eye could
endure ; great forked ribbons of fire darting into the
very bosom of the city and its crowded dwellings, or
zig-zagging through the air to an accompaniment of
short, sharp, crackling thunder, succeeded by endless,
deep, full-toned rolls that made the whole air shake
and vibrate with the heavy concussion ; pelting and
pouring rain, a perfect tornado of wind.   Heaven and
earth are all, while I write, one livid, violet-coloured
flame, and the thunder resounds through the wild
frenzy of the elements like the voice of "the Ruler of
the spirits."   My eyes ache with the incessant glare,
and I must close my letter, for it is past eleven
o'clock, and I have to rehearse to-morrow morning.
. . . I have seen Mr. Wallack since our arrival,
whom I never saw in England, either on or off the
stage.   I went the other night to see him in one of

his favourite pieces, "The Rent-Day," which made
me cry dreadfully, but chiefly, I believe, because, when
they are ruined, he asks his wife if she will go with
him to America. You see I am taking to play-going
in my old age. The theatre is very pretty, of the best
possible dimensions for me, and tolerably good for the
voice. We leave this place for Philadelphia on the
10th of October, and remain there a fortnight, and
then go on to Boston. . . .

Last Thursday we crossed the Hudson in one of
the steamers constantly plying between the opposite
shores and New York, and took a delightful walk
along the New Jersey shore to a place called Hoboken,
famous once as a duelling-ground, now the favourite
resort of a pacific society of *bon vivants,* who meet once
a week to eat turtle, or, as it is expressed on their
cards of invitation, for " spoon exercise." The
distance from our landing-point to the place where
these meetings are held is about five miles, a charming walk through a strip of forest-ground, which
crowns the banks of the river, gradually rising to a
considerable height above it. We were delighted with
the vivid, various, and strange foliage of the trees, the
magnificent river, broad and blue as a lake, with its
high and richly wooded shore, and the sparkling,
glittering town opposite. We looked down to the
Narrows, the defile through which the waters of this
noble estuary reach the Atlantic, and between whose
rocky walls two or three ships stood out against the
brilliant sky. The ebbing tide plashed on the rocks
far below us, and the warm grass through which we
walked was alive with grasshoppers, whose scarlet

wings, suddenly unfolded when they flew, made me
take them for some strange species of butterfly. It
was all indescribably bright and joyous-looking, and
the air of a transparent clearness that was one of the
most striking characteristics of the whole scene, and
one of the most delightful. . . . [In discussing the
relative merits of England and America, Dr. Channing once said to me, "The earth is yours, but the
heavens are ours;" and I quite agree with him. I
have never seen a sky comparable, for splendour of
colour or translucent purity, to that of the Northern
States.]

I have been reading your favourite book, "Sal-
monia." . . . I am rather surprised at your liking it
so very much, because, though the descriptions are
beautiful, and the natural history interesting, and the
philosophical and moral reflections scattered through
it delightful, yet there is so much that is purely
technical about fishing and its processes, and addressed only to the hook-and-line fraternity, that I
should not have thought it calculated to charm you so
greatly. However, you may have some associations
connected with it; liking is a very complex and
many-motived thing. . . .

We went through the fish and fruit markets the
other day; unfortunately it was rather late in the
morning, and of course the glory of the market was
over, but yet there remained enough to enchant us,
with their abundant plenteousness of good things.
The fruit-market was beautiful; fruit-baskets half as
high as I am, placed in rows of a dozen, filled with
peaches, and painted of a bright vermilion colour,

56

which throws a ruddy becoming tint over the downy
fruit.   It looked like something in the " Arabian
Nights ; " heaps, literally heaps of melons, apples,
pears, and wild grapes, in the greatest profusion.   I
was enchanted with the beautiful forms, bright colours,
and fragrant smell, but I saw no flowers, and I have
seen hardly any since I have been here, which is
rather a grief to me. . . .

Americans are the most extravagant people in
the world, and flowers are among them objects
of the most lavish expenditure.   The prices paid
for nosegays, wreaths, baskets, and devices of
every sort of hot-house plants, are incredible to
any reasonable mind.   At parties and balls ladies
are laden with costly nosegays which will not even
survive the evening's fatigue of carrying them.
Dinner and luncheon parties are adorned, not only
with masses of exquisite bloom as table ornaments,
but by every lady's plate a magnificent nosegay of
hot-house flowers is placed ; and I knew a lady who,
wishing to adorn her ball-room with rather more than
usual floral magnificence, had it hung round with
garlands of white camelias and myosotis.

At the theatre enormously expensive nosegays and
huge baskets of forced flowers are handed to the
favourite performers from the front of the house, till
the ceremony becomes embarrassing, and almost
ridiculous for the object of the demonstration.   The
churches at certain festivals are hung with draperies
of costly hot-house flowers ; the communion tables
heaped with them.   Weddings, of course, are natural
occasions for that species of ornament, but in America

funerals are as flowery as marriage-feasts; and I have
seen there in mid-winter, with the thermometer at
fifteen degrees below zero, large crosses, and hearts, and
wreaths, made entirely of rosebuds and lilies of the
valley, as part of the solemnities of a burial service;
and a young girl who died in the flowerless season,
was not only shrouded in blossoms, but as her coffin
was carried to the bosom of the wintry earth, a white
pall of the finest material was thrown over it, with a
great cross of double forced violets, almost the length of
the coffin, laid on it. I have had as many as a dozen
huge baskets of camelias, violets, orange-flower, and
tuberose, at one time, in my room; perishable tokens
of anonymous public and private favour, the cost of
which used to fill me with dismay: and on one occasion a table of magnificent hot-house flowers was sent
to me, of such dimensions that both sides of the street
door had to be opened to admit it. When I have
deplored the inordinate amount of money lavished
upon that which could only impart pleasure for so
brief a time, I have been answered, but not converted
from my feeling of disapprobation and regret, that the
gardeners profited by this wild extravagance. In New
York I have known a guinea paid for a gentleman's
button-hole rosebud, and three guineas for half a
dozen sprays of lily of the valley.

Good-bye, my dearest H——. I pray for you
morning and night. Is not that thinking of you, and
loving you as best I can?

Your affectionate
F. A. K.

DEAREST H——,

. . . . We are all pretty well, but all but
devoured by multitudinous and multivarious beasts of
prey—birds, I suppose they are: mosquitoes, ants,
and flies, by day; and flies, fleas, and worse, by night.
The plagues of Egypt were a joke to it. We spend
our lives in murdering hecatombs of creeping and
jumping things, and vehemently slapping our own
faces with intent to kill the flying ones that incessantly
buzz about one. It is rather a deplorable existence,
and reminds me of one of the most unpleasant circles
in Dante's "Hell," which I don't think could have
been much worse. My father began his work on
Monday last with Hamlet. Dall and I went into a
private box to see him; he acted admirably, and
looked wonderfully young and handsome. The house
was crammed, and the audience, we were assured, was
enthusiastic beyond all precedent. . . .

On Tuesday I came out in Bianca; I was rather
glad they had appointed that part for my first, because
it is one of my best; but had not the genius of
theatrical management made such a mere monologue
of the play as it has, I verily believe I should have
been "swamped" by my helpmate. My Fazio was
an unhappy man who played Romeo once with me in
London, and failed utterly: moreover, he had studied
this part in a hurry, it seems, and did not know three
words of it, and was, besides, too frightened to profit
by my prompting. The only thing that seemed to
occur to him was to go down on his knees, which he
did every five minutes. Once when I was on mine, he
dropped down suddenly exactly opposite to me, and

there we were, looking for all the world like one of those pious conjugal *vis-à-vis* that adorn antique tombs in our cathedrals. It really was exceedingly absurd. But I looked and acted well, and the play was very successful. . . . I was not nervous for my first night, till my unhappy partner made me so. My dislike to the stage would really render me indifferent to my own success, but that I am working for my livelihood; my bread depends upon success, and that is a realistic, if not an artistic, view of the case, of which I acknowledge the importance. . . .

Absolute and uncompromising vulgarity is really not very objectionable; it is rather refreshing, indeed, for it is simple, and, in that respect, rare. Vulgarity allied to pretension and the affectation of fine manners is the only real vulgarity, and is an intolerable thing. The plain rusticity, or even coarseness, of what are called the lower classes, is infinitely preferable to the assumption of *gentility* of those a little above them in the social scale. The artisan, or day-labourer, or common workman, is apt to be a gentleman, compared with a certain well-to-do small shopkeeper. . . .

On Thursday, when I went to rehearse "Romeo and Juliet," I found that the unfortunate Mr. Keppel was, by general desire, taken out of Romeo, which my father was therefore called upon, for the first time, to act with me. I was vexed at this every way. I was sorry for the poor player, whose part, of course, was money to him; and sorry for my father, who has the greatest objection to playing Romeo, for which his age, of course, disqualifies him, however much his excellent acting may tend to make one forget it; and

I was sorry for the public, who lost his admirable
Mercutio, which I do not think they were compensated
for by his taking the other part. . . .

The steward of our ship, a black—a very intelligent,
obliging, respectable servant—came here the other
morning to ask my father for an order, at the same
time adding that it must be for the gallery, as people
of colour were not allowed to go into any other part
of the theatre. Qu'en dis-tu?   The prejudice against
these unfortunate people is, of course, incomprehensible to us. On board ship, after giving that same
man some trouble, Dall poured him out a glass of
wine, when we were having our dinner, whereupon the
captain looked at her with utter amazement, and I
thought some little contempt, and said, "Ah! one can
tell by that that you are not an American;" which
sort of thing makes one feel rather glad that one is
not.

[This was in 1832, when slavery literally governed
the United States.   In 1874, when the Civil War had
washed out slavery with the blood of free men, the
prejudice engendered by it governed them still to the
following degree.   Going to the theatre in Philadelphia
one night, I desired my servant, a perfectly respectable
and decorous coloured man, to go into the house and
see the performance.   This, however, he did not succeed in doing, being informed at all the entrance doors
that persons of colour were not admitted to any part
of the theatre.   At this same time, more than half
the state legislature of South Carolina were blacks.
Moreover, at this same time, coloured children were
not received into the public schools of Philadelphia,

though coloured citizens were eligible, and in some
cases acted as members of the board of management
of these very schools. I talked of this outrageous inconsistent prejudice with some of my friends; among
others, the editor of a popular paper. They were all
loud in their condemnation of the state of things, but
strongly of opinion that to move at all in the matter
would be highly inopportune and injudicious. Time,
they said, would settle all these questions; and, without doubt, it will. Charles Sumner, who thought
Time could afford to have his elbow jogged about
them, had just gone to his grave, leaving, unfortunately, incomplete his bill of rights in behalf of the
coloured citizens of the United States.

My servant was a citizen of the United States,
having a vote, when he was turned from the theatre
door as a person of colour; and negroes had been
elected as Members of Congress at that very time.
Strangely enough, Philadelphia, once the seat of
enthusiastic and self-devoted Quaker abolitionism, the
home of that noble and admirable woman, Lucretia
Mott, who stood heroically in its vanguard, is now
one of the strongholds of the most illiberal prejudice
against the blacks.]

On Friday we acted "The School for Scandal."
Our houses have been very fine indeed, in spite of the
intolerable heat of the weather. . . . My ill-starred
Fazio of Thursday night is making a terrible stir in
the papers, appealing to the public, and writing long
letters about his having merely studied the part to
accommodate me. "Hard case—unjust partiality—
superior influence," etc., etc.—in short, an attempt at

a little cabal, the effect of which is that he has obtained leave to appear again to-morrow night in Jaffier to my Belvidera. The poor man is under a strong mental delusion, he cannot act in the least; however, we shall see what he will do with "Venice Preserved." . . .

Yesterday evening we dined with some English people who are staying in this hotel, and met Dr. Wainwright, rector of the most "fashionable" church in New York; a very agreeable, good, and clever man, who expressed great delight at having an opportunity of meeting us in private, as his congregation are so strait-laced that he can neither call upon us nor invite us to his house, much less set his foot in the theatre. The probable consequence of any of these enormities, it seems, would be deserted pews next Sunday, and perhaps eventually the forced resignation of his cure of souls. This is rather narrow-minded, I think, for this free and enlightened country. Think of my mother's dear old friend, Dr. Hughes, and Milman, and Harness, and Dyce, and all our excellent reverend friends and intimate acquaintance. . . .

To-morrow we act "Venice Preserved," on Tuesday "Much Ado about Nothing," Wednesday is a holiday, on Thursday, for my benefit, "The Stranger," and on Friday, "The Hunchback." On the 10th of next month we act in Philadelphia, where we shall remain for a fortnight, and then return here for a fortnight, after which we go on to Boston. God bless you, dear. It is past twelve at night, and I have a ten o'clock rehearsal to-morrow morning.

Ever your affectionate

F. A. K.

PART OF LETTER TO MRS. JAMESON.

New York, September 30th, 1832.

I am not sure that, upon the whole, our acting is not rather too quiet—tame, I suppose they would call it—for our present public. Ranting and raving in tragedy, and shrieks of unmeaning laughter in comedy, are not, you know, precisely our style, and I am afraid our audiences here may think us flat. I was informed by a friend of mine who heard the remark, that one gentleman observed to another, after seeing my father in "Venice Preserved," "Lord bless you! it's nothing to Cooper's acting—nothing! Why, I've seen the perspiration roll down his face like water when he played Pierre! You didn't see Mr. Kemble put himself to half such pains!" Which reminds me of the Frenchwoman's commendation to her neighbour of a performance of Dupré, the great Paris tenor of his day: "Ah! ce pauvre cher M. Dupré! ce brave homme! quel mal il se donne pour chanter cela! Regardez donc, madame, il est tout en sueur!" But this order of criticism, of course, may be met with anywhere; and the stamp-and-stare-and-start-and-scream-school has had its admirers all the world over since the days of Hamlet the Dane.

I have not seen much of either places or people yet. . . . This city is picturesque and foreign-looking; trees are much intermixed with the houses, among them a great many fine willows, and these, together with the various colours of the houses, and the irregularity of the streets and buildings, form constantly "little bits" that would gladden the eye of a painter. The sky here is beautiful; I find in it what you have seen in Italy, and I only in Angerstein's Gallery, the orange sunsets of Claude Lorraine.

We leave New York for Philadelphia after next week, and shall remain there three weeks.

I have read and noted much of your pretty book. There are one or two points which shall "serve for sweet discourses" in our time to come. I find great satisfaction in our discussions, for though I may not often confess to being convinced by your arguments in our differences (does any one ever do so ?), I derive so much information from them, that they are as profitable as pleasant to me. Are you going to be busy with your pen soon again? Write me how the world is going on yonder, and believe me ever truly yours,

F. A. K.

New York, September 30th, 1832. ',

DEAREST H——,

. . . Perhaps, as you say, it is morbid to dwell as I do upon the unreality of acting, because its tangible reality makes its appearance duly every morning with the "returns" of the preceding night; but I am not sure that it is morbid to consider wants exaggerated and necessities unreal which render insufficient, earnings that would be ample for any one's real need. A livelihood, of course, we could make in England. . . . You speak of all the various strange things I am to see, and the amount of knowledge I shall involuntarily acquire, by this residence in America ; but you know I am what Dr. Johnson would have considered disgracefully "incurious," and the lazy intellectual indifference which induced me to live in

London by the very spring of the fountain of knowledge without so much as stooping my lips to it, prevails with me here.

[Our house in Great Russell Street, which was the last at the corner of Montague Place, adjoined the British Museum, and has since been taken into, or removed for (I don't know which), the new buildings of that institution. Our friend Panizzi, the learned librarian, lived in the house that stood where ours, formerly my uncle's, did. While we were still living there, however, I was allowed a privileged entrance at all times to the library, and am ashamed to think how seldom I availed myself of so great a favour.]

Then, too, my profession occupies nearly the whole of my time; I have rehearsals every day, and act four times a week; my journalizing takes up a good deal of my leisure. Walking in the heat we still have here fatigues me, and hurts my feet very much, especially when I have to stand at the theatre all the evening. Although I have been here a month, I have seen but little either of places or people; the latter, you know, I nowhere affect, and my distaste for the society of strangers must, of course, interfere with my deriving information from them. Still, as you say, I must inevitably see and learn much that is new to me, and I take pleasure in the hope that when I return to you I shall be less distressingly ignorant than you must often have found me. . . .

I am very sorry my brother Henry and his men are going to be sent upon so odious an errand as tithe-collecting must be in Ireland. I trust in God he may meet with no mischief while fulfilling his duty; I should

be loth to think of that comely-looking young thing
bruised or broken, maimed or murdered. I hardly
think your savage Irishers would have the heart to
hurt him, he looks so like, what indeed he is, a mere
boy; but then, to be sure, his errand is not one to
recommend him to their mercy.

I have read Bryant's poetry, and like it very much.
The general spirit of it is admirable ; it is all wholesome poetry, and some of it is very beautiful.

I am going to get Graham's "History of the United
States," and Smith's " History of Virginia," to beguile
my journey to Philadelphia with. I can't fancy a savage
woman marrying a civilized man. . . . I suppose love
might bring harmony out of the discords of natures
so dissimilar, but I think if I had been a wild
she-American, I should not have been tamed by one of
the invading race, my hunters. Pocohontas thought
differently. . . .

Are you acquainted with any of Daniel Webster's
speeches ? They are very fine, eloquent, and powerful ;
and one that he delivered upon the commemoration of
the landing of the English exiles at Plymouth, in
many parts, magnificent. I was profoundly affected
by it when my father read it to us on board
ship. . . .

Bad as your mice, of which you complain so bitterly,
may be, they are civilized Christian creatures compared with the heathen swarms with which we wage
war incessantly here. Every evening, as soon as the
sun sets, clouds of mosquitoes begin their war-dance
round us ; their sting is most venomous, and as my
patience is not even skin-deep, I tear myself like a

maniac, and then, instead of oil, pour aromatic
vinegar into my wounds, and a very pretty species of
torture is produced by that means, I assure you.
Besides these winged devils, we have swarms of flies,
which also bite and sting, with a venomous rancour of
which I should have thought their frivolity incapable.
Besides these, every cupboard and drawer in our
rooms is full of moths. Besides these, we have an
army of cantankerous fleas quartered upon us. Besides
these, we have one particular closet where we keep—
our bugs, and where for the most part, I am truly
thankful to say, they keep themselves. Besides these,
we have two or three ants' nests in our bedroom, and
everything we look upon seems but a moving mass of
these red, long-legged, but always exemplary insects.
These fellow-creatures make one's life not worth much
having, and I do nothing all day long but sing the
famous entomological chorus in " Faust ; " and if this
goes on much longer, I feel as if I should take to
buzzing. Do you know that it is hard upon three
o'clock in the morning ? I must leave off and go
to bed, for I rehearse Constance to-morrow at eleven,
and act her to-morrow night. On Friday I act Bizarre
in " The Inconstant," and think I shall find it great
fun. . . . God bless you, dearest H——.
                    Ever your affectionate
                              F. A. K.

Mansion House, Philadelphia, Oct. 10th, 1832.
DEAREST H——,
        Do not let the date of this make any altera-
tion in your way of addressing your letters, which

·must still be " Park Theatre, New York ; " for before
this reaches you we shall probably have returned
thither; but I date particularly that you may follow
us with your mind's legs, and know where to find us.
My dearest H——, in spite of an often heavy heart,
and my distaste for my present surroundings, I have
reason to be most grateful, and I trust I am so, for
the benefits which we have already derived from a
visit to this far world beyond the sea.   The first and
greatest of these is the wonderful improvement in my
dear father's health.   He looks full ten years younger
than when last you saw him, and besides enjoying
better spirits from the absence of the many cares and
anxieties and vexations that weighed upon him daily
in England, he says that he is conscious since he
came away of a great increase of absolute muscular
strength and vigour; and when he said this, I felt
that my share of the unpleasant duty of coming hither
was already amply repaid. . . . We have finished
our first engagement at New York, which was for
twelve nights, and have every reason to be satisfied
with our financial, as well as professional, success.
Living here is not as cheap as we had been led to
expect, but our earnings are very considerable, and as
we labour for these, it is matter of rejoicing that we
labour so satisfactorily.

Dall is very well, except the nuisance of a bad cold.
I am very well, without exception.   The only unpleasant effect I feel from this climate is a constant
tendency to slight relaxation of the throat, but this is
nothing more than a trifling inconvenience, very en-
durable, and which probably a little more seasoning

will remove. . . . I tell you of our health first, for at
our distance from each other that is the matter of
greatest moment and anxiety. . . .

I must tell you of our future arrangements; and,
to begin like an Irishwoman, we arrived here on
Monday. My father acts to-night for the first time,
Hamlet; and I make my first appearance to-morrow
in " Fazio." We shall act here for three weeks, and
then return to New York for a month; after which we
shall proceed to Boston, whence look to receive
volumes from me about Webster, and Channing, and
our friends and fellow-passengers, the H——s, who
reside there.

I like this place better than New York; it has an
air of greater age. It has altogether a rather dull,
sober, mellow hue, which is more agreeable than the
glaring newness of New York. There are one or two
fine public buildings, and the quantity of clean, cool-
looking white marble which they use both for their
public edifices and for the doorsteps of the private
houses has a simple and sumptuous appearance, which
is pleasant. It is electioneering time, and all last
night the streets resounded with cheers and shouts,
and shone with bonfires. The present President,
Jackson, appears to be far from popular here, and
though his own partisans are determined, of course,
to re-elect him if possible, a violent struggle is likely
to take place; and here already his opponent, Henry
Clay, who is the leader of the aristocratic party in the
United States, is said to have obtained the superiority
over him.

I have got Graham's and Smith's " Histories," and

though my time for reading is anything but abundant, yet every night and morning I do contrive, while brushing the outside of my head, to cram something into the inside of it.

I cannot bear to give up any advantage which I once possessed, and therefore struggle to keep up, in some degree, my music and Italian. These, together with rehearsing every morning, and acting four times a week, besides my journal, which I very seldom neglect, make up a good deal of daily occupation. Then, one must sacrifice a certain amount of time to the conventional waste of society, receiving and returning visits, etc. . . . I like what I have read of Graham very much; the matter is very interesting, and the spirit in which it is treated ; and I am deeply in love with Captain John Smith, and wonder greatly at Pocohontas marrying anybody else. I suppose, however, the savage was not without excuse ; for Mary Stuart, who knew something of these matters, says, with a rather satirical glance at her cousin of England, "En ces sortes de choses, la plus sage de nous toutes n'est qu'un peu moins sotte que les autres."

I have been to my first rehearsal here to-day ; the theatre is small, but pretty enough. The public has high pretensions to considerable critical judgment and literary and dramatic taste, and scouts the idea of being led by the opinion of New York. . . . It is rather tiresome that fools are cut upon the same pattern all the world over. What is the profit of travelling? Oh dear! I think my Fazio has got St. Vitus's dance! . . .

Yesterday I tried some horses, which were rather terrible quadrupeds. They were not ill-bred cattle to look at, and I should think of a race that, with care and attention, might be brought to considerable perfection; but they are never properly broken for the saddle. The Americans who have spoken to me about riding say that they do not like a horse to have what we consider proper paces, but prefer a shambling sort of half-trot, half-canter, which they judiciously call a rack, and which is the ugliest pace to behold, and the most difficult to endure, possible. They never use a curb, but ride their horses upon the snaffle entirely, dragging it as tight as they can, and having the appearance of holding on for dear life by it; so that the horse, in addition to the awkward gait I have described, throws his head up, and pokes his nose out, and with open jaws "devours the road" before him. . . .

I acted here last night for the first time. Dall and my father say that I received my reception very ungraciously. I am sure I am very sorry, I did not mean to do so, but I really had not the heart or the face to smile and look as pleased and pleasant as I can at a parcel of strangers. . . . I was not well, or in spirits, and labouring under a severe cold, which I acquired on board the steamboat that brought down the Delaware. . . . Neither the Raritan nor the Delaware struck me in any way except by their great width. These vast streams naturally suggest the mighty resources which a country so watered presents to the commercial enterprise of its inhabitants. The breadth of these great rivers dwarfs their shores and

makes their banks appear flat and uninteresting,
though the large lake-like basins into which they
occasionally expand are grand from the mere extent
and volume of the sweeping mass of waters.

The colours of the autumnal foliage are rich and
beautiful beyond imagination—crimson and gold, like
a regal mantle, instead of the sad russet cloak of our
fading woods. I think, beautiful as this is, that its
gorgeousness takes away from the sweet solemnity
that makes the fall of the year pre-eminently the
season of thoughtful contemplation. Our autumn at
home is mellow and harmonious, though sometimes
melancholy; but the brilliancy of this decay strikes
one sometimes with a sudden sadness, as if the whole
world were dying of consumption, with these glittering
gleams and hectic flushes, a mere deception of disease
and death. . . . Good-bye, my dearest H——.

Philadelphia, Oct. 14th, 1832.

DEAREST H——,
        "Boston is a Yankee town, and so is
Philadelphy;" considering which, I assure you I
find the latter quite a civilized place. The above
quotation is from "Yankee-doodle," the National
Anthem of the Americans, which I will sing to you
some day when I am within hearing.

We have just returned from church. Dall and I
being too late this morning for the service, which
begins at half-past ten, sallied forth in search of
salvation this afternoon, and after wandering about
a little, entered a fine-looking church, which we found
was a Presbyterian place of worship. . . . The

preaching to-day was extemporaneous, and extremely
feeble and commonplace, occasionally reminding me
of your eloquent friend at Skerries. . . . I shall try,
on my return to New York, to settle to some work
in earnest, as I hope there that we shall repeat the
plays we have already acted, and so need no rehearsals. . . . To-morrow I act Juliet to my father's
Romeo; he does it still most beautifully. . . . In
spite of his acting it with his own child (which puts
a manifest absurdity on the very face of it), the
perfection of his art makes it more youthful, graceful,
ardent, and lover-like—a better Romeo, in short,
than the youngest pretender to it nowadays.   It is
certainly simple truth when he says, "I am the
youngest of that name, for lack of a better," when
the nurse asks for young Romeo.

Wednesday we act "The School for Scandal," and
Friday "Venice Preserved." So there's your play-
bill. . . .

At this moment a great political excitement pervades the country; it is the time of the Presidential
Election, and the most vehement efforts are being
made by the democratic party to maintain the
present President, General Jackson, in his post.   The
majority, I believe, is in his favour, though we are
told that the "better classes" (whatever that may
mean where no distinctions of class exist) embrace
the cause of his opponent, Henry Clay.

It seems curious, if it is true, as we have been
assured, that in this one state of Pennsylvania, eight
thousand persons out of fifty who have the right of
voting were all who in this last election exercised

it; so that the much-vaunted privilege of universal suffrage does not seem to be highly prized where it is possessed.

From all the opinions that I hear expressed upon the subject, it does not seem as though the system of election prevalent here works much better, or is much freer from abuses, than the well-vilified one which England has just been reforming. Bribery and corruption are familiar here as elsewhere, to those who have, and those who wish to have, power; and I have not yet heard a single American speak of our Radical reformers without uplifted hands at what they consider their folly in not "letting well alone," or, as they say, in substituting one set of abuses for another, as they declare we shall do if we adopt their vote by ballot system.

I have now written you a philosophical, moral, and political letter, and beg you will score up my attempt to write rationally against the loads of gibberish I have from time to time discoursed to you. God bless you, dearest H——. Three thousand miles away, I am still

Always your affectionate

F. A. K.

Philadelphia, Oct. 22nd, 1832.

DEAR H——;

My first news is deplorable, and I beg you will lament over it accordingly. I eat little, drink less, rehearse six mornings and act five nights a week; in spite of all which, and riding a heavy-going, jolting, shambling, hard-pulling horse, I have grown so fat that I really cannot perceive that there is any shape in particular about me. Grotesque things sometimes are melancholy too, and it is so with me, for I am both. . . . My father and Dall are very well; at this moment he is busy saying, and she hearing him say, the part of Fazio, which he is to act with me to-morrow night. I dread it dreadfully; acting anything painful with him always tries my nerves extremely. Bianca is a part of terrible excitement in itself, without the addition of having to act it to his Fazio. I cannot get rid of his being he, and it agonizes me really to see his sham agony; however, "'tis my vocation, Hal." It is very well that our audiences should look at us as mere puppets, for could they sometimes see the real feelings of those for whose false miseries their sympathies are excited, I believe sufficiently in their humanity to think they would kindly give us leave to leave off and go home. Ours is a very strange trade, and I am sorry to say that every day increases my distaste for it. . . . I do not think that during my father's life I shall ever leave the stage; it is very selfish to feel regret at this, I know, but it sometimes seems to me rather dreary to look along my future years, and think that they will be devoted to labour that I dislike and despise. . . . For many years—ever since I entered upon my first girlhood, indeed—a quiet, lonely life upon a small independence has been the aim of my desires and my notion of happiness. Italy and the south of France formerly constantly solicited my imagination, as offering pleasant places wherein to build a solitary nest. . . . And now a cottage near Edinburgh, with an

income of two hundred a year, seems to me the most
desirable of earthly possessions; but, though this is
certainly not a very wild vision of wealth or magnificence, I fear it is quite as little within my reach as
southern palaces, or villas on the Mediterranean.

My father has hitherto been able to lay by nothing,
and my assistance is absolutely necessary to him,
. . . and as long as I can in any way serve my
father's interests by remaining in my profession I
shall do so, and must naturally look forward to a
prolonged period of my present exertions. It is
useless pondering upon this, but I have been led to
do so lately from a letter which my father received
from Mr. Bartley, the stage manager of Covent
Garden, the other day, which contained the plan
of a new theatrical speculation, in which he is most
anxious to engage us. I know not how my father feels
upon this subject. . . . I, however, am well determined that neither Mr. L——'s opinion, nor that
of the whole world besides, should induce me to own
the value of a truss of straw in any theatre. My
father's whole life has been given over to trouble and
anxiety in consequence of his proprietorship and
involvement in that ruinous concern, Covent Garden;
and now, when his remaining health and strength
will no more than serve to lay up the means of
subsistence when health and strength are gone, the
idea of his loading himself with such a burden of
bitterness as the proprietorship of a new theatre
makes me perfectly miserable. For my own part,
I am determined to own neither part nor lot in any
such venture : I will lend or give anything that I

may earn to it, and I will act, at half the price
I might get elsewhere, for it, if my father wishes me
to do so; but not a demonstrable cent. per cent. profit
should induce me to run such a risk of cursing the
day that I was born, as to become owner of a theatre.
I write you all this (and I have written more than
enough about it) because it has been lately a subject
of much anxious meditation to me. The matter is
at present without settled form or plan, but the
proposal of such a scheme has caused me deep regret
and anxiety. . . . I am going to act to-morrow
in "The Hunchback;" Thursday, Mrs. Beverley;
Friday, Lady Townley; Saturday, Juliet; Monday,
Julia again; and Tuesday, Bizarre in "The Inconstant;" which ends our engagement here. This
is pretty hard work, is it not? besides always one,
and sometimes two rehearsals of a morning.

We begin our second engagement in New York on
the 7th of November. Don't forget that the 27th of
that month is my birthday, and that if you neglect to
drink my health, I shall probably die, for want of
your good wishes to keep me alive.

We act in Boston on the 3rd of December; "further
than that the deponent sayeth not."

I told you in my last letter that Philadelphia was
the cleanest place in the world. The country along
the banks of the Schuylkill (one of the rivers on
which it stands; the other is the Delaware) is wild
and beautiful, and the glory of the autumn woods
what an eye that hath not seen can by no manner of
means conceive. I have for the last week had my
room full of the most delicious flowers that could only

be seen with us at midsummer, and here, in these
last days of autumn, they are as abundant and
fragrant, and the sun is as intensely hot and brilliant,
as it should be, but never is, with us, in the month of
July. . . .

Dall went into a Quaker's shop here the other day,
when, after waiting upon her with the utmost attention
and kindness, the master of the shop said, "And how
doth Fanny? I was in hopes she might have wanted
something; we should have great pleasure in attending upon her." Was not that nice? So to-day I
went thither, and bought myself a lovely sober-
coloured gown. This place, as you know, is the head-
quarters of Quakerdom, and all the enchanting nosegays come from " a Philadelphia friend," the latter
word dashed under, as if to indicate a member of the·
religious fraternity always called by that kindly title
here. . . .

I think my father has some idea of bringing out
" The Star of Seville " here, and if he does, I shall
break my heart that it was not brought out first in
England. Emily always reproaches me with want of
patriotism. I have more than helps to make me
cheerful here, and leaving England—not home, and
not you, but England, England—for two years, seems
to me now ridiculous, and fabulous, and preposterous,
and disastrous.

I have finished my first volume of Graham, and I
have finished this letter. God bless you !

Ever your affectionate

F. A. K.

Philadelphia, Nov. 2nd, 1832.

DEAREST H——,

I received your fifth letter to-day, and one from Dorothy, and one from Emily Fitzhugh. . . . My last letter to you was a sad one, and sad in a fashion that does not often occur to me. I was troubled and anxious about my professional labour and its results, and that may be called a small sadness compared with some other with which I have lately become familiar. Of course none of these anxieties have been removed, for some time must elapse before I can know on what plan my father determines with regard to Mr. Bartley's proposal about this new theatre. It does not affect me personally, because I am thoroughly determined to take no part in any speculation of the kind; but the possibility of my father entering into any such scheme is care enough to " kill a cat," and make a kitten miserable besides. . . . In all matters, but especially in matters of business, I hold frankness, straightforwardness, and decision as conducive to success, as consonant with right feeling; but I think men are much more cowardly than women, and believe a great deal more in policy, temporizing, and expediency than we do. " Managing " is supposed to be a feminine tendency; it has no place in my composition; perhaps I might be the better for a little of it—but only perhaps, and only a little. . . . This letter, as you will perceive by its date, was begun on the banks of the Delaware; here we are, however, once more in New York. It is Monday evening, the 5th of November, and you are firing squibs and burning mannikins *en action de grâces* that the Houses of Parliament were not blown

up by the Roman Catholics, instead of living to be
reformed by the Whigs, and (peradventure) blowing
up the nation.

The Presidential Election is going on here, and
creates immense excitement. General Jackson, they
say, will certainly be re-elected.

Our last fortnight in Philadelphia has been one of
incessant and very hard work, rehearsing every morning and acting every night. I rejoiced heartily when
our engagement drew to a close, for I was fairly worn
out, and money bought with health is bought too
dear, I think. . . . I have taken some very pleasant
rides during our stay in Philadelphia; the horses are
none of them properly broken for riding, which makes
it a pleasure of no small fatigue to ride them for
three or four hours. Luckily, I do not object to
severe exercise, and the weather and the country were
both charming. . . .

I am glad you have been re-reading the " Tempest."
. . . What exquisite pleasure that fine creation has
given me! I like it better than any of the other
plays; it is less "of the earth, earthy" than any of
the others; for though the "Midsummer Night's
Dream" is in some sort, as it were, its companion,
the mortal element in the latter poem is far less
noble and lovely than in the "Tempest." Prospero
and Miranda, the dwellers on the enchanted island,
are statelier and fairer than any of the human
wanderers in the mazes of the Athenian wood. There
is a deep and indescribable melancholy to me in the
" Tempest " that mingles throughout with its beauty,
and lends a special charm to it. I so often contem-
plate in fancy that island, lost in the unknown seas,

just in the hour of its renewed solitude, after the
departure of its "human mortal" dwellers and
visitors, when Prospero and his companions had
bade farewell to it, when Caliban was grunting and
grubbing and grovelling in his favourite cave again,
when Ariel was hovering like a humming-bird over
the flower draperies of the woods, where the footprints
of men were still stamped on the wet sand of the
shining shore, but their voices silent and their forms
vanished, and utter solitude, and a strange dream of
the past, filling the haunts where human life, its sin
and sorrow, and joy and hope, and love and hate, had
breathed and palpitated, and were now for ever gone.
The notion of that desert once, but now deserted,
paradise, whose flowers had looked up at Miranda,
whose skies had shed wisdom on Prospero, always
seems to me full of melancholy. The girl's sweet
voice singing no more in the sunny, still noon, the
grave, tender converse of the father and child charming no more the solemn eventide, the forsaken island
dwells in my imagination as at once desecrated and
hallowed by its mortal sojourners; no longer savage
quite, and never to be civilized; the supernatural
element disturbed, the human element withdrawn; a
sad, beautiful place, stranger than any other in the
world. Perhaps the sea went over it; it has never
been found since Shakespeare landed on it. I love
that poem beyond words. . . .

I shall ruin you in postage; if there is any chance
of that, keep Mrs. Norton's five guineas to pay for my
American epistles.

Ever your affectionate

F. A. K.

DEAREST H——,

I have received your letter, acknowledging
my first to you. . . . As for letters, they are like everything else we experience here, sources of to the full as
much suffering as satisfaction. Who has not felt their
whole blood run backwards at sight of one of these
folded fate-bearers? I declare, breaking an envelope
always has something of the character of pulling a
shower-bath string over one's own head; I wonder
anybody ever has the courage to do it. . . .

Your dread of our finding New York quite a desert
would have been literally fulfilled had we reached it
a fortnight sooner; but the dreadful malady, the
cholera, had taken its departure, and though private
bereavements and general stagnation of business
rendered the season a very unfavourable one for our
experiment, yet, upon the whole, we have every reason
to be well satisfied with the result of it, and think we
did well not to postpone the beginning of our
campaign. . . . The first serious experiences of our
youth seem to me like the breaking asunder of some
curious, beautiful, and mystical pattern or device. All
our lives long we are more or less intent on replacing
the bright scattered fragments in their original shape:
most of us die with the bits still scattered round us—
that is to say, such of the bits as have not been ground
into powder, or soiled and defaced beyond recognition,
in the life-process. The few very wise find and place
them in a coherent form at last, but it is quite another
curious, beautiful, and mystical device or pattern from
the original one. . . .

The deaths of the young Napoleon, the Duke of

Reichstadt, and Walter Scott have excited universal
interest here, naturally of a very dissimilar kind.
One's heart burns to think of that young eagle falling
like a weakly winter flower, or a faded, sickly girl, into
his untimely grave. . . . There was nothing for him
but death. If he had been anything, it could only
have been a wild spark of the mad meteor from which
he sprang; and as Heaven in its wisdom forbade that,
I think it much of its mercy that it extinguished him
early and utterly, and did not leave him to flare and
flicker and burn himself out with foul gunpowder smoke,
and smell of dead men slain in battle, in the middle
of the smouldering ashes of his father's European
empire.

My admiration and respect for Walter Scott are
unbounded, and were I the noblest, richest, and
charmingest man in the world, I would lay myself
at Anne Scott's feet out of sheer love and veneration
for her father. . . .

You ask me if I wrote anything on board ship?
Nothing but odds and ends of doggerel. Since I have
been here I have written some verses on the beautiful
American autumn, which have been published with
commendation. I am thinking of writing a prose
story, if ever again I can get two minutes and a half
of leisure. . . . Your entreaties for minute details of
our life make me sad, for how little of what we do,
be, or suffer can be conveyed to you in this miserable
scrap of paper! . . . Our dinner-hour is three when
we are actors, five when we are ladies and gentlemen.
The food we get here in New York is very indifferent.
It was excellent in quality in Philadelphia, but

wherever we have been there is a want of niceness
and refinement in the cooking and serving everything
that is very disagreeable. . . .

Thursday, Nov. 27th. This is my birthday—in
England always one of the gloomiest days of this
gloomy month; here my windows are all open, and
the warm sun streaming in as it might on the finest
of early September days with us. I am to-day three
and twenty. Where is my life gone to? As the child
said, "Where does the light go when the candle is
out?" . . . Since last I wrote to you I have been
forty miles up the Hudson, and seen such noble waters
and beautiful hills, such glory of colour and magnificent breadth in the grand river and its autumn
woods, as I cannot describe.

This is our last night but one of acting here. We
play "The Hunchback" on Saturday, and on Monday go back to Philadelphia for three weeks; thence
to Baltimore and Washington, and then return here.
I must go now and rehearse Katharine and Petruchio.

I have just finished Graham's "History," and am
beginning John Smith. By-the-by, a gentleman here
is writing a play, in which I am to act Pocohontas
and my father Captain Smith. Come out and see it,
won't you? Good-bye, dear. Think always of your
affectionate

F. A. K.

December 9th, 1832.

MY DEAREST H——,
        I received yours of October 16th yester-
day. . . . You are not healthily natured enough to

be inconstant. Yours is one of those morbid organi-
zations for whom the present never does its wholesome,
proper office of superseding the past, and your thoughts
and feelings, your whole inner life, in short, is always
out of perspective, because your background is for ever
your foreground, and with you, half the time, nothing
is but what is not; not in consequence of looking
forward, like Macbeth, but the reverse. . . . I am
delighted that you are going to Scotland to know
my dear Mrs. Harry Siddons. . . . Before this letter
reaches you, however, you will have returned to your
castle, and your visit to Edinburgh will be over. . . .
Mercy on me! what disputations you and Mr. Combe
will have had—on matters physiological, psychological,
phrenological, and philosophical! My brains ache to
imagine them. . . . Spurzheim, you know, is dead
lately in Boston. It is a matter of regret to me not
to have seen him, and his death will be a grief to the
Combes, who venerate him highly. . . . Making trial
of people is running a foolish risk, and they who get
disappointment by it reap the most probable result
from such experiments. I am quite willing to trust
my friends; God forbid I should ever try them! . . .

We have not yet been to Boston, and therefore
I myself know nothing of Channing, and cannot
answer your questions about him. All that I hear
inclines me to like as well as respect him. His
gentleness and kindness, his weak health, brought on
by over-study, his perfect simplicity and unaffected-
ness,—these are the usual details that follow any
mention of him, and accord with the impression his
writings produced upon me; but of his theological
treatises I know nothing.

I am glad anything so universal as the blessed
sunshine reminds you of me, because my remem-
brance must be present with you almost daily.   The
lights of heaven shine more glowingly here than
through the misty veils that curtain our islands.   The
moon and stars are wonderfully bright, and there
is an intensity, an earnestness, and a translucent
purity in the sky here that delights me. . . . Four
months are already gone out of the two years we are
to pass out of England.   Dear England!   My heart
dwells with affectionate pride upon the beauty and
greatness and goodness of my own country—that
wonderful little land, that mere morsel of earth as it
seems on the map—so full of power, of wealth, of
intellectual vigour and moral worth! . . .

I found Graham a little too much of a Republican
for me, though his "History" seemed to me upon the
whole good and very impartial.   I am now half-way
through Smith's "Virginia," which pleases me by its
quaint old-world style.   I am myself much inclined
to be in love with Captain Smith.   A man who fights
three Turks and carries their heads on his shield is to
me an admirable man. . . .

I answer the propositions in your letters in regular
rotation as they come; and so, with regard to the
peaches, those that I have tasted on this side of the
Atlantic I should say were not comparable to fine hot-
house peaches in England and fine French espalier
peaches; but then the peach trees here are standard
trees, and there are whole orchards of them.   Their
chief merit, therefore, is their abundance, and some
of that abundance is certainly fit for nothing but to

feed pigs withal.   [It is by no means a luxury to be
despised, however, to have, in the American fashion,
on a hot summer's day, a deep plate presented to you
full of peaches, cut up like apples for a pie, that have
been standing in ice, and are then snowed over with
sugar and frozen cream.]

    We are now in Philadelphia, whence we go to Balti-
more, Washington, and Charleston.   The Southern
States are at this moment in a state of violent excitement, which seems almost to threaten a dissolution
of the Union.   The tariff question is the point of dis-
agreement; and as the interests of the North and
South are in direct opposition on this subject, there
is no foretelling the end.

    Our success is very great, and we have every reason
to be satisfied with and grateful for it.   Our houses
are full, and eke our pockets, and we have hitherto
managed to live in tolerable privacy and very tolerable
discomfort.   But I believe the western part of the
country has yet to teach us the extent of inconvenience to which travellers in America are sometimes liable.   God bless you, dearest H——.

        I am, ever yours affectionately,

                                           F. A. K.

    My father and I took a moonlight walk the other
night, from ten o'clock till half-past twelve, during
which we neither of us uttered six words.

                      Baltimore, January 2nd, 1833.
    MY DEAREST H——,

        You are the first to whom I date this new
year. . . . I told you in one of my letters to keep the

five guineas Mrs. Norton has paid you for my scribble-
ments to pay the postage of my letters—do so. . . .

We arrived in this place on Monday, at half-past
four, having left Philadelphia at six in the morning.
We have just terminated a second engagement there
very successfully. If the roads and carriages are bad,
and the land travelling altogether detestable, the
speed, facility, and convenience of the steamboats, by
which one may really be conveyed from one end to
another of this world of vast waters, are very admirable. Vast waters indeed they are! We came
down the Delaware on Monday, and (open your Irish
eyes!) sometimes it was six, sometimes thirteen miles
wide, and never narrower than three or four miles
at any part of it that we saw. So wide an expanse of
fresh running water is in itself a fine object. We
crossed the narrow neck of land between the Delaware
and the Chesapeak on a railroad with one of Stephenson's engines. . . . The railroad was full of knots
and dots, and jolting and jumping and bumping and
thumping places. The carriages we were in held
twelve people very uncomfortably. Baltimore itself,
as far as I have seen it, strikes me as a large,
rambling, red-brick village on the outskirts of one of
our manufacturing towns, Birmingham or Manchester.
It covers an immense extent of ground, but there are
great gaps and vacancies in the middle of the streets,
patches of gravelly ground, parcels of meadow land,
and large vacant spaces—which will all, no doubt, be
covered with buildings in good time, for it is growing
daily and hourly—but which at present give it an
untidy, unfinished, straggling appearance. . . .

While my father and I were exploring about together yesterday, we came to a print shop, whose window exhibited an engraving of Reynolds' Mrs. Siddons as the Tragic Muse, and Lawrence's picture of my uncle John in Hamlet. We stopped before them, and my father looked with a good deal of emotion at these beautiful representations of his beautiful kindred, and it was a sort of sad surprise to meet them in this other world where we are wandering, aliens and strangers.

This is the newest-looking place we have yet visited, the youngest in appearance in this young world; and I have experienced to-day a disagreeable instance of its immature civilization, or at any rate its small proficiency in the elegancies of life. I wanted to ride, but although a horse was to be found, no such thing as a side-saddle could be procured at any livery-stable or saddler's in the town, so I have been obliged to give up my projected exercise. . . .

I have been to my first rehearsal here this morning, and wretched enough all things were. I act for the first time to-morrow night Bianca, which they have everywhere chosen for my opening part; and it is a good one for that purpose, as I generally act and look well in it, and it is the sort of play that all sorts of people can comprehend. There is a foreign—I mean continental—custom here, which is pleasant. They have a *table d'hôte* dinner at two o'clock, and while it is going on a very tolerable band plays all manner of Italian airs and German waltzes, and as there is a fine long corridor into which my room door opens, with a window at each end, I have a very agreeable promenade, and take my exercise to this musical accompaniment. . . .

I have at this moment on my table a lovely nosegay—roses, geraniums, rare heaths, and perfect white camelias. Our windows are all wide open; the heat is intense, and the air that comes in at them like a sirocco. It is unusual weather for the season even here, and very unwholesome.

In a week's time we are going on to Washington, where we shall find dear Washington Irving, whom I think I shall embrace, for England's sake as well as his own. We have letters to the President, to whom we are to be presented, and to his rival, Henry Clay, and to Daniel Webster, whom I care more to know than either of the others.

After a short stay in Washington we return here, and then back to Philadelphia and New York, till the 20th of February, after which we sail for Charleston. There has been, and still exists at present, a very considerable degree of political alarm and excitement in this country, owing to the threat of the South Carolinians to secede from the Union if the tariff is not annulled, and the country was in hourly expectation of being involved in a civil war. However, the prevailing opinion among the wise seems to be that the Northern States will be obliged to give up the tariff, as the only means of preserving the Union; and if matters come to a peaceable settlement, we shall proceed in February to Charleston; if not, South Carolina will have other things to think of besides plays and play-actors. The summer we shall probably spend in Canada; the winter, perhaps in

Jamaica, to which place we have received a most pressing invitation from Lord Mulgrave. The end of the ensuing spring will, I trust in God, see us embarked once more for England. . . .

We are earning money very fast, and though I think we work too incessantly and too hard, yet, as every night we do not act is a certain loss of so much out of my father's pocket, I do not like to make many objections to it, although I think it is really not unlikely to be detrimental to his own health and strength. . . .

I spent yesterday evening with some very pleasant people here, who are like old-fashioned English folk, the Catons, Lady Wellesley's father and mother. They are just now in deep mourning for Mrs. Caton's father, the venerable Mr. Carroll, who was upwards of ninety-five years old when he died, and was the last surviving signer of the Declaration of Independence. I saw a lovely picture by Lawrence of the eldest of the three beautiful sisters, the daughters of Mrs. Caton, who have all married Englishmen of rank. [The Marchioness of Wellesley, the Duchess of Leeds, and Lady Stafford. The fashion of marrying in England seems to be traditional in this family. Miss McTavish, niece of these ladies, married Mr. Charles Howard, son of the Earl of Carlisle.]

The Baltimore women are celebrated for their beauty, and I think they are the prettiest creatures I have ever seen as far as their faces go ; but they are short and thin, and have no figures at all, either in height or breadth, and pinch their waists and feet most cruelly, which certainly, considering how small they are by nature, is a work of supererogation, and does

not tend to produce in them a state of grace. . . . We
act every night this week, and as we are obliged
to rehearse every morning, of course I have no time
for any occupations but my strictly professional ones.
I do not approve of this quantity of hard work for either
my father or myself, but I do not like to make any
further protest upon the subject. . . .

Good-bye, dearest H——.

I am ever your affectionate

F. A. K.

To MRS. JAMESON.

Baltimore, January 11th, 1833.

Thank you across the sea, dear Mrs. Jameson, for
your letter of the 1st of November. I had been wondering, but the day before it reached me, whether you
had ever received one I wrote to you on my first
arrival in New York, or whether you were accusing me
of neglect, ingratitude, forgetfulness, and all the tur-
pitudes that the delay of a letter sometimes causes
folk to give other folk credit for. My occupations are
incessant, or rather, I should say, my occupation, for
to my sorrow I have but one. 'Tis not with me now
as in the fortunate days when, after six rehearsals, a
piece ran, as the saying is, twenty nights, leaving me
all the mornings and three evenings in the week at my
own disposal. Here we rush from place to place, at
each place have to drill a new set of actors, and every
night to act a different play; so that my days are
passed in dawdling about cold, dark stages, with
blundering actors who have not even had the conscience to study the words of their parts, all the

morning. All the afternoon I pin up ribbons and
feathers and flowers, and sort out theatrical adorn-
ments, and all the evening I enchant audiences,
prompt my fellow-mimes, and wish it had pleased
Heaven to make me a cabbage in a corner of a
Christian kitchen-garden in—well, say Hertfordshire,
or any other county of England; I am not particular
as to the precise spot. . . . Whenever I can I get on
horseback; it is the only pleasure I have in this
world; for my dancing days are drawing to a close.
But I mean to ride as long as I have a hand to hold
a rein, or a leg to put over a pommel. By-the-by, I
ought to beg your pardon for the last sentence; I
ought to have said a foot to put into a stirrup; for if
you are not ashamed of having legs you ought to be—
at least, we are in this country, and never mention, or
give the slightest token of having such things, except
by wearing very short petticoats, which we don't consider
objectionable. . . . I am glad you have furbished up
and completed your little room, because it is a sign
you mean to stay where you are, and I like to know
where to find you in my imagination. . . . I have
just seen dear Washington Irving, and it required all
my sense of decent decorum to prevent my throwing
my arms round 'his neck, he looked so like a bit of
home, England.

You will be glad to hear that we are thriving, in
body and estate. We are all well, and our work is
very successful. The people flock to see us, and
nothing can exceed the kindness which we meet with
everywhere and from everybody. . . . I read nothing
whatever since I am in this blessed land. The only

books I have accomplished getting through have been
Graham's "History of North America," Knicker-
bocker's "History of New York," which nearly killed
me with laughing; "Contarini Fleming," which is
very affected and very clever; sundry cantos of Dante,
sundry plays of Shakespeare, sundry American poems
[which are very good], and old Captain John Smith's
quaint "History of Virginia." As fast as I gather my
wits together for any steady occupation, I am whisked
off to some new place, and do not recover from one
journey before I have to take another. The roads
here shake one's body, soul, thoughts, opinions, and
principles all to pieces; I assure you they are wicked
roads.

Our theatre, Covent Garden, is, we understand,
going to the dogs. I cannot help it any more, that is
certain, and feel about that as about all things that
have had their day—it must go. Taglioni is like
a dream, and you must not abuse Mademoiselle Mars
to me. I never saw her but twice—in "L'Ecole des
Vieillards" and "Valérie"—and I thought her perfection in both. . . . If I do not leave off, you will
be blind for the next fortnight with reading this
crossed letter. I wish you success most heartily in all
you undertake, and am truly and faithfully yours,

FANNY KEMBLE.

[Washington Irving was intimately acquainted with
my father and mother, and a most kind and condescending friend to me. He often told me that when
first he went to England, long before authorship or
celebrity had dawned upon him, he was a member of

a New York commercial house, on whose affairs he
was sent to Europe. It was when he was a mere
obscure young man of business in London that he
had been introduced to my mother, whose cordial
kindness to him in his foreign isolation seemed
to have made a profound impression on him; for
when I knew him, in the days of his great literary
celebrity and social success, he often referred to it
with the warmest expressions of gratitude. I think,
of all the distinguished persons I have known, he was
one of the least affected by the adulation and admiration of society. He remained quite unchanged by
his extreme social popularity. Simple, unaffected, unconstrained, genial, kindly, and good, he seemed so
entirely to forget his own celebrity, that one almost
forgot it too in talking to him. I remember his
coming, the day after my first appearance at Covent
Garden, to see us, and congratulated my parents on
the success of that terrible experiment. I, who was
always delighted to see him, ran to fetch the pretty
new watch I had received from my father the night
before, and displayed its beauties with an eager
desire for his admiration of them. He took it and
slowly turned it about, commending its fine workman-
ship and pretty enamel and jewellery; then putting it
to his ear, with a most mischievous look of affected
surprise, he exclaimed, as one does to a child's watch,
" Why, it goes, I declare ! "

To my great regret and loss, I saw Mademoiselle
Mars only in two parts, when, in the autumn of her
beauty and powers, she played a short engagement in
London. The grace, the charm, the loveliness, which

she retained far into middle age, were, even in their
decline, enough to justify all that her admirers said of
her early incomparable fascination.   Her figure had
grown large and her face become round, and lost
their fine outline and proportion ; but the exquisite
taste of her dress and graceful dignity of her deportment, and sweet radiance of her expressive countenance, were still indescribably charming ; and the
voice, unrivalled in its fresh melodious brilliancy, and
the pure and perfect enunciation, were unimpaired,
and sounded like the clear liquid utterance of a young
girl of sixteen.   Her Celimène and her Elmire I
never had the good fortune to see, but can imagine,
from her performance of the heroine in Casinier de la
Vigne's capital play of " L'Ecole des Vieillards," how
well she must have deserved her unrivalled reputation
in those parts.

It is remarkable that one of the most striking
points in Madame d'Orval was suggested by herself
to the author.   De la Vigne, according to the
frequent usage of French authors, was reading his
piece to the great actress, upon whom its success was
mainly to depend, and when he came to the scene
where the offended but unjustly suspicious husband
recounts to his wife the details of his duel with the
young duke whose attentions to her had excited his
jealousy, and that when, full of the tenderest anxiety
for his safety, she flies to meet him, and is repulsed
by the bitter irony of his speech, beginning, " Rassurez-vous, madame, le duc n'est point blessé,"
Mademoiselle Mars, having listened in silence till
the end of D'Orval's speech, exclaimed, " Mais, quoi !

je ne dis rien, elle ne dit rien!" De la Vigne, who
had made the young woman listen in speechless
anguish to the bitter and unjust reproach conveyed by
her husband's first words and his subsequent account
of the duel, said, in some surprise at Mademoiselle
Mars' suggestion, "Mais quoi encore—que peut-elle
dire? que voudriez-vous qu'elle dise?" "Ah,
quelquechose!" cried Mademoiselle Mars, clasping
her hands in the imagined distress of the situation;
"rien—deuxmots seulement. 'Ah, monsieur!' quand
il dit, 'Rassurez-vous, madame, le duc n'est point
blessé.'" "Eh bien! dites, dites comme cela," cried
De la Vigne, amazed at all the expression the exquisite
voice and face had given to the two words. And so
the scene was altered, and the long recital of D'Orval
was broken by the reproachful "Ah, monsieur!" of his
wife, and seldom has the utterance of such an insignificant exclamation affected those who heard it so
keenly. For myself, I never can forget the sudden,
burning blush that spread tingling to my shoulders at
all the shame and mortification and anguish conveyed
in the pathetic protest of that "Ah, monsieur!" of
Mademoiselle Mars.

Dr. Gueneau de Mussy, who knew her well, and
used to see her very frequently in her later years
of retirement from the stage, told me that he had
often heard her read, among other things, the whole
play of "Le Tartuffe," and that the coarse flippancy of
the honest-hearted Dorinne, and the stupid stolidity
of the dupe Orgon, and the vulgar, gross, sensual
hypocrisy of the Tartuffe, were all rendered by her
with the same incomparable truth and effect as her

own famous part of the heroine of the piece, Elmire.
On one of the very last occasions of her appearing
before her own Parisian audience, when she had
passed the limit at which it was possible for a woman
of her advanced age to assume the appearance of
youth, the part she was playing requiring that she
should exclaim "Je suis jeune! je suis jolie!" a loud,
solitary hiss protested against the assertion with
bitter significance. After an instant's consternation,
which held both the actors and audience silent, she
added, with the exquisite grace and dignity which
survived the youth and beauty to which she could no
longer even pretend, "Je suis Mademoiselle Mars!"
and the whole house broke out in acclamations, and
rang with the applause due to what the incomparable
artiste still was, and the memory of all that she had
been.]

New York, February 21st, 1833.

It is a long time since I have written to you, my
dearest H——. . . . My work is incessant, . . . and
there is no end to the breathless hurry of occupation
we pass our days in. Here is already a break since
I began this letter, for we are now in Philadelphia, on
our way to Washington, and it is Thursday, the 3rd
of March. . . . It has been matter of serious regret
to me that I have not, from the very first day of my
becoming a worker for wages, looked more into the
details of my earnings and spendings. I have felt
this particularly lately from circumstances relative to
V——'s position, which is a very sad one, from
which I have been very anxious to relieve her. . . .

All I know at present is, that since we have been
here in America our earnings have already been
sufficient to enable us to live in tolerably decent
comfort on the Continent. . . . Do you know, dearest
H——, that it is not impossible that I may never
return to England to reside there. See it again, I
will, please God to grant me life and eyes, but
the state of my father's property in Covent Garden
is such that it seems more than likely that he
may never be able to return to England without
risking the little which these last toilsome years will
have enabled him to earn for the support of his own
and my mother's old age. He will be compelled, in
all likelihood, to settle and die abroad, as my uncle
John did, by the liabilities of that ruinous possession
of theirs, the first theatre of London.   When first
my father communicated this chance to me, and
expressed his determination, should the affairs of the
theatre remain in their present situation, to buy
a small farm in Normandy, and go and live there, my
heart sank terribly. This was very different from my
girlish dream of a life of lonely independence among
the Alps, or by the Mediterranean ; and the idea of
living entirely out of England seems to me now very
sad for all of us. . . . However, there are earth and
skies out of England.   What does Imogen say ?—
    " I prithee think, there's livers out of Britain ; "
and if God vouchsafe me my faculties, and I can bid
farewell to this life of distasteful toil, I have visions
of studies and pursuits which I think might make
existence very happy in a farm in Normandy, though
such might not have been my own choice. . . . What

special inquiries did you wish me to make about
General Washington? I was, when at Washington,
within fifteen miles of Mount Vernon, his home and
burying-place, but could not make time to go thither.
I have one of his autograph letters, and if there be
any indication of character in handwriting—which I
hope to goodness there is not—it certainly exists
in his, for a firmer, clearer, and fairer hand I never
saw—an excellent, honest handwriting. His likeness
confronts one at every corner here; not only at every
street corner, where he lends his countenance to the
frequenters of drinking-houses, but over every chim-
ney-piece in every sitting-room. He is like the frogs
of the old Egyptian plague, except that they were in
the king's chamber, where he was too good a Republican ever to have been. '

I am amused at your summing up your account of
the restless and perturbed state of poor Ireland by saying, "After all, I believe America is the land of peace
and quiet." It seems to me, who am here, that everything at this moment threatens change and disin-
tegration in this country. It is impossible to imagine
more menacing elements of discord and disunion than
those which exist in the opposite and antagonistic
interests of its southern and northern provinces, and
the anomalous mixture of aristocratic feeling and
democratic institutions. . . . God bless you, my dear
H——. I will write to you soon again; if possible,
before the breathing time this snow-storm is giving
us is over.

Ever affectionately yours,

F. A. K.

New York, April 3, 1833.

My dearest H——,

. . . . I am working very hard, what with
rehearsing, acting, studying new parts, devising new
dresses, and attending—which, of course, I am obliged
also to do—to the claims of the society in which we
are living, and my time is so full that I barely contrive to fulfil all my duties and answer all the claims
made upon me. . . . The spring is in the sky, and in
the air her soft smile and sweet breath are gladdening
the world; but the process of vegetation is much later
in beginning, and much more rapid in its operations
when they do begin here, than with us.   Though the
last three days have been as hot as our midsummer
weather, the trees are yet leafless and budless—as dry
and unpromising-looking as they were in mid-winter;
and, indeed, the transition from winter to summer is
almost instantaneous here.   The spring does not
stand coaxing and beckoning the shy summer to the
woods and fields as in our country, but while winter
yet seems lord of the ascendant, and his white robes
are still covering land and water, suddenly the
summer looks down upon the earth from the cloudless sky, and, as by magic, the ice melts, the snow
evaporates, the trees are clothed with green, the woods
are full of flowers, and the whole world breaks out
into a hallelujah of warmth, beauty, and blossoming
like mid-July in our deliberate climate.   This again
lasts, as it were, but a day; the sun presently becomes
so powerful that the world withers away under the
intense heat, the flowers and shrubs fade, and instead
of screening and refreshing the earth, are themselves

scorched and parched with the glaring fierceness of
the sky ; the ground cracks, the watercourses dry up,
the rivers shrink in their beds, and every human
creature that can flies from the lowlands and the
cities to go up into the north or to the mountains to
find breath, shelter, and refreshment from the sultry
curse.   Then comes the autumn, and that is most
glorious ; not soft and sad as ours, but to the very
threshold of winter bright, warm, lovely, and gorgeous.
Two seasons remain to our earthly year, remem-
brances, I think, of Paradise ; the spring in Italy, and
autumn in America. . . .

You ask me how I "fit in" to my American
audiences ?   Why, very kindly indeed.   At first
they seemed to me rather cold, and I felt this more
with regard to my father than myself, but I think
they have grown to like us ; I certainly have
grown to like them, and their applause satisfies
me amply. . . . I heard yesterday of one of Sir
Thomas Lawrence's prints of me which was carried
by a pedlar beyond the Alleghany Mountains [the
Alleghany Mountains then were further than the
Rocky Mountains are now from the Atlantic seaboard],
and bought at an egregious price by a young engineer,
who with fifteen others went out there upon some
railroad construction business, were bidding for it at
auction in that wilderness, where they themselves
were gazed at, as prodigies of strange civilization, by
the half-savage inhabitants of the region.   That
touched and pleased me very much. . . . We are
going to act here till the 12th of this month, when we
go to Boston, where we shall remain for a month ;

after which we return here for a week, and then proceed to Philadelphia by the 1st of June, where we intend closing our professional labours for the summer. Thence we shall probably go to Niagara and the Canadas. My father has talked of spending a little quiet time in Rhode Island, where the weather is cool and we' might recruit a little; but there does not seem much certainty about our plans at present. In the autumn we shall begin our progress towards New Orleans, where we shall probably winter, and act our way back here by the spring, when I hope and trust we shall return to England. . . . The book of Harriet Martineau's which you bade me read is delightful. I have not quite finished it yet, for I have scarcely any time at all for reading; for want of the habit of thinking and reading on such subjects I find the political economy a little stiff now and then, though the clearness and simplicity with which it is treated in this story are admirable. I did not know that I was supposed to be the original of Letitia. . . . God bless you, my dearest H——.

I am ever your most affectionate,

F. A. K.

" For Each and for All " was, I think, the name of the volume taken from Miss Martineau's admirable series of political economy tales, which my friend, Miss S——, sent me. The heroine of the story is a young actress, and Miss Martineau once told me that she had derived some slight suggestion of the character from me.

New York, Friday, April 10th, 1833.

My dearest H——,

. . . . On Monday last I acted Lady
Macbeth; on Tuesday, Lady Townley; on Wednesday,
Belvidera; and last night, Portia, and Mary Copp in
"Charles II." This is pretty hard work. To-morrow
we start for Boston, which we shall reach on Sunday,
and Monday our work begins there. . . . I think
four nights a week as much as either my father or
myself ought to work, and as much as we really can
work profitably, the rest being money taken from our
capital, *i.e.*, our health. But in Boston we shall act
for three weeks or a month every night but the
Saturdays. [The days when four or five performances a week were considered a sufficient exertion for
popular actors or singers are far enough in the past,
and now there seems to be no limit to the capacity of
such artists for earning money by the exercise of their
talents. Five and six performances a week are the
normal number now expected from great European
stars, or rather those which great European stars
expect to give and to be paid for. Their health is
one invariable sacrifice to this over-work, and their
artistic excellence a still more grievous one. It has
been asked why artists invariably return to Europe
comparatively coarse and vulgar in the style of their
performances, and the result is attributed to the want
of refined taste and critical judgment of the American
audiences—in my opinion very unjustly, for if want of
knowledge and nice perception in the public induces
carelessness and indifference in performers, the grasping greed of gain and incessant over-exertion, mental

and physical, for the sake of satisfying it, is a far more certain cause of artistic deterioration. During Madame Ristori's last visit to America, I went to see a morning performance of "Elizabeta d' Inglterra" by her. Arriving at the theatre half an hour before the time announced for the performance, I found notices affixed to the entrances, stating that the beginning was unavoidably delayed by Madame Ristori's non-arrival. The crowd of expectant spectators occupied their seats and bore this prolonged postponement with American—*i.e.*, unrivalled—patience, good-temper, and civility. We were encouraged by two or three pieces of information from some official personage, who from the stage assured us that the moment Madame Ristori arrived (she was coming by railroad from Baltimore) the play should begin. Then came a telegram, she was coming; then an announcement, she was come; and driving from the terminus straight to the theatre, tired and harassed herself with the delay, she dressed herself and appeared before her audience, went through a part of extraordinary length and difficulty and exertion—almost, indeed, a monologue—including the intolerable fatigue and hurry of four or five entire changes of costume, and as the curtain dropped rushed off to disrobe and catch a train to New York, where she was to act the next morning, if not the evening, of that same day. I had seen Madame Ristori in this part in England, and was shocked at the great difference in the merit of her performance. Every particle of careful elaboration and fine detail of work-manship was gone; the business of the piece was hurried through, with reference, of course, only to the

time in which it could be achieved; and of Madame
Ristori's once fine delineation of the character, which,
when I first saw it, atoned for the little merit of the
piece itself, nothing remained but the broad claptrap
points in the several principal situations, made coarse,
and not nearly even as striking, by the absence of due
preparation and working up to them, the careless
rendering of everything else, and the slurring over of
the finer minutiæ and more delicate indications of the
whole character. It was a very sad spectacle to me.]

Besides your letter, the poor old *Pacific* (the ship
that brought us to America) brought me something
else to-day. While Washington Irving was sitting
with me, a message came from the mate of the
Pacific with a large box of mould for me. I had
it brought in, and asking Irving if he knew what it
was, "A bit of the old soil," said he; and that
it was. . . . Washington Irving was sure to have
guessed right as to my treasure, and I was not
ashamed to greet it with tears before him. . . . He
is so sensible, sound, and straightforward in his way
of seeing everything, and at the same time so full
of hopefulness, so simple, unaffected, true, and good,
that it is a privilege to converse with him, for which
one is the wiser, the happier, and the better. . . .

Here is Monday, April 15th, Boston, my dear
H——. We arrived here yesterday evening, and in
the course of this morning I have already received
fourteen visitors, all of whom I shall have to go and
waste my time with in return for their kind waste
of theirs upon me. . . . To-morrow I begin my work
with " Fazio " and go to a party afterwards. . . .

Tuesday, 16th.

. . . This morning I have been to rehearsal, and
out shopping, and received crowds of strangers who
come and call upon us. . . . To-night I make my first
appearance here in "Fazio," and we hear the theatre
will be crammed, and I am going to a party after
that dreadful play; not by way of delight, but of
duty, and a severe one it will be. To-morrow I act
Mrs. Haller, Thursday, Lady Teazle, and Friday,
Bianca again; Saturday is a blessed holiday. . . .
I have finished Smith's "Virginia," which I found
rather tiresome towards the end. I have finished
Harriet Martineau's political economy story, which
I liked exceedingly. I am reading a small volume
of Brewster's on "Natural Magic," which entertains
me very much; but I am dreadfully cramped for
time, and my poor mind goes like a half-tended
garden, which every now and then makes me feel sad.

You would have been pleased, dear H——, if you
had heard Washington Irving's answer to me the
other day when, in talking with him of my profession
and my distaste for it, I complained of the little
leisure it left me for study and improving myself,
for reading, writing, and the occupations that were
congenial to me. "Well," he said, "you are living,
you are seeing men and things, you are seeing the
world, you are acquiring materials and heaping
together observations and experience and wisdom,
and by-and-by, when with fame you have acquired
independence and retire from these labours, you will
begin another and a brighter course with matured
powers. I know of no one whose life has such a

promise in it as yours." Oh! H——, I almost felt hopeful while he spoke so to me. . . .

[Alas! my kind friend was no prophet. Not many months after, sitting by him at a dinner-party in New York, he said to me, "So I hear you are engaged to be married, and you are going to settle in this country. Well, you will be told that this country is like your own, and that living in it is like living in England: but do not believe it; it is no such thing, it is nothing of the sort; which need not prevent your being very happy here if you make the best of things as you find them. Above all, whatever you do, don't become a creaking door." "What's that?" asked I, laughing. He then told me that his friend Leslie, the painter, who was, I believe, like his cotemporary and charming rival artist, Gilbert Stewart Newton, an American by birth, had married an Englishwoman, whom he had brought out to America, "but who," said Irving, "worried and tormented his and her own life out with ceaseless complaints and comparisons, and was such a nuisance that I used to call her 'the creaking door.'"]

Good-bye, and God bless you, dearest H——.

I am affectionately yours,

FANNY KEMBLE.

Boston, Sunday, April 21st, 1833.

DEAR MRS. JAMESON,

There lies in my desk, and has lain, I am ashamed to say, for a long time now, an unanswered letter of yours, which smites my conscience every

time I open that useful receptacle (desk, not conscience), where it has, I am sorry to say, many
companions in its own predicament. My time is
like running water, and the quickest, but the rapids
of Niagara, that ever ran, I think; and every hour,
as it flies away, is filled with so much that must
be done, letting alone so much that I would wish
to do, that I am fairly out of breath, and feel as if
I were flying myself in a whirling high wind, and
if ever I stop for a moment, shan't be surprised to
find that I have gone crazy. I think I should like
to spend a few days entirely alone in a dark room,
secluded from every sight and sound, for my senses
are almost worn out, and my sense exhausted, with
looking, hearing, feeling, going, doing, being, and
suffering. Our work is incessant; we never remain
a month in any one place, and we are scarce off our
knees from putting things into drawers than we are
down on them again to take them out and put them
all back into trunks. My health has not suffered
hitherto from this constant exertion, but I am occasionally oppressed with the dreadful unquietness of
our life, and long for a few moments' rest of body
and of mind.

This is our first visit to this place, and I am
enchanted with it. As a town, it bears more re-
semblance to an English city than any we have yet
seen; the houses are built more in our own fashion,
and there is a beautiful walk called the Common,
the features of which strongly resemble the view over
the Green Park just by Constitution Hill. The
people here take more kindly to us than they have

done even elsewhere, and it is delightful to act to audiences who appear so pleasantly pleased with us. . . .

Only think! a book was sent to me from Philadelphia the other day which proved to be the "Diary of an Ennuyée." I have no idea who it came from, or who made so good a guess at that old predilection of mine. I fell to forthwith—for that book has always had a most powerful charm for me—and read, and read on, though I have read it many a time through before, and though I had been acting Bianca, and my supper was in my plate before me.

I heard the other day mention of another work of yours, since the Shakespeare book. If you are not weary of writing to me, with such long intervals between your question and my reply, tell me something of this new work in your next letter.

Our plans for the summer are yet unsettled. . . . I was much disappointed on arriving here to find that Dr. Channing has left Boston for the South. His health is completely broken, and the bleak and bitter east wind that blows perpetually here is a formidable enemy to life, even in stronger frames than his. . . .

The hotel in which we are lodging here is immediately opposite the box-office, and it is a matter of some agreeable edification to me to see the crowds gathering round the doors for hours before they open, and then rushing in, to the imminent peril of life and limb, pushing and pommelling and belabouring one another like madmen. Some of the lower class of purchasers, inspired by the thrifty desire for gain said to be a New England characteristic, sell these tickets, which they buy at the box-office price, at an enormous advance, and smear their clothes with treacle and sugar and other abominations, to secure, from the fear. of their contact of all decently-clad competitors, freer access to the box-keeper. To prevent, if possible, these malpractices, and secure, to ourselves and the managers of the theatre any such surplus profit as may be honestly come by, the proprietors have determined to put the boxes up to auction and sell the tickets to the highest bidders. It was rather barbarous of me, I think, upon reflection, to stand at the window while all this riot was going on, laughing at the fun; for not a wretch found his way in that did not come out rubbing his back or his elbow, or showing some grievous damage done to his garments. The opposite window of my room looks out upon a churchyard and burial-ground; the reflections suggested by the contrast between the two prospects are not otherwise than edifying. . . . Good-bye ; God bless you !

I am ever yours, most truly,
FANNY KEMBLE.

New York, Friday, May 24, 1833.

MY DEAREST H——,

I received your last letter, dated the 22nd March, a week ago, when I was in Boston, which we have left, after a stay of five weeks, to return here, where we arrived a few days ago. . . .

Boston is one of the pleasantest towns imaginable. It is built upon three hills, which give it a singular, picturesque appearance, and I suppose suggested the

name of Tremonte Street, and the Tremonte Hotel,
which we inhabited. The houses are many of them
of fine granite, and have an air of wealth and solidity
unlike anything we have seen elsewhere in this
country. Many of the streets are planted with trees,
chiefly fine horse-chestnuts, which were in full leaf
and blossom when we came away, and which har-
monize beautifully with the grey colour and solid
handsome style of the houses. They have a fine
piece of ground, like a park, in one part of the town,
which, together with the houses round it, reminded
me a good deal of the Green Park and the walk at the
back of Arlington Street.

[The addition of the new part of Boston, stretching
beyond the Common and the public Gardens, has
added immensely to the beauty of the city, and the
variety of the buildings and alternate views at the
end of the vistas of the fine streets, looking towards
Dorchester Heights, and those ending in the blue
waters of the bay and Charles River, not unfrequently
reminded me both of Florence and Venice, under a
sky as rich, and more pellucid, than that of Italy.]

The country all round the neighbourhood of Boston
is charming. The rides I took in every direction
were lovely, and during the last fortnight of our stay
nothing could exceed the exquisite brightness of the
spring weather. The apple trees were all in bloom,
the lilacs in flower, and everything as sweet, fresh,
and enchanting as possible. . . . How I wish you
could have seen the glorious Hudson with me the
other day, now that the woods on its banks are dark
with the shade of their thick and varied foliage !

How you would have rejoiced in the beautiful and
noble river scenery ! This is "a brave new world,"
more ways than one, and we are every way bound to
like it, for our labour has been most amply rewarded
in its most important result, money ; and the universal
kindness which has everywhere met us ever since we
first came to this country ought to repay us even for
the pain and sorrow of leaving England. . . . We
are to remain here about ten days longer, and then
·proceed to Philadelphia, where we shall stay a fortnight, and then we start for cool and Canada, taking
the Hudson, Trenton Falls, and Niagara on our way ;
act in Montreal and Quebec for a short time, and then
adjourn, I hope, to Newport in Rhode Island, to rest
and recruit till we begin our autumnal work. . . .
And now I have done grumbling at "the state of life
into which it has pleased God to call me." My dear
H——, I began this letter yesterday, and am this
moment returned from a long visit to Dr. Channing.
. . . The outward man of the eloquent preacher
and teacher is rather insignificant, and produces no
impression at first sight of unusual intellectual
supremacy ; and though his eyes and forehead are
fine, they did not seem to me to do justice to the
mind expressed in his writings ; for though Shakespeare says,

"There is no art to read the mind's construction in the face,"

I think the mental qualities are more often detected
there than the moral ones. He is short and slight in
figure, and looks, as indeed he is, extremely delicate,
an habitual invalid ; his eyes, which are grey, are

well and deeply set, and the brow and forehead fine,
though not, perhaps, as striking as I had expected.
The rest of the face has no peculiar character, and is
rather plain.

He talked to me a great deal about the stage,
acting, the dramatic art; and, professing to know
nothing about it, maintained some theories which
proved he did not, indeed, know much. As far as
knowledge of the stage and acting goes, of course
this was not surprising, his studies, observation, and
experience certainly not having lain in that direction ;
indeed, if they had, he might not have shown more
comprehension of the subject. Sir Thomas Lawrence
is the only unprofessional person I ever heard speak
upon it whose critical opinion and judgment seemed
to me worth anything ; but it appeared to me that, in
the course of the discussion, some of Dr. Channing's
opinions (with all respect be it spoken) betrayed an
ignorance of human nature itself, upon which, after
all, dramatic literature and dramatic representation
are founded. He asked me if at the present day, and
in our present state of civilization, such a character
as Juliet could be imagined possible ; so that I believe
I was a little disappointed, in spite of his greatness,
his goodness, and my reverence and admiration for
him.

I went to call on him with a Miss Sedgwick, a
person of considerable literary reputation here, and
whose name and books you may perhaps have heard
of. One of them, " Hope Leslie," is, I think, known
in England. Though she is a good deal older than
myself, I have formed a great friendship with her ;

she is excellent, as well as very clever and charming. She knows Dr. Channing intimately, and is a member of his church. . . .

It is now Monday morning, dear H——, and I am presently going to set off to the races. American races! only think of that! I who never saw but one in my own country, and was totally uninterested by it! But I am going chiefly to please a nice little woman who is just married, and whose husband has several horses that are to run, so perhaps I shall find these more exciting than I did the races I attended at home. They are very little supported or resorted to here; the religious and respectable part of the community disapprove of them. There is a general prejudice against them, and they are even preached against; so that they are entirely in the hands of a few gentlemen of fortune, who keep them up, partly for their amusement, and partly with a view to the improvement of the breed of horses in this country. The running is said to be very good, the show is nothing. . . . However, I am going, and therefore you may look hereafter to hear—what you shall hear now —because I'm just come back, and am happy to inform you that my friend's husband's horse won the race. The stake was only £2000—no very great matter— but still enough to make the result interesting, if not important; though I think the hazard we ran of our lives at starting was the most exciting part of the day.

The race-course is on Long Island, and, to reach it, one crosses the arm of the sea that divides that strip of land from New York in a steam ferry-boat. All these transports were so thronged to-day with carriages, horses, and a self-governed, enlightened, and very free people, that in all my life I never saw anything so frightful as the confusion of the embarking and disembarking. . . .

Dr. Channing was talking to me the other day of Harriet Martineau's writings, and has sent me " Ella of Garvelock," recommending it highly as an interesting story, though he does not seem to think Miss Martineau's principles of political economy sufficiently sound to make her works as useful upon that subject, or to do all the good which she herself evidently hopes to produce by these tales. . . .

God bless you, dear friend ! I am ever most truly yours,

F. A. K.

New York, Sunday, June 24th, 1833.

Great was my surprise, dear Mrs. Jameson, to find accompanying your letter of April 9th a card of Mr. Jameson's. My father called upon him almost immediately, but had not the good fortune to find him at home, and I presume he is now gone on to Canada, whither we are ourselves proceeding, and where we may very possibly meet him. Our spring engagements are all over, and we are now going away from the hot weather to Niagara, into which, if all tales be true, I expect to fall headlong, with sheer surprise and admiration ; after which I shall accompany my father to Montreal and Quebec, where we shall resume our professional labours. . . .

I am very sorry you have been ill. You do not speak of your eyes, from which I argue that you were

not painfully conscious of the existence of those
valuable luminaries at the time you wrote. . . .

The accounts, public and private, that we receive of
the state of England are not encouraging, and the
trouble seems such as neither Tory, Whig, nor even
Radical, can cure. You talk of bringing out a colony
to this country ; bring out half of England, and those
who starve at home will have to eat, and to spare,
here. How I do wish our poor labouring people could
be made to know how easily they might exchange
their condition for a better one !

I wish you could have heard what my father was
reading to us this morning out of Stewart's "North
America ;" not Utopian dreams of some imaginary
land of plenty and fertility, but sober statements of
authentic fact, telling of the existence of unnumbered
leagues of the richest soil that ever rewarded human
industry an hundredfold ; wide tracts of lovely wilderness, covered with luxuriant pasture, and adorned
profusely with the most beautiful wild-flowers ; great
forests of giant timber, and endless rolling prairies of
virgin earth, untouched by axe or plough ; a world
of unrivalled beauty and fertility, untenanted and
empty, waiting to receive the over-brimming popula-
tions of the crowded lands of Europe, and to repay
their labour with every species of abundance. It is
strange how slow those old-world, weary, working
folk have hitherto been to avail themselves of God's
provision for them here. . . . You tell me you are
working hard, but you do not say at what. Innumerable are the questions I have been asked about
you, and a Philadelphian gentleman, a very intelli-

gent and clever person, who is a large bookseller and publisher here, bade me tell you that you and your works were as much esteemed and delighted in in America as in your own country. He was so enthusiastic about you that I think he would willingly go over to England for the sole purpose of making your acquaintance.

[It is a pity that the American law on the subject of copyright should have rendered Mr. Carey's admiration of my friend and her works so barren of any useful result to her. Any tolerably just equivalent for the re-publication of her books in America would have added materially to the hardly earned gains of her laborious literary life.]

I am already half moulded into my new circumstances and surroundings; and though England will always be home to my heart, it may be that this country will become my abiding-place; but if you come out to Canada we shall meet on this side of the Atlantic instead of the other. . . .

Believe me ever yours truly,

F. A. K.

To Miss Fitzhugh.

Montreal, July 24, 1833.

My dearest Emily,

Within the last fortnight we have progressed, as we say in this country, over about nine hundred and fifty miles of land and water. We have gone up the Hudson, seen Trenton, the most beautiful, and Niagara, the most awful, of waterfalls. As for Niagara, words cannot describe it, nor can any imagination, I think, suggest even an approximate idea of its terrible loveliness. I feel half crazy whenever I think of it. I went three times under the sheet of water; once I had a guide as far as the entrance, and twice I went under entirely alone. If you fancy the sea pouring down from the moon, you still have no idea of this glorious huge heap of tumbling waters. It is worth crossing the Atlantic to see it. . . . As I stood upon the brink of the abyss when I first saw it, the impulse to jump down seemed all but an irresistible necessity, and but for the strong arm that held mine fast, I think I might very well have taken the same direction as the huge green glassy mountain of water that was pouring itself headlong into—what no eye can penetrate. It literally seemed as if everything was going down there, and one must go along with everything. The chasm into which the cataract falls is hidden by dense masses of snowy foam and spray, rising in an everlasting creation of cloud up into the sky, and veiling the frantic fury of the cauldron below, where the waves churn and tread each other underfoot in the rocky abyss that receives them, in darkness which the sun's rays cannot penetrate nor the strongest wind for a moment disperse; a mystery, of which its thousand voices reveal nothing. It is nonsense writing about it—seeing and hearing are certainly, in this case, the only reasons for believing. I think it would be delightful to pass one's life by this wonderful creature's side, and quite pleasant to die and be buried in its bosom. . . .

We left that wonderful place a few days ago, steamed across Lake Ontario, came down the rapids

of the St. Lawrence in an open boat, sang the
Canadian boat song, and are now safe and sound,
only half roasted, in his Majesty's dominions.   Of
all that we have seen, Niagara is, of course, the old
object beyond all others, but we were delighted with
the softness and beauty of a great deal of the scenery
that we saw in traversing the state of New York.
One of twenty states, not the largest of the twenty,
but large enough to hold England in its lap.

The rapids of the St. Lawrence, though, I believe,
really rather dangerous to descend, have so little
appearance of peril, that I derived none of the excitement I had expected, and which a little danger always
produces, from going through them.   Instead of
shooting down long sheets of rushing water, which
was what I expected, we were tossed and tumbled and
shaken up and down, in the midst of a dozen con-
flicting currents and eddies, which break the whole
surface of the river into short pitching waves, and
dance about in frantic white whirligigs, like the
circles of the bad nuns' ghosts, in Meyerbeer's
devilish Opera. . . .

Good-bye, my dearest Emily.   I am always affectionately yours,

F. A. K.

Steamboat St. Patrick, on the St. Lawrence,
August 17, 1833.

MY DEAREST H——,

There is lying in my desk an unfinished
letter to you, begun about a week ago, which is
pausing for want of an opportunity to go on with it;

but here I am, a prisoner in a steamboat, destined to pass the next four and twenty hours on the broad bosom of the St. Lawrence, and what can I do better than begin a fresh chapter to you, leaving the one already begun to be finished on my next holiday. My holidays, indeed, are far from leisure time, for when I have nothing to do I have all the more to see ; so that I am as busy and more weary than if I were working much harder.

We have been staying for the last fortnight in Quebec, and are now on our way back to Montreal, where we shall act a night or two, and then return to the United States, to New York and Boston. . . . The greater part of these poems of Tennyson's which you have sent me we read together. The greater part of them are very beautiful. He seems to me to possess in a higher degree than any English poet, except, perhaps, Keats, the power of writing pictures. "The Miller's Daughter," "The Lady of Shallot," and even the shorter poems, "Mariana," "Eleonore," are full of exquisite form and colour ; if he had but the mechanical knowledge of the art, I am convinced he would have been a great painter. There are but one or two things in the volume which I don't like. "The little room with the two little white sofas," I hate, though I can fancy perfectly well both the room and his feeling about it ; but that sort of thing does not make good poetry, and lends itself temptingly to the making of good burlesque.

I have much to tell you, for in the last two months I have seen marvellous much. I have seen Niagara. I wish you had been there to see it with me. How-

ever, Niagara will not cease falling; and you may,
perhaps, at some future time, visit this country. You
must not expect any description of Niagara from me,
because it is quite unspeakable, and, moreover, if it
were not, it would still be quite unimaginable. The
circumstances under which I saw it I can tell you,
but of the great cataract itself, what can be told
except that it is water?

I confess the sight of it reminded me, with additional admiration, of Sir Charles Bagot's daring
denial of its existence; having failed to make his
pilgrimage thither during his stay in the United
States, he declared on his return to England that he
had never been able to find it, that he did'nt believe
there was any such thing, and that it was nothing
but a bragging boast of the Americans.

At Albany, our first resting-place from New York,
we had been joined by Mr. Trelawney, who had been
introduced to me in New York, and turned out to be
the well-known friend of Byron and Shelley, and
author of "The Adventures of a Younger Son,"
which is, indeed, said to be the story of his own life.

[His wild career of sea-adventure with De Ruyter,
who was supposed to have left him at his death all
his share of the results of their semi-bucaneering
exploits, his friendship and fellowship with Byron
and Shelley, the funeral obsequies he bestowed upon
the latter on the shore of the Gulf of Spezzia, his
companionship in the mountains of Greece with the
patriot chief, Odysseus, and his marriage to that
chief's sister, are all circumstances given with more
or less detail in his book, which was Englished for

him by Mary Shelley, the poet's widow, who was much attached to him; Trelawney himself being quite incapable of any literary effort which required a knowledge of common spelling. . . . He was strikingly handsome when first I knew him, with a countenance habitually serene, and occasionally sweet in its expression, but sometimes savage with the fierceness of a wild beast. His speech and movements were slow and indolently gentle, his voice very low and musical, and his utterance deliberate and rather hesitating; he was very tall, and powerfully made, and altogether looked like the hero of a wild life of adventure, such as his had been. I hear he is still alive, a very wonderful-looking old man, who sat to Millais for his picture, exhibited in 1874, of the " Old Sea-Captain."]

We all liked him so well that my father invited him to join our party, and travel with us to Niagara, whither he was bound as well as ourselves. He had seen it before, and though almost all the wonders of the world are familiar to him, he said it was the only one that he cared much to see again.

We reached Queenstown, on the Niagara river, below the falls, at about twelve o'clock, and had three more miles to drive to reach them. The day was serenely bright and warm, without a cloud in the sky, or a shade in the earth, or a breath in the air. We were in an open carriage, and I felt almost nervously oppressed with the expectation of what we were presently to see. We stopped the carriage occasionally to listen for the giant's roaring, but the sound did not reach us until, within three miles over the thick

woods which skirted the river, we saw a vapoury
silver cloud rising into the blue sky. It was the spray,
the breath of the toiling waters ascending to heaven.
When we reached what is called the Niagara House,
a large tavern by the roadside, I sprang out of the
carriage and ran through the house, down flights of
steps cut in the rock, and along a path skirted with
low thickets, through the boughs of which I saw the
rapids running a race with me, as it seemed, and
hardly faster than I did. Then there was a broad,
flashing sea of furious foam, a deafening rush and
roar, through which I heard Mr. Trelawney, who was
following me, shout, " Go on, go on; don't stop ! "
I reached an open floor of broad, flat rock, over which
the water was pouring. Trelawney seized me by the
arm, and all but carried me to the very brink; my
feet were in the water and on the edge of the precipice,
and then I looked down. I could not speak, and I
could hardly breathe; I felt as if I had an iron band
across my breast. I watched the green, glassy,
swollen heaps go plunging down, down, down; each
mountainous mass of water, as it reached the dreadful
brink, recoiling, as in horror, from the abyss; and
after rearing backwards in helpless terror, as it were,
hurling itself down to be shattered in the inevitable
doom over which eternal clouds of foam and spray
spread an impenetrable curtain. The mysterious
chasm, with its uproar of voices, seemed like the
watery mouth of hell. I looked and listened till the
wild excitement of the scene took such possession of
me that, but for the strong arm that held me back,
I really think I should have let myself slide down into

the gulf. It was long before I could utter, and as I began to draw my breath I could only gasp out, "O God! O God!" No words can describe either the scene itself, or its effect upon me.

We stayed three days at Niagara, the greater part of which I spent by the water, under the water, on the water, and more than half in the water. Wherever foot could stand I stood, and wherever foot could go I went. I crept, clung, hung, and waded; I lay upon the rocks, upon the very edge of the boiling cauldron, and I stood alone under the huge arch over which the water pours with the whole mass of it, thundering over my rocky ceiling, and falling down before me like an immeasurable curtain, the noonday sun looking like a pale spot, a white wafer, through the dense thickness. Drenched through, and almost blown from my slippery footing by the whirling gusts that rush under the fall, with my feet naked for better safety, grasping the shale broken from the precipice against which I pressed myself, my delight was so intense that I really could hardly bear to come away.

The rock over which the rapids run is already scooped and hollowed out to a great extent by the action of the water; the edge of the precipice, too, is constantly crumbling and breaking off under the spurn of its downward leap. At the very brink the rock is not much more than two feet thick, and when I stood under it and thought of the enormous mass of water rushing over and pouring from it, it did not seem at all improbable that at any moment the roof might give way, the rock break off fifteen or twenty feet, and the whole huge cataract, retreating back, leave a still wider basin for its floods to pour themselves into. You must come and see it before you die, dear H——.

After our short stay at Niagara, we came down Lake Ontario and the St. Lawrence to Montreal and Quebec. Before I leave off speaking of that wonderful cataract, I must tell you that the impression of awe and terror it produced at first upon me completely wore away, and as I became familiar with it, its dazzling brightness, its soothing voice, its gliding motion, its soft, thick, furry beds of foam, its veils and draperies of floating light, and gleaming, wavering diadems of vivid colours, made it to me the perfection of loveliness and the mere magnificence of beauty. It was certainly not the "familiarity" that "breeds contempt," but more akin to the "perfect love" which "casteth out fear;" and I began at last to understand Mr. Trelawney's saying that the only impression it produced on him was that of• perfect repose; but perhaps it takes Niagara to mesmerize him.

[The first time I attempted to go under the cataract of Niagara I had a companion with me, and one of the local guides, who undertook to pilot us safely. On reaching the edge of the sheet of water, however, we encountered a blast of wind so violent that we were almost beaten back by it. The spray was driven against us like a furious hailstorm, and it was impossible to open our eyes or draw our breath, and we were obliged to relinquish the expedition. The next morning, going down to the falls alone, I was seduced by the comparative quietness and calm, the

absence of wind or atmospheric disturbance, to
approach gradually the entrance to the cave behind
the water, and finding no such difficulty as on the
previous day, crept on, step by step, beneath the
sheet, till I reached the impassable jutting forward
of the rock where it meets the full body of the
cataract. My first success emboldened me to two
subsequent visits, the small eels being the only unpleasant incident I encountered. The narrow path I
followed was a mere ledge of shale and broken particles of the rock, which is so frayable and crumbling,
either in its own nature, or from the constant action
of the water, that as I passed along and pressed
myself close against it, I broke off in my hands the
portions of it that I grasped.]

A few miles below the falls is a place called the
whirlpool, which, in its own kind, is almost as fine as
the fall itself. The river makes an abrupt angle in its
course, when it is shut in by very high and rocky
cliffs—walls, in fact—almost inaccessible from below.
Black fir trees are anchored here and there in their
cracks and fissures, and hang over the dismal pool
below, most of them scathed and contorted by the
fires or the blasts of heaven. The water itself is of
a strange colour, not transparent, but a pale blue-
green, like a discoloured turquoise, or a stream of
verdigris, streaked with long veins and angry swirls
of white, as if the angry creature couldn't get out of
that hole, and was foaming at the mouth; for, before
pursuing its course, the river churns round and round
in the sullen, savage, dark basin it has worn for itself,
and then, as if it had suddenly found an outlet,

rushes on its foaming, furious way down to Ontario.
We had ridden there and alighted from our horses,
and sat on the brink for some time. It was the most
dismal place I ever beheld, and seemed to me to grow
horribler every moment I looked at it: drowning in
that deep, dark, wicked-looking whirlpool would be
hideous, compared to being dashed to death amid
the dazzling spray and triumphant thunder of
Niagara.

[There are but three places I have ever visited that
produced upon me the appalling impression of being
accursed, and empty of the presence of the God of
nature, the Divine Creator, the All-loving Father:
this whirlpool of Niagara, that fiery, sulphurous, vile-
smelling wound in the earth's bosom, the crater of
Vesuvius, and the upper part of the Mer de Glace at
Chamouni. These places impressed me with horror,
and the impression is always renewed in my mind
when I remember them: God-forsaken is what they
looked to me.]

I do not believe this whirlpool is at all as generally
visited as the falls, and perhaps it might not impress
everybody as it did me.

Quebec, where we have been staying, is beautiful.
A fortress is always delightful to me; my destructive-
ness rejoices in guns and drums, and all the circumstance of glorious war. The place itself, too, is so
fiercely picturesque—such crags, such dizzy, hanging
heights, such perpendicular rocky walls, down to the
very water's edge, and such a broad, bright bay. The
scenery all round Quebec is beautiful, and we went to
visit two fine waterfalls in the neighbourhood, but of

course to us just now there is but one waterfall in the
world. . . . God bless you, dear!
Ever affectionately yours,
F. A. K.

To MRS. JAMESON.
New York, Tuesday, October 15th, 1833.

You are wandering, dear Mrs. Jameson, in the land
of romance, the birthplace of wild traditions, the
stronghold of chivalrous legends, the spell-land of
witchcraft, the especial haunt and home of goblin,
spectre, sprite, and gnome; all the beautiful and
fanciful creations of the poetical imagination of the
Middle Ages. You are, I suppose, in Germany; intel-
lectually speaking, almost the antipodes of America.
Germany is now the country to which my imagination
wanders oftener than to any other. Italy was my
wishing land eight years ago, but many things have
dimmed that southern vision to my fancy, and the
cloudier skies, wilder associations, and more solemn
spirit of Germany attract me more now than the
sunny ruin-land. . . .

I shall not return to England, not even to visit it
now—certainly never to make my home there again.
" The place that knew me will know me no more,"
and you will never again have the satisfaction of
coming to me after a first night's new part to say all
manner of kind things about it to me. My feelings
about the stage you know full well, and will rejoice
with me that there is a prospect of my leaving it
before its pernicious excitements had been rendered
necessary to me by habit. Yet when I think of my

"farewell night," I cannot help wishing it might have taken place in London, before my own people, who received my first efforts so kindly, and where I stood in the very footprints, as it were, of my kindred. . . . Thank you for your long and entertaining letter, and for the copy of the second edition of " Shakespeare's Women." You cannot think how extremely popular you are in this country. A lady assured me the other day, that when you went to heaven, which you certainly would, Shakespeare would meet you and kiss you for having understood, and made others understand, him so well. If ever you do come to this side of that deep, dividing ditch, which you speak of as not an improbable event, you will find as much admiration waiting for you here as you can have left behind; whether it is equally valuable, it is for you to judge. . . . I have seen Niagara since last I wrote to you, and it was in a balcony almost overhanging it that I saw your husband, and that he gave me long accounts of your literary plans.

Dear Mrs. Jameson, this is a short and stupid letter, but I have been working awfully hard, and have not been well for the past month, and am not capable of much exertion. It is quite a novelty to me, and not an agreeable one, to feel myself weak, and worn out, and good for nothing. Good-bye; write to me from some of your halting-places, and believe me ever yours truly,

F. A. K.

I noted the altered frontispiece of my little book.

Boston, April 16th, 1834.

DEAR MRS. JAMESON,

I received a kind and interesting letter from you, dated "Munich," some time past, and lately, another from London, telling me of the alarm you experienced with regard to your father's health, and your sudden return from Germany, which I regretted very much, for selfish as well as sympathetic motives. You were not only enjoying yourself there, but were gathering materials for the enjoyment of others; and I am as loath to lose the benefit of your labours as sorry that your pleasant holiday was thus interrupted.

It is now probable, unless the Atlantic should like me better going than it did coming, and that it should take me to its bosom, that I may be in London in July, when I hope I shall find you there. . . . I am coming back to England, after all, and shall, I think, remain on the stage another year. . . .

I received, a few days ago, a letter from dear H——, in which she mentioned that you had an intention of writing a memoir or biographical sketch of " the Kemble family," in which, if I understood her right, you thought of introducing the notice which you wrote for Hayter's drawings of me in Juliet. She said that you wished to know whether I had any objection or dislike to your doing so, and I answered directly to yourself, " None in the world." I had but one fault to find with that notice of me, that it was far too full of praise; I thought it so sincerely. But, without wishing to enter into any discussion about my merits or your partiality, I can only repeat that you are free to write of me what you will, and as you will; but,

for your own sake, I wish you to remember that praise
is, to the majority of readers, a much more vapid thing
than censure, and that if you could admire me less
and criticize me more, I am sure, as the housemaids
say, you would give more satisfaction.   However, keep
your conscience by you; praise or blame, it is none
of my business.   Talking of that same Juliet, I
received a letter from Hayter the other day which
gave me some pain.   He tells me that he has all those
sketches on his hands, and asks me if I am inclined
to take them of him.   I fear his applying to me, at
such a distance, on this subject, is a sign that he is
not prosperous or doing well.   He is an amiable,
clever little man, and I shall feel very sorry if my
surmise proves true.   My father wishes to have the
collection, and I shall write to tell him so forthwith.

It is no slight illustration to me of the ephemeral
nature of the popularity which I enjoyed, to think that
those drawings, which, as works of art, were singularly
elegant and graceful, should go a-begging for a pur-
chaser.   Verily, "all is vanity!"

[My friend, Lord Ellesmere, purchased the series
of drawings Mr. Hayter made from my performance
of Juliet; and on my last visit to Lady Ellesmere at
Hatchford, she pointed them out to me round a small
hall that led to her private sitting-room, over the
writing-table of which hung a miniature of me copied
from a drawing of Mrs. Jameson's by that charming
and clever woman, Miss Emily Eden.]

You will be sorry for me and for many when I tell
you that our good, dear friend Dall is dangerously ill.
I am writing at this moment by her bed. . . . This

is the only trial of the kind I have ever undergone;
God has hitherto been pleased to spare all those whom
I love, and to grant them the enjoyment of strength
and health. This is my first lonely watching by a sick
bed, and I feel deeply the sadness and awfulness of
the office. . . . Now that I am beginning to know
what care and sorrow really are, I look back upon my
past life and see what reason I have to be thankful
for the few and light trials with which I have been
visited. My poor dear aunt's illness is giving us a
professional respite, for which my faculties, physical
and mental, are very grateful. They needed it sorely;
I was almost worn out with work, and latterly with
anxiety and bitter distress.

We terminated our last engagement here on Friday
last, when the phlegmatic Bostonians seemed almost
beside themselves with excitement and enthusiasm:
they shouted at us, they cheered us, they crowned me
with roses. Conceive, if you can, the shocking contrast between all this and the silent sick-room, to which
I went straight from the stage. . . . Surely, our profession involves more intolerable discords between the
real human beings who exercise it, and their unreal
vocation, than any in the world! . . . In returning to
England, two advantages, which I shall value much,
will be obtained: a fortnight's rest during the passage,
and, I hope, not quite such hard work when I resume
my labours. . . . As for the hollowness and heartless-
ness of the world, by which one means really the
people that one has to do with in it, I cannot say that
I trouble my mind much about it. In their relations
with me I commit every one to their own conscience;

if they deal ill by me, they deal worse by themselves.
. . . I hope you may be in London when we reach it.
Farewell.

I am ever yours truly, ·

FANNY KEMBLE.

New York, Thursday, April 24th, 1834.

MY DEAR H——,

This will be but a short letter, the first short
one you will have received from me since we parted.
Dear Dall has gone from us. She is dead ; she died in
my arms, and I closed her eyes. . . . I cannot attempt
to speak of this now, I will give you all details in my
next letter. It has been a dreadful shock, though it
was not unexpected ; but there is no preparation for
the sense of desolation which oppresses me, and which
is beyond words. . . . I wrote you a long letter a few
days ago, which will perhaps have led you to anticipate
this. We shall probably be in England on the 10th
of July. . . . The sole care of my father, who is
deeply afflicted, and charge of everything, devolves
entirely on me now. . . . We left Boston on Tuesday.
. . . I act here to-night for the first time since I lost
that dear and devoted friend, who was ever near at
hand to think of everything for me, to care for me in
every way. I have almost cried my eyes out daily for
the last three months ; but that is over now. I am
working again, and go about my work feeling stunned
and bewildered. . . .

I saw Dr. Channing on Monday ; he has just lost a
dear and intimate connection. With what absolute
faith he spoke of her ! Gone ! to the Author of all

good. That which was good must return to Him. It is true, and I believe it, and know it; but at first I was lost. . . . God bless you, dear H———. We shall meet ere long, and in the midst of great sorrow that will be a great joy to

Yours ever affectionately,

F. A. K.

We have buried dear Dall in a lonely, lovely place in Mount Orban's cemetery, where ——— and I used to go and sit together last spring, in the early time of our intimacy. I wished her to lie there, for life and love and youth and death have their trysting-place at the grave.

My aunt died in consequence of an injury to the spine, received by the overturning of our carriage in our summer tour to Niagara.

———

I was married in Philadelphia on the 7th of June, 1894, to Mr. Pierce Butler, of that city.

THE END.

PRINTED AT THE CAXTON PRESS, BECCLES. *L. & Co.*

61